JET FIGHTERS
INSIDE & OUT

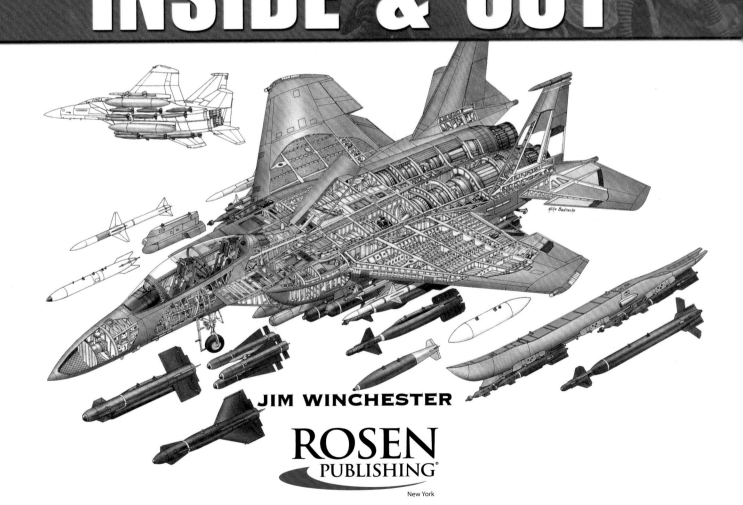

JIM WINCHESTER

ROSEN
PUBLISHING®

New York

This edition first published in 2012 by:

The Rosen Publishing Group, Inc.
29 E. 21st Street
New York, NY 10010

Additional end matter copyright © 2012 by The Rosen Publishing Group, Inc.

Project Editor: James Bennett
Picture Research: Terry Forshaw
Design: Zoë Mellors

Library of Congress Cataloging-in-Publication Data

Winchester, Jim.
Jet fighters: inside & out/Jim Winchester.
        p. cm.—(Weapons of war)
Includes bibliographical references and index.
ISBN 978-1-4488-5982-5 (library binding)
1. Fighter planes—Juvenile literature. I. Title.
UG1242.F5W55 2012
623.74'64—dc23

2011030891

Manufactured in the United States of America

CPSIA Compliance Information: Batch #W12YA: For further information, contact Rosen Publishing, New York, New York, at 1-800-237-9932.

Copyright © 2010 by Amber Books Ltd. First published in 2010 by Amber Books Ltd.

Contents

Classic Jets 1945–1960

"Only the spirit of attack born in the brave heart can bring the success to any fighter plane, no matter how developed it may be."
– Lieutenant General Adolf Galland, *The First and the Last*

Above: The Messerschmitt Me 262 was the first and last jet many Allied airmen ever saw, but it was too late and too unreliable to influence the outcome of World War II or win back even local air superiority for the Germans.

In 1945, when Adolf Galland was flying his last missions in the Messerschmitt Me 262, only six countries (United Kingdom, United States, Germany, Japan, Sweden and the Soviet Union) had active jet fighter aircraft programs, and two of those were soon closed down by the Axis defeat. In the 1950s and 1960s, various other countries tried, often with the help of former German designers, to build indigenous fighters, including Switzerland, India, Egypt and Argentina.

But the great cost of such programs and the increasing sophistication of avionics and missiles meant that they usually turned out both more expensive and less competitive than their contemporaries. Almost every Western or non-aligned nation except the United Kingdom, France and Sweden gave up on totally home-grown fighters, and chose to buy outright or produce under license the products of Lockheed, Dassault or Hawker. Communist or Moscow-leaning nations had a choice of Mikoyan-Gurevich MiGs (or their Chinese copies) or Sukhois. India, Pakistan and some Arab nations hedged their bets by buying aircraft of both Western and Soviet or Chinese origin.

THE FIGHTER'S GOLDEN AGE

The 1950s, in particular, proved to be a golden age for fighter design, with new prototypes appearing seemingly every month. Some of these even made it into production, a process in those days which could often be achieved in a relatively short time and reasonably close to budget. Increasing capability, sophistication and more rigorous testing and evaluation, as well as political interference, have helped to extend development programs close to two decades between design freeze and initial operational capability.

Today's analysts and marketing departments recognize five generations of jet fighters. The term "fifth-generation fighter" was coined in Russia in the 1990s as a way of describing the top-secret program to develop a competitor to the Joint Strike Fighter of the United States and its allies. It seems to have stuck, and postwar fighters can be allocated to previous generations, although the placement of some is debatable.

The first-generation fighters were characterized by gun and occasionally rocket armament, straight or swept wings, single unaugmented (non-afterburning) engines and hence

Above: The F-86 Sabre pilot had an excellent outside view when he was not busy monitoring the multitude of instruments typical of first-generation jets.

Above: Mikoyan-Gurevich's MiG-21 proliferated through the 1960s and 1970s, and it is the last second-generation fighter still to be found in large numbers.

subsonic speeds in all flight regimes except a dive from altitude. Radar, if present, was usually a simple ranging set for gun aiming. Examples of first-generation fighters include the North American F-86 Sabre, Gloster Meteor, Mikoyan-Gurevich MiG-15, Grumman F9F Panther/Cougar and de Havilland Vampire/Venom. Today, the only survivors of the era remaining airworthy fly in air shows, not air combat.

EVER-GROWING SOPHISTICATION

Supersonic performance in level flight came with second-generation jets, as did basic guided missiles and air-to-air radar. Some fighters such as the Convair F-102 Delta Dagger and F-106 Delta Dart could be flown hands-off to an interception by signals from ground control. Swept or delta wings became universal and afterburning engines widespread. Second-generation fighters included all of the "Century Series" from the North American F-100 Super Sabre to the F-106 Delta Dart, Mikoyan-Gurevich MiG-19 and MiG-21, Vought F-8 Crusader, Saab 35 Draken, Dassault Mirage III/V, Hawker Hunter, English Electric Lightning and Gloster Javelin. Apart from some MiGs and their Chinese equivalents, the second generation has all but vanished from active service.

Third-generation fighters sometimes eliminated gun armament altogether in favor of "fire-and-forget" and beyond-visual-range missiles. In actual combat, rules of engagement often prevented firing until positive visual identification was made, which drew the missile-armed fighter into a close-in fight with smaller, nimbler enemies and their cannon. In Vietnam, the United States prevailed in the air-to-air arena, but not before it was taught some important lessons. Representative third-generation fighters include the McDonnell Douglas F-4 Phantom, Panavia Tornado, Mikoyan-Gurevich MiG-23, Saab 37 Viggen and others with analog control systems, conventional dial cockpit instrumentation and in many cases different variants for different roles such as air interdiction and suppression of enemy air defenses.

TESTED IN ACTION

The third generation saw significant combat in Southeast Asia and over the Middle East. Considerable numbers remain in service, particularly Phantoms, Dassault Mirage F1s and Northrop F-5s. Upgrade programs have kept these older aircraft viable with multimode radars, "glass" cockpits and integration of precision weapons such as AMRAAMs (advanced medium-range air-to-air missiles) and the later versions of the venerable Sidewinder. Often the technical advances developed for the next generation have been fed

Above: Marking the peak of single-seat fighter size and mechanical complexity, the F-105's main defense was its speed at low level.

Above: For smaller air arms such as Brazil's navy, the purchase and eventual upgrade of older aircraft such as the Douglas A-4 Skyhawk is a way to maintain a fairly cheap fighter capability.

back into the existing fighter fleets, which on one hand has served to keep fighters competitive while the air arms await their (often delayed) replacements, but on the other sometimes reduces the need for the planned number of new fighters. In this way, some fighter manufacturers have found that their biggest competitors are their own "legacy" products. Controlling access to the software codes that allow export customers to upgrade their expensive fighters has become as important to the balance sheet as the supplying of spare parts has traditionally been for the few remaining fighter makers.

The 1950s, in particular, proved to be a golden age for jet fighter design, with new prototypes appearing seemingly every month.

Messerschmitt Me 262

The Me 262 was the world's first operational jet fighter. Politics and technical difficulties prevented the 262 from reaching its full potential, and only a small number actually saw combat in the last months of World War II.

ME 262 A-1A/B SPECIFICATION

Dimensions

Length: 34 ft 9 in (10.58 m)
Height: 12 ft 7 in (3.83 m)
Span: 40 ft 11 in (12.5 m)
Wing area: 234 sq ft (21.73 m²)
Wing leading-edge sweepback: 18° 32'

Power plant

Two Junkers Jumo 004B-1, -2 or -3 axial-flow turbojets each rated at 1,984 lb st (8.83 kN)

Weights

Empty: 3,778 lb (3795 kg)
Empty equipped: 9,742 lb (4413 kg)
Maximum takeoff: 14,080 lb (6387 kg)

Performance

Maximum speed at sea level: 514 mph (827 km/h)
Maximum speed at 9,845 ft (3000 m): 530 mph (852 km/h)
Maximum speed at 19,685 ft (6000 m): 540 mph (869 km/h)
Maximum speed at 26,245 ft (8000 m): 532 mph (856 km/h)
Initial climb rate: 3,937 ft (1200 m) per minute
Service ceiling: over 40,000 ft (12,190 m)
Range: 652 miles (1050 km) at 29,530 ft (9000 m)
Landing speed: 109 mph (175 km/h)

Armament

Four 1.18-in (30-mm) Rheinmetall-Borsig Mk 108A-3 cannon with 100 rounds per gun for the upper pair and 80 rounds per gun for the lower pair, and aimed with a Revi 16.B gunsight or EZ.42 gyro-stabilized sight. Provision for 12 R4M air-to-air rockets under each wing (Me 262A-1b).

Cutaway Key

1 Flettner-type geared trim tab
2 Mass-balanced rudder
3 Rudder post
4 Tail fin structure
5 Tailplane structure
6 Rudder tab mechanism
7 Flettner-type servo tab
8 Starboard elevator
9 Rear navigation light
10 Rudder linkage
11 Elevator linkage
12 Tailplane adjustment mechanism
13 Fuselage break point
14 Fuselage construction
15 Control runs
16 FuG 25a loop antenna (IFF)
17 Automatic compass
18 Aft auxiliary self-sealing fuel tank (159 gal/600-liter capacity)
19 FuG 16zy R/T
20 Fuel filler cap
21 Aft cockpit glazing
22 Armored aft main fuel tank (238-gal/900-liter capacity)
23 Inner cockpit shell
24 Pilot's seat
25 Canopy jettison lever
26 Armored 0.59-in (15-mm) headrest
27 Canopy (hinged to starboard)
28 Canopy lock
29 Bar-mounted Revi 16B sight (for both cannon and R4M missiles)
30 Armor glass windshield 3.54 in (90 mm)
31 Instrument panel
32 Rudder pedal
33 Armored forward main fuel tank (238-gal/900-liter capacity)
34 Fuel filler cap

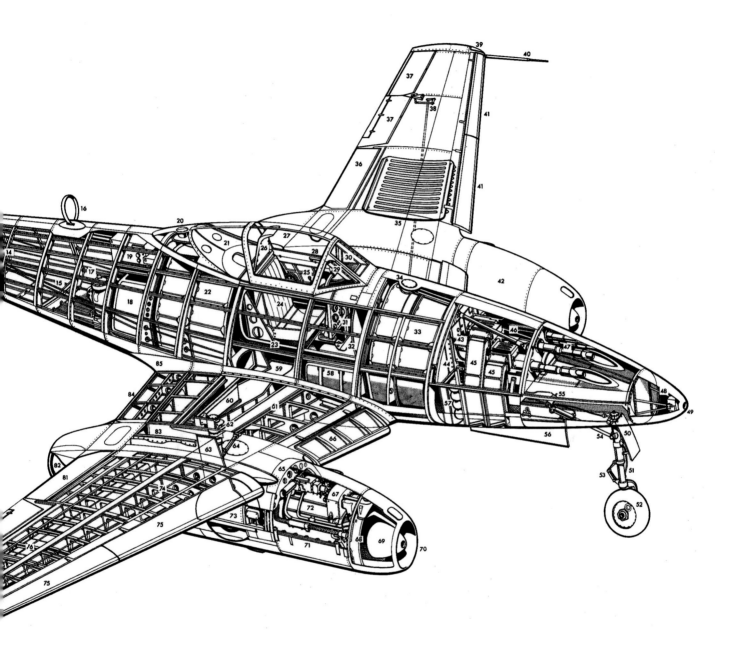

35 Underwing wooden rack for 12 R4M 2.17-in (55-mm) rockets (Me 262A-1b)
36 Port outer flap section
37 Frise-type aileron
38 Aileron control linkage
39 Port navigation light
40 Pitot head
41 Automatic leading-edge slats
42 Port engine cowling

43 Electrical firing mechanism
44 Firewall
45 Spent cartridge ejector chutes
46 Four 1.18-in (30-mm) Rheinmetall Borsig Mk 108 cannon (100 rpg belt-fed ammunition for upper pair and 80 rpg for lower pair)
47 Cannon muzzles
48 Combat camera

49 Camera aperture
50 Nosewheel fairing
51 Nosewheel leg
52 Nosewheel
53 Torque scissors
54 Retraction jack
55 Hydraulic lines
56 Main nosewheel door (starboard)
57 Compressed air bottles
58 Forward auxiliary fuel tank (45-gal/170-liter capacity)

59 Mainwheel well
60 Torque box
61 Main spar
62 Mainwheel leg pivot point
63 Mainwheel door
64 Mainwheel retraction rod
65 Engine support arch
66 Leading-edge slat structure
67 Auxiliaries gearbox
68 Annular oil tank
69 Riedel starter motor housing

70 Engine air intake
71 Hinged cowling section
72 Junkers Jumo 004B-2 axial-flow turbojet
73 Starboard mainwheel
74 Wing structure
75 Automatic leading-edge slats
76 Mainspar
77 Starboard navigation light
78 Frise-type ailerons

79 Trim tab
80 Flettner-type geared tab
81 Starboard outer flap section
82 Engine exhaust orifice
83 Engine support bearer
84 Starboard inner flap structure
85 Faired wing root

"It was as if an angel were pushing me."
– Major General Adolf Galland after his first
  flight in the Me 262

MESSERSCHMITT ME 262 – VARIANTS

WARTIME VARIANTS

Me 262 A-0: Pre-production aircraft fitted with two Jumo 004B turbojet engines.

Me 262 A-1a "Schwalbe": Production version, fighter and fighter-bomber.

Me 262 A-1a/R-1: Equipped with provisions for R4M air-to-air rockets.

Me 262 A-1a/U1: Single prototype with six nose-mounted guns.

Me 262 A-1a/U2: Single prototype with FuG 220 Lichtenstein SN-2 90 MHz radar transceiver and Hirschgeweih antenna array, for trials as a night fighter.

Me 262 A-1a/U3: Reconnaissance version.

Me 262 A-1a/U4: Bomber-destroyer version.

Me 262 A-1a/U5: Heavy jet fighter with six MK 108s in the nose.

Me 262 A-1b: As A-1a but powered with BMW 003 engines.

Me 262 A-2a "Sturmvogel": Definitive bomber version.

Me 262 A-2a/U1: Single prototype with advanced bombsight.

Me 262 A-2a/U2: Two prototypes with glazed nose for accommodating a bombardier.

Me 262 A-3a: Proposed ground-attack version.

Me 262 A-4a: Reconnaissance version.

Me 262 A-5a: Definitive reconnaissance version.

Me 262 B-1a: Two-seat trainer.

Me 262 B-1a/U1: Me 262 B-1a trainers converted into provisional night fighters, FuG 218 Neptun radar, with Hirschgeweih antenna array.

Me 262 B-2: Proposed night-fighter version with stretched fuselage.

Me 262 C-1a: Single prototype of rocket-boosted interceptor (Heimatschützer I) with Walter HWK 109-509 rocket in tail.

Me 262 C-2b: Single prototype of rocket-boosted interceptor (Heimatschützer II).

Me 262 C-3a: Never completed. Possible Heimatschützer III prototype of rocket-boosted interceptor with Walter rocket motor in belly pack.

Me 262 S: Zero-series model for Me 262 A-1a.

Me 262 V: Test model for Me 262.

POSTWAR VARIANTS

Avia S-92: Czechoslovak-built Me 262A.

Avia S-92: Czechoslovak-built Me 262 A-1a.

Avia CS-92: Czechoslovak-built Me 262 B-1a (fighter trainer, two seats).

MESSERSCHMITT ME 262

The Me 262 A-1a was the first production model of the "Schwalbe" (Swallow), followed by the Me 262 A-2a "Sturmvogel" (Stormbird) fighter-bomber. This Me 262 A-1a of 3./JG 7 was found by Allied forces in April 1945 in a hangar at Stendal, Germany, having been damaged by anti-aircraft fire, possibly German. Although it was considered for repair and evaluation, better examples were available and it was scrapped. Jagdgeschwader 7 was the only wing to fully equip with Me 262s and claimed more than 135 victories against Allied aircraft before the war's end. On March 18 , 1945, it managed to get 37 Me 262s airborne for the type's biggest mission, during which it used the R4M rocket for the first time.

German research into jet engines began in the late 1930s, leading to the first flight of the Heinkel He 178 and He 180 test aircraft in 1939 and 1940, respectively. By 1942, Ernst Heinkel had fallen out of favor with the Nazi hierarchy, and the war seemed to be going well enough for Germany that defensive fighters would be unnecessary, no matter how superior. Willi Messerschmitt was working on his own design, to be powered by either a BMW or Junkers axial-flow turbojet.

Above: With two bombs mounted under the fuselage, the Me 262A-2a "Sturmvogel" was a fast but inaccurate fighter-bomber.

In ground testing, the proposed power plants failed to produce enough thrust, but Messerschmitt proceeded with the airframes regardless, and the first Messerschmitt 262 with a Junkers Jumo 210G piston engine fitted in the nose flew in April 1941.

PROTOTYPE CONFIGURATIONS

The fully jet-powered Me 262 V3 with BMW 003s retained the tailwheel undercarriage of the V1. This proved a mistake because the thrust line and wing incidence combined to prevent enough airflow over the wing to allow flying speed. The temporary solution required the pilot to tap the brakes during the takeoff roll, which raised the tail and allowed liftoff. Subsequent aircraft had the undercarriage changed to a nosewheel configuration. The first flight on jet power alone was in July 1942.

The production model Me 262 A was powered by Jumo 004s, and it was armed with either two or four 1.8-in

Above: Me 262s belonging to a test unit in the summer of 1944. Soon the aircraft would have to be dispersed and camouflaged to avoid roaming Allied ground-attack aircraft on the lookout for German targets.

Above: The simple and well-laid-out instrument panel of an Me 262. The engine instruments on the right-hand side had to be carefully watched so that the pilot could take measures to prevent the turbines from overheating.

(30-mm) MK 108 cannon. Later aircraft were capable of carrying racks of R4M unguided rockets. The leading-edge sweep of 18.5 degrees was not enough to really call it a swept-wing aircraft by later standards.

When shown the Me 262 in November 1943, Adolf Hitler asked if it could carry bombs. Willi Messerschmitt lied, but immediately set his engineers to modifying the Me 262 to carry a pair of bombs under the forward fuselage. It is debatable whether this actually delayed its service entry appreciably, but it proved harder than anticipated and produced a very short-ranged and inaccurate bomber that was to have no effect on the Allied invasion of France.

The first test unit began business in May 1944 and spawned the first operational jet squadron in September, called Kommando Nowotny after its leader, 283-victory ace Walter Nowotny. Nowotny himself lived only until November 1944, before he was brought down by P-51 Mustangs. Despite their superiority at high speed and altitude, the Me 262s were extremely vulnerable on their landing approaches, and their concrete-paved runways were easy for roving Allied fighters to find.

DEVASTATING EFFECT

Several units were formed, but the largest rarely had more than 30 aircraft operational at one time. The Me 262 scored its first confirmed victories in August 1944. Where they were able to be concentrated against USAAF bombers, their effect could be devastating. A total of 27 Luftwaffe pilots became jet aces by scoring five or more kills with the Me 262, although many were already *experten* on propeller-driven fighters. One such pilot was Adolf Galland, who added seven U.S. aircraft to his total score of 104.

The Me 262 was in the end hampered by Allied attacks on its supply lines, particularly fuel for support vehicles, and by its unreliable engines, made with materials unsuitable for prolonged high temperatures.

Gloster Meteor

The Meteor was the Allies' first operational jet fighter and the only one to see active combat in World War II. Later variants were used in Korea and served well into the 1960s.

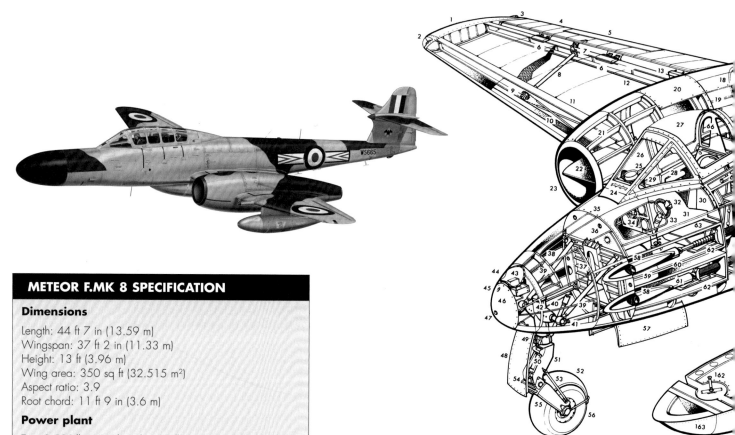

METEOR F.MK 8 SPECIFICATION

Dimensions

Length: 44 ft 7 in (13.59 m)
Wingspan: 37 ft 2 in (11.33 m)
Height: 13 ft (3.96 m)
Wing area: 350 sq ft (32.515 m²)
Aspect ratio: 3.9
Root chord: 11 ft 9 in (3.6 m)

Power plant

Two 3,500-lb (15.5-kN) thrust Rolls-Royce Derwent 8 turbojets

Weights

Empty: 10,684 lb (4846 kg)
Maximum overload: 15,700 lb (7122 kg)

Performance

Maximum speed at sea level: 592 mph (953 km/h)
Maximum speed at 30,000 ft (9144 m): 550 mph (885 km/h)
Climb to 30,000 ft (9144 m): 6 minutes 30 seconds
Service ceiling: 44,000 ft (13,410 m)
Range without wing drop tanks: 690 miles (1111 km)
Endurance at 40,000 ft (12,192 m) with 504 gal (1909 liters) of fuel: 592 mph (953 km/h)

Armament

Four fixed 0.79-in (20-mm) British Hispano cannon in the nose with 195 rounds per gun

Cutaway Key

1 Starboard detachable wingtip
2 Starboard navigation light
3 Starboard recognition light
4 Starboard aileron
5 Aileron balance tab
6 Aileron mass balance weights
7 Aileron control coupling
8 Aileron torque shaft
9 Chain sprocket
10 Crossover control runs
11 Front spar
12 Rear spar
13 Aileron (inboard) mass balance
14 Nacelle detachable tail section
15 Jet pipe exhaust
16 Internal stabilizing struts
17 Rear spar "spectacle" frame
18 Fire extinguisher spray ring
19 Main engine mounting frame
20 Engine access panel(s)
21 Nacelle nose structure
22 Intake internal leading-edge shield
23 Starboard engine intake
24 Windshield de-icing spray tube
25 Reflector gunsight
26 Cellular glass bulletproof windshield
27 Aft-sliding cockpit canopy
28 Demolition incendiary (cockpit starboard wall)
29 RPM indicators (left and right of gunsight)
30 Pilot's seat
31 Forward fuselage top deflector skin
32 Gun wobble button
33 Control column grip
34 Main instrument panel
35 Nosewheel armored bulkhead
36 Nose release catches (10)
37 Nosewheel jack bulkhead
38 Nose ballast weight location
39 Nosewheel mounting frames
40 Radius rod (link and jack omitted)
41 Nosewheel pivot bearings
42 Shimmy-damper/ self-centering strut
43 Gun camera
44 Camera access
45 Aperture
46 Nose cone
47 Cabin cold-air intake
48 Nosewheel leg door
49 Picketing rings
50 Tension shock absorber
51 Pivot bracket
52 Mudguard
53 Torque strut
54 Doorhoop
55 Wheel fork
56 Retractable nosewheel
57 Nosewheel doors
58 Port cannon trough fairings
59 Nosewheel cover
60 Intermediate diaphragm
61 Blast tubes
62 Gun front mount rails
63 Pilot's seat pan
64 Emergency crowbar
65 Canopy demisting silica gel cylinder
66 Bulletproof glass rear-view cutouts
67 Canopy track
68 Sea bulkhead
69 Entry step
70 Link ejection chutes
71 Case ejection chutes
72 0.79-in (20-mm) Hispano Mk III cannon
73 Belt-feed mechanism
74 Ammunition feed necks
75 Ammunition tanks

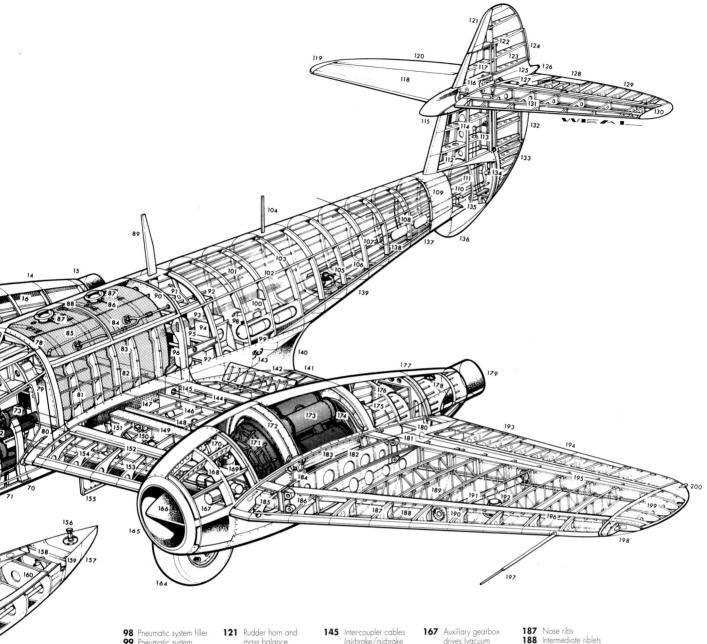

76 Aft glazing (magazine bay top door)
77 Leading ramp
78 Front spar bulkhead
79 Oxygen bottles (2)
80 Front spar carry-through
81 Tank bearer frames
82 Rear spar carry-through
83 Self-sealing (twin compartment) main fuel tank, capacity 198 gal (750 liters) in each half
84 Fuel connector pipe
85 Return pipe
86 Drain pipes
87 Fuel filler caps
88 Tank doors (2)
89 T.R.1143 aerial mast
90 Rear spar bulkhead (plywood face)
91 Aerial support frame
92 R.3121 (or B.C.966M) IFF installation
93 Tab control cables
94 Amplifier
95 Fire extinguisher bottles (2)
96 Elevator torque shaft
97 T.R.1143 transmitter/receiver radio installation

98 Pneumatic system filler
99 Pneumatic system (compressed) air cylinders
100 Tab cable fairlead
101 Elevator control cable
102 Top longeron
103 Fuselage frame
104 IFF aerial
105 DR compass master unit
106 Rudder cables
107 Starboard lower longeron
108 Cable access panels (port and starboard)
109 Tail section joint
110 Rudder linkage
111 Tail ballast weight location
112 Fin spar/fuselage frame
113 Rudder tab control
114 Fin structure
115 Torpedo fairing
116 Tailplane spar/upper fin attachment plates
117 Upper fin section
118 Starboard tailplane
119 Elevator horn and mass balance
120 Starboard elevator

121 Rudder horn and mass balance
122 Rudder upper hinge
123 Rudder frame
124 Fixed tab
125 Rear fairing
126 Tail navigation light
127 Elevator torque shaft
128 Elevator trim tab
129 Elevator frame
130 Elevator horn and mass balance
131 Tailplane structure
132 Rudder combined balance trim tab
133 Rudder lower section
134 Elevator push-rod linkage
135 Rudder internal/lower mass balance weight
136 Emergency landing tailskid
137 Tail section riveted joint
138 Port lower longeron
139 Fuselage stressed skin
140 Wing root fairing
141 Inboard split flap
142 Airbrake (upper and lower surfaces)
143 Flap indicator transmitter
144 Rear spar

145 Inter-coupler cables (airbrake/airbrake and flap/flap)
146 Port mainwheel well
147 Roof rib station
148 Front diaphragm
149 Undercarriage beam
150 Undercarriage retraction jack
151 Undercarriage sidestay/downlock
152 Front spar
153 Nose ribs
154 Aileron control runs
155 Mainwheel door inner section
156 Ventral tank transfer pipe
157 Tank rear fairing
158 Filler stack pipes
159 Ventral tank attachment strap access doors
160 Anti-surge baffles
161 Fixed ventral fuel tank, capacity 126 gal (477 liters)
162 Air pressure inlet
163 Tank front fairing
164 Port mainwheel
165 Starboard engine intake
166 Intake internal leading edge shield

167 Auxiliary gearbox drives (vacuum pump/generator)
168 Nacelle nose structure
169 Starter motor
170 Oil tank
171 Rolls-Royce W.2B/23C Derwent I
172 Main engine mounting frame
173 Combustion chambers
174 Rear spar spectacle frame
175 Jet pipe thermo-coupling
176 Nacelle aft frames
177 Nacelle detachable tail section
178 Jet pipe suspension link
179 Jet pipe exhaust
180 Gap fairing tail section
181 Rear-spar outer wing fixing
182 Outer wing rib No.1
183 Engine end rib
184 Engine mounting/removal trunnion
185 Gap fairing nose section
186 Front-spar outer wing fixing

187 Nose ribs
188 Intermediate riblets
189 Wing ribs
190 Aileron drive chain sprocket
191 Aileron torque shaft
192 Retractable landing lamp
193 Port aileron
194 Aileron balance tab
195 Rear spar
196 Front spar
197 Pitot head
198 Port navigation light
199 Outer wing rib No.10/wingtip attachment
200 Port recognition light

"All I want for Christmas is my wings swept back."
– song sung by Australian Meteor pilots in Korea, 1951

"It's a very sweet airplane. It's beautiful to fly, lovely to
operate, a real honey."
– Meteor ejection-seat testbed pilot Dan Griffith

GLOSTER METEOR – VARIANTS AND MILITARY OPERATORS

VARIANTS

F: First production aircraft built between 1943 and 1944.

F 1: One-off engine testbed, built 1945, designated EE227, for the new and highly successful Rolls-Royce Trent turboprop engine, making it the world's first turboprop-powered aircraft.

F 2: One model built of alternative-engined version.

F 3: Derwent I powered version with sliding canopy.

F 4: Derwent 5 powered version with strengthened fuselage.

FR 5: One-off fighter reconnaissance version of the F 4.

T 7: Two-seat trainer.

F 8: Greatly improved from the F 4. Longer fuselage, greater fuel capacity, standard ejection seat and modified tail.

F 8 Prone Pilot: One-off experimental prone pilot F8, WK935 modified by Armstrong Whitworth. The sole "prone pilot" experimental testbed.

FR 9: Fighter reconnaissance version of the F 8.

PR 10: Photo reconnaissance version of the F 8.

NF 11: Night-fighter variant with Airborne Intercept radar.

NF 12: Longer-nosed version of the NF 11 with American radar.

NF 13: Tropicalized version of the NF 11 for overseas service.

NF 14: NF 11 with new two-piece canopy.

U 15: Drone conversion of the F 4.

U 16: Drone conversion of the F 8.

TT 20: High-speed target towing conversion of the NF 11.

U 21: Drone conversion of the F 8.

MILITARY OPERATORS
Argentine Air Force
Royal Australian Air Force
Belgian Air Force
Brazilian Air Force
Royal Canadian Air Force
Royal Danish Air Force
Ecuadorian Air Force
Royal Egyptian Air Force
French Air Force
Israeli Air Force
Royal Netherlands Air Force
Royal New Zealand Air Force
Royal Norwegian Air Force
South African Air Force
Swedish Air Force
Syrian Air Force
UK Royal Air Force and Royal Navy Fleet Air Arm

GLOSTER METEOR

The Meteor night fighters were developed and built by Armstrong Whitworth in Coventry, England. The NF 14 was the last to enter service. Unlike earlier models, which inherited a heavily framed canopy from the T 7 trainer, the NF 14 had a clear bubble canopy for the pilot and radar operator. Compared to the original Meteor NF 11, the Mk 14 had a taller tail, longer wings and a longer nose. WS600 was delivered to the RAF in 1954. In 1959, it was serving with No. 60 Squadron at Tengah, Singapore. When 60 Squadron re-equipped with Gloster Javelins, it was struck off charge (withdrawn from use) in August 1961 at RAF Seletar and later scrapped.

Jet-engine pioneer Sir Frank Whittle worked through the 1930s to develop a practical gas turbine (jet) aircraft engine. The British Air Ministry issued a request for an operational fighter based around a Whittle W2 engine in 1940, and this was preceded by the E28/39 test aircraft, sometimes called the Gloster Whittle, which flew in May 1941. The low power and questionable reliability of Whittle's original engine suggested that a twin-engined layout would be wise for an operational aircraft. Whittle's own small Power Jets company was not in a position to build aircraft or mass-produce engines. Gloster proposed an aircraft called the G41, and Rolls-Royce took on engine development and produced the W2 as the Welland, although the prototype G41, soon named Meteor, flew in March 1942 with de Havilland Halford H1 engines.

Above: The Meteor T 7 remained in use as an advanced trainer long after the fighter versions were retired from the RAF. They suffered a high accident rate when training pilots to cope with engine failures.

Two years of testing and training followed before the Meteor F 1 entered service with the RAF in July 1944 at Manston in Kent. Immediately they were thrown into action against the V-1 flying bombs being launched against London. More than a dozen were destroyed by the Meteor's four 0.79-in (20-mm) cannon or by tipping them out of control with their wingtips. At first Meteors were forbidden from flying over enemy-held territory in order to preserve their secrets, but this restriction was soon abandoned. By World War II's end, Meteors had had a few inconclusive encounters with manned Luftwaffe aircraft, but had scored no victories nor suffered any losses, being mostly used for ground attack. On these missions, they destroyed numerous aircraft and vehicles on the ground.

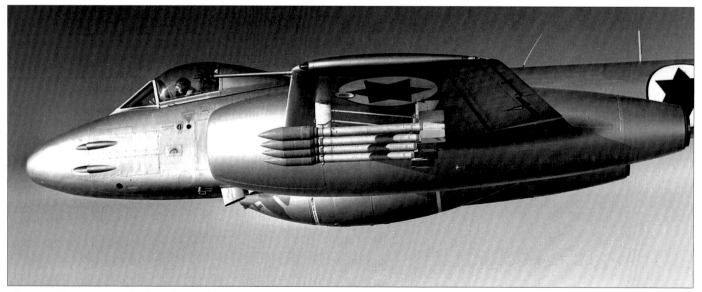

Above: Israel's Meteor F 8s fought with and defeated Egyptian Vampires in 1955. From 1956 until 1961, when they were retired, the aircraft were mainly used in the ground-attack role, with rockets (seen here) and bombs.

Above: A factory-fresh Meteor F 3, the first version produced in large quantities. This F 3 was later converted into a U 16 target drone.

Meteors were developed through a succession of fighter/ground-attack and reconnaissance models. The most important was probably the F 8, with Derwent 8 engines, a taller tail and longer fuselage. The Royal Australian Air Force used them in Korea, but by then the swept-wing Mikoyan-Gurevich MiG-15 was on the scene, and the Aussies suffered a poor kill-to-loss ratio.

DIFFICULT HANDLING

The Meteor had very poor handling at low speed with one engine out. Training for an engine failure on takeoff or landing caused more accidents than did actual engine failures. There was no radar in most models, and flying into bad weather followed by the ground caused further accidents. The two-seat models lacked ejection seats, as did the early

fighters. In RAF service alone, there were 890 Meteors lost in total, 150 of them in 1952 alone.

A series of night-fighter variants were produced by Armstrong Whitworth from 1949. The NF 11 had a long nose with an American-built radar inside, a second seat for a radar operator, and cannon in the outer wings rather than the fuselage. An NF 13 model suited to tropical conditions and an improved NF 14 followed. As well as the RAF, Israel, Egypt and Syria used the night-fighter Meteors. Single-seaters and trainers were exported to nine countries: Australia, Belgium, Denmark, Ecuador, Egypt, France, Israel, the Netherlands and Syria. Others were used by civilian organizations as target tugs and ejection-seat testbeds. The last fully military Meteors were probably those of the Israeli Air Force, used as trainers until 1970.

Lockheed P-80 Shooting Star

The P-80 was the United States' first successful jet fighter, although it was quickly superseded by swept-wing aircraft. It was adapted to become the most successful jet trainer ever built and eventually evolved into the Lockheed F-94 Starfire.

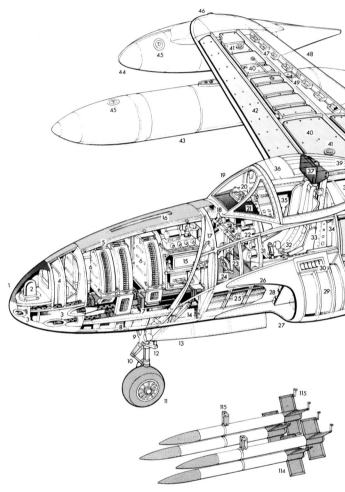

F-80C SHOOTING STAR (EARLY) SPECIFICATION

Dimensions

Length: 34 ft 5 in (10.49 m)
Height: 11 ft 3 in (3.42 m)
Wingspan: 38 ft 9 in (11.81 m)
Wing area: 237.5 sq ft (22.07 m²)

Power plant

One Allison J33-A-23/35 turbojet rated at 4,600 lb st (20.7 kN) dry, and 5,200 lb st (23.4 kN) with water injection

Weights

Empty: 8,420 lb (3819 kg)
Gross: 12,200 lb (5534 kg)
Maximum takeoff: 16,856 lb (7646 kg)

Fuel

Fuel (normal): 425 gal (1609 liters)
Fuel (maximum): 755 gal (2858 liters) including drop tanks

Performance

Maximum level speed at sea level: 594 mph (956 km/h)
Maximum level speed at 25,000 ft (7620 m): 543 mph (874 km/h)
Cruising speed: 439 mph (707 km/h)
Landing speed: 122 mph (196 km/h)
Climb to altitude: climb to 25,000 ft (7620 m) in 7 minutes
Rate of climb: 6,870 ft (2094 m) per minute
Service ceiling: 46,800 ft (14,265 m)

Range

Range: 825 miles (1328 km)
Maximum range: 1,380 miles (2221 km)

Armament

Four 0.50-in (12.7-mm) Colt-Browning M3 machine guns each with 300 rounds, plus ten 5-in (127-mm) HVARs or two 1,000-lb (454-kg) bombs

Cutaway Key

1 Nose antenna fairing
2 D/F loop aerial
3 Machine-gun muzzles
4 Oxygen tank
5 Nose compartment access panel
6 Port and starboard ammunition boxes, 300 rounds per gun
7 0.5-in (12.7-mm) machine guns
8 Spent cartridge case and link ejector chutes
9 Landing and taxiing lamps
10 Nosewheel leg torque scissors
11 Nosewheel
12 Steering linkage
13 Nosewheel doors
14 Retraction strut
15 Radio and electrical equipment bay
16 External canopy-
release handle
17 Cockpit front bulkhead
18 Windshield heater duct
19 Bulletproof windshield panel
20 Reflector gunsight
21 Instrument panel shield
22 Instrument panel
23 Rudder pedals
24 Cockpit floor level
25 Nosewheel bay
26 Intake lip fairing
27 Port air intake
28 Boundary layer bleed air duct
29 Intake ducting
30 Boundary layer air exit louvers
31 Engine throttle control
32 Safety harness
33 Pilot's ejection seat
34 Cockpit rear bulkhead
35 Starboard side console panel
36 Sliding cockpit canopy cover
37 Ejection seat headrest
38 Canopy aft decking
39 D/F sense antenna
40 Starboard wing fuel tanks
41 Fuel filler caps
42 Leading-edge tank
43 Fletcher-type tip tank, capacity 265 gal (1003 liters)
44 Tip tank, capacity 165 gal (625 liters)
45 Tip-tank filler cap
46 Starboard navigation light
47 Aileron balance weights
48 Starboard aileron
49 Aileron hinge control
50 Trailing-edge fuel tank

51 Starboard split trailing-edge flap
52 Flap control links
53 Fuselage fuel tank, total internal capacity 657 gal (2487 liters)
54 Fuselage main longeron
55 Center fuselage frames
56 Intake trunking
57 Main undercarriage wheel well
58 Wing spar attachment joints
59 Pneumatic reservoir
60 Hydraulic accumulator
61 Control access panel

62 Spring-loaded intake pressure relief doors
63 Allison J33-A-23 centrifugal-flow turbojet engine
64 Rear fuselage break point
65 Rear fuselage attachment bolts (three)
66 Elevator control rods
67 Jet pipe bracing cable
68 Fin-root fillet
69 Elevator control link
70 Starboard tailplane
71 Starboard elevator
72 Fin construction
73 Pitot tube

74 Fintip communications antenna fairing
75 Rudder mass balance
76 Rudder construction
77 Fixed tab
78 Elevator and rudder hinge control
79 Tail navigation light
80 Jet pipe nozzle
81 Elevator tabs
82 Port elevator construction
83 Elevator mass balance
84 Tailplane construction
85 Fin/tailplane attachment joints

86 Tailplane fillet fairing
87 Jet pipe mounting rail
88 Rear fuselage frame and stringer construction
89 Gyrosyn radio compass flux valve
90 Fuselage skin plating
91 Jet pipe support frame
92 Trailing-edge wing root fillet
93 Flap drive motor
94 Port split trailing-edge flap
95 Flap shield ribs
96 Trailing-edge fuel tank bay

97 Rear spar
98 Trailing-edge ribs
99 Port aileron tab
100 Aileron hinge control
101 Upper-skin panel aileron hinge line
102 Aileron construction
103 Wingtip fairing construction
104 Tip tank
105 Port navigation light
106 Tip-tank mounting and jettison control
107 Detachable lower wing skin panels
108 Port wing fuel-tank bays

109 Inter tank bay ribs
110 Front spar
111 Corrugated leading-edge inner skin
112 Port stores pylon
113 1,000-lb (454-kg) HE bomb
114 5-in (127-mm) HVAR ground-attack rockets (10 rockets maximum load)
115 HVAR mountings
116 Port mainwheel
117 Mainwheel doors
118 Wheel brake pad
119 Main undercarriage leg strut

120 Retraction jack
121 Upper skin panel wing stringers
122 Wing root leading-edge extension
123 Port ventral airbrake

"The name 'Shooting Star' fit the P-80 well. I felt that I was riding on a shooting star, that all my training and flying up to now were to prepare me for this airplane."
– Don Lopez, USAAF (US Army Air Forces) test pilot

FACTS

- Shooting Stars were the first U.S. jets to see operational service.

- Early P-80s had no ejection seats and a number of wartime aces were killed in test flying accidents.

- Many F-80s ended their careers by being turned into QF-80 pilotless drones, to act as targets and take air samples from atomic test sites.

P-80 SHOOTING STAR – VARIANTS

EF-80: Prone-pilot test aircraft.

XP-80: Prototype, one built.

XP-80A: Second prototype variant, two built.

YP-80A: 12 pre-production aircraft built.

XF-14: One built from YP-80A order. USAAF photo-reconnaissance prototype.

P-80A: 344 block 1-LO aircraft; 180 block 5-LO aircraft. Block 5 and all subsequent Shooting Stars were natural metal finish.

F-80A: USAF (US Air Force) designation of P-80A.

EF-80: Modified to test "prone pilot" cockpit positions.

F-14A: Conversions from P-80A, all redesignated FP-80A.

XFP-80A: Modified P-80A 44-85201 with hinged nose for camera equipment.

F-80A: Test aircraft with twin 0.5-in (12.7-mm) machine guns in oblique mount (similar to World War II German Schräge Musik), to study the ability to attack Soviet bombers from below.

F-80: With Schräge Musik configuration at full elevation.

FP-80A: 152 block 15-LO; operational photo-reconnaissance aircraft.

RF-80A: USAF designation of FP-80A; 66 F-80As modified to RF-80A standard.

ERF-80A: Modified P-80A 44-85042 with experimental nose contour.

XP-80B: Reconfigured P-80A with improved J-33 engine. One model built as a prototype for the P-80B.

P-80B: 209 block 1-LO; 31 block 5-LO; first model fitted with ejection seat.

F-80B: USAF designation of P-80B.

XP-80R: Modification of XP-80B to racer.

P-80C: 162 block 1-LO; 75 block 5-LO; 561 block 10-LO.

F-80C: USAF designation. Major P-80 production version.

RF-80: Upgraded photo-reconnaissance plane.

DF-80A: F-80As converted into drone directors.

QF-80A/QF-80C/QF-80F: Project Bad Boy F-80 conversions to target drones.

TP-80C: First designation for TF-80C trainer prototype.

TF-80C: Prototype for T-33.

TO-1: US Navy variant of F-80C.

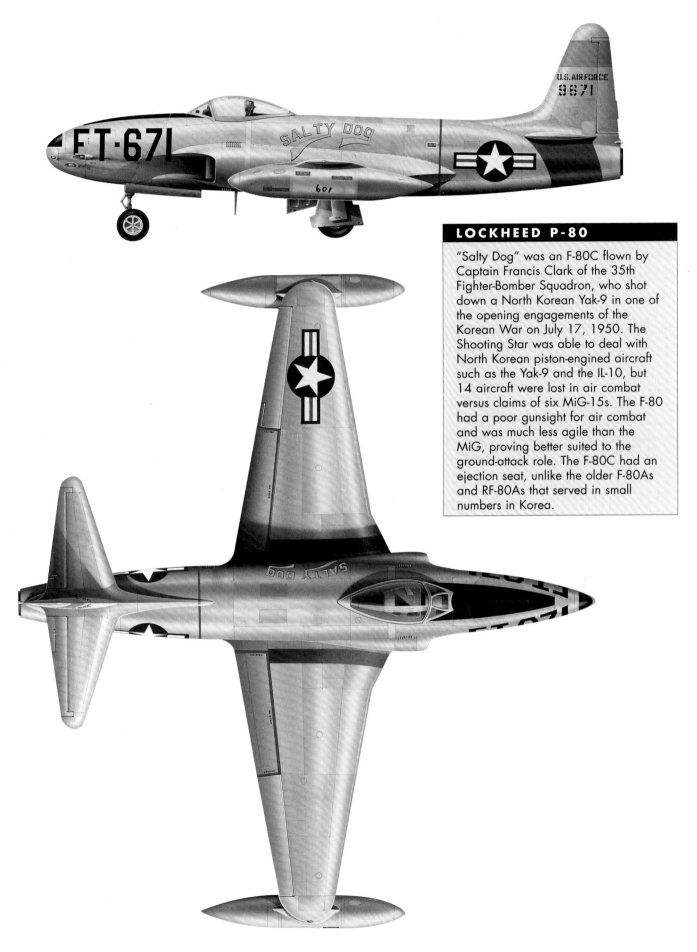

LOCKHEED P-80

"Salty Dog" was an F-80C flown by Captain Francis Clark of the 35th Fighter-Bomber Squadron, who shot down a North Korean Yak-9 in one of the opening engagements of the Korean War on July 17, 1950. The Shooting Star was able to deal with North Korean piston-engined aircraft such as the Yak-9 and the IL-10, but 14 aircraft were lost in air combat versus claims of six MiG-15s. The F-80 had a poor gunsight for air combat and was much less agile than the MiG, proving better suited to the ground-attack role. The F-80C had an ejection seat, unlike the older F-80As and RF-80As that served in small numbers in Korea.

The Unites States lagged behind Europe in jet aircraft development during World War II. The Bell XP-59 Airacomet flew in October 1942, before the Gloster Meteor, but was something of a dead end and Bell did not have the capacity to continue development.

In the spring of 1943, Lockheed offered its own design, which was accepted by the USAAF, which called for a flyable prototype in 180 days. Designer Clarence "Kelly" Johnson assembled a top team of engineers and began work in a warehouse in Burbank, Los Angeles. This was the start of the famous "Skunk Works," which was to develop many successful combat and reconnaissance aircraft over the years.

PROTOTYPE AND DEVELOPMENT

The bottle-green XP-80 prototype, named "Lulu Belle," flew from Muroc Dry Lake (later to become Edwards Air Force Base) in January 1944, only 143 days after the go-ahead. Its appearance was little different to all the P-80s and F-80s to follow, although after early testing the wing and tail tips were rounded off in a move to improve stability. The XP-80 was powered by a British engine, the Halford H1B, supplied as a goodwill gesture. The following aircraft used the General Electric I-40, a license-built Whittle engine later mass-produced as the J33 by both GE and Allison. Four YP-80A development aircraft were sent to Europe in late 1944 and two went on to Italy, where they flew a few operational missions before the war's end, although they never met any opposition.

The P-80A was the first major production version. Armament was less than most U.S. piston-engined wartime

Above: The P-80 pilot's view was dominated by the large gunsight, which proved inadequate for use in air combat at jet speeds.

fighters – four 0.50-in (12.7-mm) machine guns, with the ability to carry a couple of bombs. The P-80B introduced the first ejection seat in a production U.S. aircraft, as well as other improvements. In June 1948, the new United States Air Force revised its designation system, exchanging "P" for "pursuit" for "F" for "fighter." The P-80C was heavier and more powerful, and the main U.S. jet aircraft in Asia at the time of the outbreak of the Korean War.

F-80s destroyed several North Korean Il-10 propeller-driven attack aircraft in some of the first aerial action of the war in July 1950, and helped to win battlefield air superiority until that situation was reversed with the introduction of Soviet-built MiG-15s in November. The F-80 soon scored the first victory in aerial combat between two jet-propelled

Above: The XP-80R was a modified P-80B used to set the first speed record of more than 623 mph (1,000 km/h) in June 1947.

Above: The F-80 was used for the first U.S. jet display team, the "Acrojets," from 1948 to 1950. These aircraft all have their ventral airbrakes deployed.

aircraft when Lieutenant Russell Brown shot down a MiG-15 over Korea, but generally the MiG outclassed the Shooting Star, which was largely relegated to ground-attack missions.

TWO-SEAT CONVERSION

The F-80 was supplied to a number of Latin American air forces from the late 1940s, including those of Peru, Uruguay and Chile, but was otherwise not widely exported. The T-33 trainer, however, a straightforward two-seat conversion of the F-80, was a huge export success. More than 30 nations used T-33s and, despite its fixed armament of only two machine

guns, the aircraft were sometimes used as fighters. While the last F-80s were retired by Uruguay in the 1970s, T-33s continue to serve with a handful of nations.

A development of the T-33 was the Lockheed F-94, which entered service in 1950. The YF-94 prototypes were rebuilt T-33 airframes, but later models diverged from the original design. The ultimate F-94C Starfire had a new wing and tail, and large fixed wingtip tanks and mid-wing rocket pods, as well as rockets and radar mounted in the nose and an afterburning J33 engine. F-94s served only with the USAF's Air Defense Command.

De Havilland Vampire and Venom

The Vampire, the second jet fighter to enter service with the Royal Air Force, may not have seen active combat in World War II, but it achieved several important aviation milestones. The Venom was developed from the Vampire and was intended to be its replacement.

Cutaway Key

1 Ciné camera port
2 Cockpit fresh air intake
3 Nosewheel leg door
4 Pivoted axle nosewheel suspension
5 Anti-shimmy nosewheel tire
6 Nose undercarriage leg strut
7 Nosewheel door
8 Cannon muzzle blast trough
9 Nosewheel hydraulic jack
10 Nose undercarriage pivot fixing
11 Radio
12 Gun camera
13 Windshield fluid de-icing reservoir
14 Armored instrument access panel
15 Cockpit front bulkhead
16 Rudder pedals
17 Cockpit floor level
18 Nosewheel housing
19 Instrument panel
20 Reflector gunsight
21 Windshield panels
22 Side console switch panel
23 Control column
24 Engine throttle
25 Tailplane trim handwheel
26 Undercarriage and flap selector levers
27 Control linkage
28 Cannon barrels beneath cockpit floor
29 Pull-out boarding step
30 Control system cable compensator
31 Emergency hydraulic hand pump
32 Pilot's seat
33 Safety harness
34 Sliding canopy rails
35 Cockpit heater
36 Cockpit canopy cover
37 Pilot's head and back armor
38 Hydraulic system reservoir
39 Radio equipment bay
40 Ammunition tanks (150 rounds per gun)
41 Plywood/balsa/plywood fuselage skinning
42 Boundary layer splitter
43 Port engine air intake
44 Ventral gun bay (4 x 0.79-in [0.79-in (20-mm)] Hispano cannon)
45 Spent cartridge case and link ejector chute
46 Cannon bay access panel
47 Cockpit heating and pressurizing intake
48 Intake ducting
49 Fuselage/front spar attachment joint
50 Fuselage/main spar attachment joint
51 Engine bay fire wall
52 Fuselage fuel tank (total internal system capacity 480 gal/1818 liters)
53 Fuel filler cap
54 Wooden skin section fabric covering
55 Cockpit air heat exchanger
56 Engine bearer struts
57 de Havilland Goblin DGn 2 centrifugal-flow turbojet
58 Cabin blower
59 Engine accessories
60 Engine bay access panels
61 Starboard wing root fuel tank

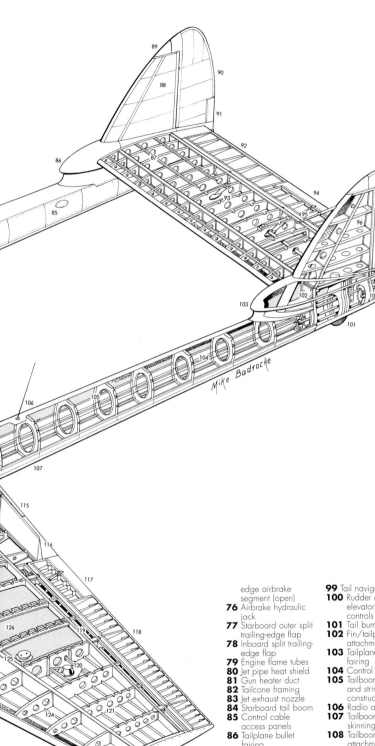

Mike Badrocke

VAMPIRE F MK III SPECIFICATION

Dimensions

Length: 30 ft 9 in (9.37 m)
Height: 8 ft 10 in (2.69 m)
Wingspan: 40 ft (12.19 m)
Wing area: 266 sq ft (24.71 m²)
Wing loading: 39.4 lb/sq ft (192 kg/m²)

Power plant

One de Havilland Goblin 2 centrifugal-flow turbojet
   rated at 3,100 lb st (14 kN)

Weights

Empty: 7,134 lb (3236 kg)
Maximum takeoff: 12,170 lb (5520 kg)

Fuel

Internal fuel: 636 gal (2409 liters)
External fuel: 240 gal (909 liters) in drop tanks

Performance

Maximum level speed at sea level: 531 mph
   (855 km/h)
Maximum level speed at 17,500 ft (5334 m):
   525 mph (845 km/h)
Maximum level speed at 30,000 ft (9144 m):
   505 mph (813 km/h)
Rate of climb at sea level: 4,375 ft (1334 m) per minute
Rate of climb at 20,000 ft (6096 m): 2,500 ft
   (762 m) per minute
Rate of climb at 40,000 ft (1,2192 m): 990 ft (302 m)
   per minute
Service ceiling: 43,500 ft (13,259 m)
Takeoff run to 50 ft (15.24 m) at maximum weight:
   3,540 ft (1079 m)
Landing run from 50 ft (15.24 m): 3,300 ft (1006 m)

Range and endurance

Range at sea level: 590 miles (949 km) at 350 mph
   (463 km/h)
Range at 30,000 ft (9144 m): 1,145 miles (1843 km)
   at 350 mph (463 km/h)
Patrol duration at sea level: 2 hours at 220 mph
   (354 km/h)
Patrol duration at 30,000 ft (9144 m): 2 hours 35 mins
   at 220 mph (354 km/h)

Armament

Four 0.79-in (20-mm) Hispano cannon mounted in the
front of the lower fuselage. Ammunition of 150 rounds
per gun, giving a total of 600 rounds

edge airbrake
segment (open)
76 Airbrake hydraulic
jack
77 Starboard outer split
trailing-edge flap
78 Inboard split trailing-
edge flap
79 Engine flame tubes
80 Jet pipe heat shield
81 Gun heater duct
82 Tailcone framing
83 Jet exhaust nozzle
84 Starboard tail boom
85 Control cable
access panels
86 Tailplane bullet
fairing
87 Tailplane
construction
88 Starboard fin
89 Rudder mass
balance
90 Starboard rudder
91 Rudder trim tab
92 Elevator construction
93 Ventral elevator
mass balance
weights
94 Elevator tab
95 Pitot tube
96 Port fin construction
97 Port rudder
98 Rudder trim tab

99 Tail navigation light
100 Rudder and
elevator hinge
controls
101 Tail bumper
102 Fin/tailplane
attachment joint
103 Tailplane bullet
fairing
104 Control cable runs
105 Tailboom frame
and stringer
construction
106 Radio aerial mast
107 Tailboom
skinning
108 Tailboom
attachment
ring joint
109 Trailing-edge
root fillet
110 Port inboard split
trailing-edge flap
111 Flap
interconnection
112 Hydraulic flap
jack
113 False rear spar
114 Flap shield ribs
115 Port outboard split
trailing-edge flap
116 Rotating trailing-
edge segment
airbrake, open

117 Aileron tab
118 Port aileron
construction
119 Aileron mass
balance weights
120 Retractable
landing/taxiing
lamp
121 Wingrib and
stringer
construction
122 Wingtip fairing
123 Port navigation
light
124 Leading-edge
nose ribs
125 Fuel filler cap

126 Port wing main
fuel tanks
127 Fuel tank
interconnection
128 Pylon attachment
rib
129 Port 134-gal
(509-liter) drop
tank
130 Drop-tank pylon
131 Port mainwheel
132 Mainwheel door
actuating linkage
133 Port mainwheel
bay
134 Retraction linkages
and locks

135 Main
undercarriage leg
strut pivot fixing
136 Wing root fuel
tank
137 Fuel filler cap
138 Main spar
139 Wing stringers
140 Leading-edge
fuel tank
141 Rocket launcher
rail
142 60-lb (27-kg)
unguided ground-
attack rocket
143 500-lb (227-kg)
HE bomb

62 Starboard main
undercarriage,
retracted position
63 Leading-edge
fuel tank
64 Starboard drop
tank (134 gal/
509 liters)
65 Drop-tank pylon
66 Starboard wing
fuel tanks
67 Fuel filler cap

68 Gyrosyn compass
remote transmitter
69 Starboard
navigation light
70 Wingtip fairing
71 Starboard aileron
72 Aileron mass
balance weights
73 Trim tab
74 Aileron hinge
control
75 Starboard trailing-

"As used by the RAF, the single-seat Vampires were one of the few series-produced jet fighters to not have ejection seats."

Above: The first production Vampire was the F1. The example seen here is carrying two underwing drop tanks.

FACTS

- The Vampire had a wooden fuselage covered with doped fabric, but the wings and tail section were mainly aluminium.

- In 1948, the Vampire became the first jet aircraft to cross the Atlantic Ocean.

- The Vampire was also the first jet aircraft to land on and take off from an aircraft carrier.

DE HAVILLAND DH 100 VAMPIRE – VARIANTS

DH 100: Three prototypes.

Mk I: Single-seat fighter version for the RAF.

Mk II: Three prototypes, with Rolls-Royce Nene turbojet engine.

F 3: Single-seat fighter for the RAF.

Mk IV: Nene-engined project, not built.

FB 5: Single-seat fighter-bomber version.

FB 6: Single-seat fighter-bomber. Powered by a Goblin 3 turbojet.

Mk 8: Ghost-engined, one conversion from Mk 1.

FB 9: Tropicalized fighter-bomber through air-conditioning a Mk 5.

Mk 10 or DH 113 Vampire: Goblin-powered two-seat prototype.

NF 10: Two-seat RAF night-fighter version.

Sea Vampire Mk10: Prototype for deck trials. One conversion.

Mk 11 or DH 115 Vampire Trainer: Private venture, two-seat jet trainer prototype.

T 11: Two-seat RAF training version for the RAF.

Sea Vampire F 20: Naval version of the FB 5.

Sea Vampire Mk 21: Three aircraft converted for trials.

Sea Vampire T 22: Two-seat training version for the Royal Navy.

FB 25: B 5 variants.

F 30: Single-seat RAAF fighter-bomber.

FB 31: Nene-engined.

F 32: One Australian conversion with air-conditioning.

T 33: Two-seat training version. Powered by the Goblin turbojet.

T 34: Two-seat training version for the Royal Australian Navy.

T 34A: Vampire T 34s fitted with ejector seats.

T 35: Modified two-seat training version.

T 35A: T33 conversions to T35 configuration.

FB 50: Exported to Sweden as the J 28B.

FB 51: Export prototype (one conversion) to France.

FB 52: Export version of Mk 6.

FB 52A: Single-seat fighter-bomber for the Italian Air Force.

FB 53: Single-seat fighter-bomber for France's Armée de l'Air as the Sud-Est SE 535 Mistral.

NF 54: Export version of Vampire NF 10 for the Italian Air Force.

T 55: Export version of the DH 115 trainer.

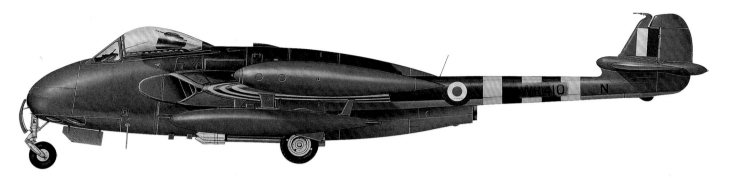

DE HAVILLAND VENOM FB MK 4

The Venom was a development of the Vampire with numerous refinements. Obvious recognition features were the swept-wing leading edge and the wingtip fuel tanks. Unlike the RAF's Vampires and the Mk 1 Venom, the FB 4 model, illustrated, had an ejection seat. This FB 4 wears the "Suez" stripes applied to all British and French tactical aircraft as a recognition feature during the Suez Campaign in October 1956, when Venoms were flown from Cyprus and Jordan. It carries eight rocket projectiles (RPs) on rails under the intakes. In 1957, Venom WR410 went on to No. 6 Squadron at RAF Benson, Oxfordshire. It ended its career in 1960, being struck off at RAF Eastleigh (Nairobi), Kenya.

Above: The FB 5 was the definitive RAF Vampire version. The ports for the four 0.79-in (20-mm) Hispano cannon can be clearly seen in this view.

While Gloster worked on the twin-engined Meteor, de Havilland was designing a very different single-engined fighter based around the Halford H1 centrifugal-flow engine. This was another design by Frank Whittle, differing from the axial-flow engines of the Meteor in having a large impeller fan with combustion chambers arranged around the outside, which gave it a large diameter.

The prototype DH 100 was first flown in September 1943, but the second aircraft was delayed when its intended engine was sent to the United States to replace one Lockheed had damaged in early trials of the XP-80. At this time, the aircraft was code-named "Spider Crab," but was officially named "Vampire" in May 1944. The H1 engine became the de Havilland Goblin.

The pilot, engine and armament were all enclosed in a central pod to which the wings were attached, as were the tail booms, which were connected by a tailplane and elevator. Under the cockpit were four 0.79-in (20-mm) Hispano cannon, in the same configuration as the Mosquito fighter-bombers. The same design team was behind both aircraft, and there were many other common features, not least that the fuselage was made of wood. The Vampire nosewheel and leg were the same as the Mosquito tailwheel, and the canopy of the two-seat T 11 was the same as a Mosquito's as well.

As used by the RAF, the single-seat Vampires were one of the few series-produced jet fighters to not have ejection seats. Later export fighters and twin-seaters usually had Martin Baker Mk 3 seats.

OPERATIONAL SQUADRONS

With priority given to getting the Meteor into service, the Vampire did not reach operational squadrons before World War II's end. The first Vampire F 1s joined RAF squadrons from March 1946 as interceptors. F 2s with the Rolls-Royce Nene engine were built under license in Australia and France (as the Sud-Est Mistral). The F 3 had increased internal fuel and provision for drop tanks.

The definitive single-seater, the FB 5, was intended more as a fighter-bomber, with underside armor plate and pylons for rockets and bombs. As well as being supplied in large numbers to the RAF (more than 1,200), it became the basis of numerous export models such as the FB 6 (Switzerland), FB 51 (France) and FB 52 (India and others.) The FB 9 had an air conditioner for use in hot climates and was mainly operated by the RAF, although Rhodesia (now Zimbabwe) also used them.

Vampires rarely engaged in actual air-to-air combat. Although they were nimble and delightful to fly, they were quickly outmoded by Mikoyan-Gurevich MiG-15s and other swept-wing jets. Israeli Mystéres claimed a number of Egyptian Vampires over the Sinai in 1956. The RAF used them in conflicts in Aden and Kenya against various rebel groups. The rocket armament proved particularly effective in the ground-attack role.

TWO-SEAT TRAINER

The two-seat trainer version, the T 11, was first flown in 1950. With side-by-side seats it had a wide nose, which was used for an airborne intercept (AI) radar in the NF 10 night-fighter variant, which was sold to India and Italy, as well as used by the RAF. Armament remained four cannon. T 11s and their derivatives were used by most of the export customers as jet trainers and weapons trainers.

Vampires were phased out of frontline RAF service in the 1960s, but remained with some export customers, including Switzerland, into the 1980s. In many cases, they

Above: Instrumentation on the Vampire was largely the same as most wartime British fighters, including the standard six-instrument blind flying panel situated in the center.

were replaced by the DH 112 Venom, a larger and more powerful outgrowth of the Vampire design. With its thinner wing with swept leading edge and more powerful engine, the Venom was 100 mph (160 km/h) faster than the Vampire.

Above: The main visual difference between the F 1, seen here, and the FB 5 was found in the tailfin shapes.

North American F-86 Sabre

The F-86 Sabre was the classic jet fighter of the early Cold War era. Although it was soon superseded in frontline USAF service, it went on to find use around the world in a myriad of different versions.

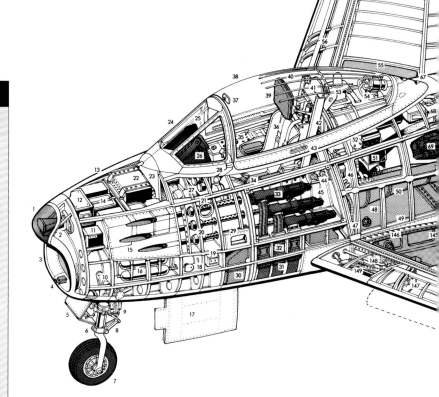

F-86E SABRE SPECIFICATION

Dimensions

Length: 37 ft (11.27 m)
Height: 14 ft (4.26 m)
Wingspan: 37 ft (11.27 m)
Wing area: 288 sq ft (26.75 m²)

Power plant

One General Electric J47-GE-13 turbojet rated at 5,450 lb (24.24 kN) static thrust

Weights

Empty: 10,555 lb (4788 kg)
Normal loaded: 16,346 lb (7414 kg)
Maximum takeoff: 17,806 lb (8077 kg)

Fuel

Normal internal fuel: 435 gal (1646 liters)
Maximum internal fuel: 675 gal (2555 liters)

Performance

Maximum level speed clean at 35,000 ft (10,688 m): 601 mph (967 km/h)
Maximum level speed clean at low level: 679 mph (1093 km/h)
Cruising speed: 537 mph (864 km/h)
Stalling speed: 123 mph (198 km/h)
Climb to 30,000 ft (9144 m): 6 minutes 18 seconds
Service ceiling: 47,200 ft (14,387 m)
Range: 848 miles (1365 km)
Maximum range: 1,022 miles (1645 km)

Armament

Primary armament consisted of six 0.5-in (12.7-mm) Colt-Browning machine guns mounted in the forward fuselage with a total of 1,800 rounds; provision for either two 1,000-lb (454-kg) bombs or 16 0.5-in (12.7-mm) rocket projectiles mounted on underwing racks, in place of two 120-gal (454-liter) drop tanks, a variety of other ordnance loads could also be carried.

Cutaway Key

1 Radome
2 Radar antenna
3 Engine air intake
4 Gun camera
5 Nosewheel leg doors
6 Nose undercarriage leg strut
7 Nosewheel
8 Torque scissor links
9 Steering control valve
10 Nose undercarriage pivot fixing
11 Sight amplifier
12 Radio and electronics equipment bay
13 Electronics bay access panel
14 Battery
15 Gun muzzle blast troughs
16 Oxygen bottles
17 Nosewheel bay doors
18 Oxygen servicing point
19 Canopy switches
20 Machine-gun barrel mountings
21 Hydraulic system test connections
22 Radio transmitter
23 Cockpit armored bulkhead
24 Windshield panels
25 A-1CM radar gunsight
26 Instrument panel shield
27 Instrument panel
28 Control column
29 Kick-in boarding step
30 Used cartridge case collector box
31 Ammunition boxes (267 rounds per gun)
32 Ammunition feed chutes
33 0.5-in (12.7-mm) Colt Browning machine guns
34 Engine throttle
35 Starboard side console panel
36 North American ejection seat
37 Rear-view mirror
38 Sliding cockpit canopy cover
39 Ejection seat headrest
40 ADF sense aerials
41 Pilot's back armor
42 Ejection-seat guide rails
43 Canopy handle
44 Cockpit pressure valves
45 Armored side panels
46 Tailplane trim actuator
47 Fuselage/front spar main frame
48 Forward fuselage fuel tank (total internal fuel capacity 435 gal/1646 liters)
49 Fuselage lower longeron
50 Intake trunking
51 Rear radio and electronics bay
52 Canopy emergency release handle
53 ADF loop aerial
54 Cockpit pressure relief valve
55 Starboard wing fuel tank
56 Leading-edge slat guide rails
57 Starboard automatic leading-edge slat, open
58 Cable drive to aileron actuator
59 Pitot tube
60 Starboard navigation light
61 Wingtip fairing
62 Starboard aileron
63 Aileron hydraulic control unit
64 Aileron balance
65 Starboard slotted flap, down position
66 Flap guide rail
67 Upward identification light
68 Air-conditioning

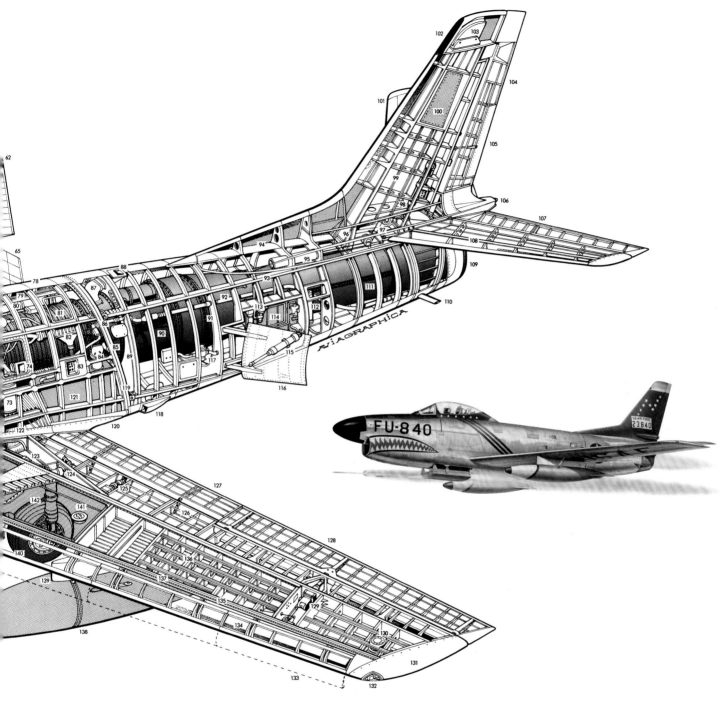

AiAGRAPHiCA

FU·840

23840

plant	**80** Starboard side oil tank	**92** Fuel jettison pipe	**105** Rudder trim tab	**117** Hydraulic system emergency pump
69 Intake fairing starter/generator	**81** General Electric J47-GE-27 turbojet	**93** Fuselage top longeron	**106** Tail navigation light	**118** Cooling air intake
70 Fuselage/rear spar main frame	**82** Bleed air system primary heat exchanger	**94** Fin/tailplane root fillet fairing	**107** Port elevator/ tailplane flap	**119** Lower longeron joint
71 Hydraulic system reservoirs	**83** Ground power connections	**95** Control cable duct	**108** All-moving tailplane construction	**120** Trailing-edge root fillet
72 Longeron/main frame joint	**84** Fuel filler cap	**96** Fin spar attachment joint	**109** Engine exhaust nozzle	**121** Aft main fuel tank
73 Fuel filter de-icing fluid tank	**85** Fuselage break point sloping frame (engine removal)	**97** Tailplane/rudder control cables	**110** Fuel jettison pipe	**122** Main undercarriage wheel bay
74 Cooling air outlet	**86** Upper longeron joint	**98** All-moving tailplane hydraulic jack	**111** Heat-shielded jet pipe	**123** Hydraulic retraction jack
75 Engine equipment access panel	**87** Engine bay air cooling duct	**99** Tailfin construction	**112** Power control compensator	**124** Main undercarriage pivot fixing
76 Heat exchanger exhaust duct	**88** Cooling air outlet	**100** Flush HF aerial panel	**113** Emergency hydraulic valves	**125** Hydraulic flap jack
77 Engine suspension links	**89** Engine firewall bulkhead	**101** Starboard tailplane	**114** Airbrake housing	**126** Flap shield ribs
78 Fuselage skin plating	**90** Engine flame cans	**102** Fintip dielectric aerial fairing	**115** Airbrake hydraulic jack	**127** Port slotted flaps
79 Engine withdrawal rail	**91** Rear fuselage framing	**103** ADF aerial	**116** Port airbrake (open)	**128** Port aileron construction

129 Aileron hydraulic power control unit	**139** Drop-tank pylon
130 Gyro compass remote transmitter	**140** Port main wheel
131 Wingtip fairing	**141** Fuel filler cap
132 Port navigation light	**142** Main undercarriage leg strut
133 Port automatic leading-edge slat, open position	**143** Fuel-tank bay corrugated double skin
134 Leading-edge slat rib construction	**144** Port wing fuel tank
135 Front spar	**145** Tank interconnectors
136 Wing rib and stringer construction	**146** Skin panel attachment joint strap
137 Wing skin/ leading-edge piano-hinge attachment joint	**147** Slat guide rails
138 120-gal (454-liter) drop tank	**148** Fuel feeders
	149 Aileron cable drive

"For my money, the F-86E is the greatest jet aircraft I have ever flown from a pure handling aspect. It set standards in stability and control which are still held up as ideals to attain."
– Captain Eric "Winkle" Brown, Royal Navy

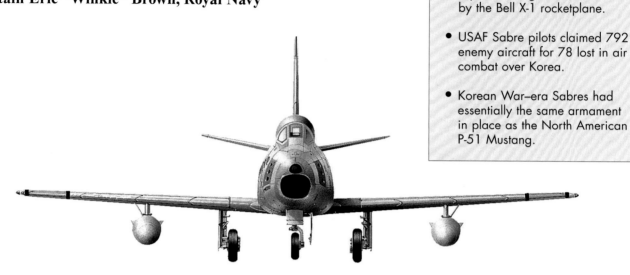

NORTH AMERICAN F-86 SABRE – VARIANTS

XF-86: Three prototypes, originally designated XP-86, North American model NA-140.

YF-86A: This was the first prototype fitted with a General Electric J47 turbojet engine.

F-86A: North American model NA-151 and NA-161.

DF-86A: A few F-86A conversions as drone directors.

RF-86A: F-86A conversions with three cameras for reconnaissance.

F-86B: Upgraded A-model with wider fuselage and larger tires, but delivered as F-86A-5, North American model NA-152.

F-86C: Original designation for the YF-93A. North American model NA-157.

YF-86D: Prototype all-weather interceptor originally ordered as YF-95A; two built but designation changed to YF-86D. North American model NA-164.

F-86D: Production interceptor originally designated F-95A.

F-86E: Improved flight control system and an "all-flying tail." North American model NA-170 and NA-172 (essentially the F-86F airframe with the F-86E engine).

F-86E(M): Designation for ex-RAF Sabres diverted to other NATO air forces.

QF-86E: Designation for surplus RCAF Sabre Mk. Vs modified to target drones.

F-86F: Uprated engine and larger "6-3" wing without leading-edge slats. North American model NA-172.

F-86F-2: Designation for aircraft modified to carry the M39 cannon in place of the M3 0.50-caliber machine gun "six-pack."

QF-86F: Former JASDF F-86F airframes converted to drones for use as targets by the U.S. Navy.

RF-86F: F-86F-30s converted with three cameras for reconnaissance.

TF-86F: Two F-86F converted to two-seat training configuration with lengthened fuselage and slatted wings under North American model NA-204.

YF-86H: Extensively redesigned fighter-bomber model with deeper fuselage, uprated engine, longer wings and power-boosted tailplane. Two built as North American model NA-187.

F-86H: Production model with Low Altitude Bombing System (LABS) and provision for nuclear weapon. North American model NA-187 and NA-203.

QF-86H: Target conversion of 29 airframes for use at the United States Naval Weapons Center.

F-86J: Single F-86A-5-NA flown with Orenda turbojet under North American model NA-167.

F-86E SABRE

This F-86E "Elenore 'E'" in the colors of the 25th Fighter Interceptor Squadron, 51st Fighter Wing, was flown by Major William T. Whisner from Suwon Air Base, South Korea, in 1952. Whisner was credited with 15½ victories in flying P-51s over Europe in World War II and added a further 5½ in Korea for a total of 21, although only 9½ are marked here. "Half" kills were credited when more than one pilot made damaging hits on an enemy that subsequently went down. The F-86E was an improvement on the F-86A, with an all-moving tailplane and leading-edge slats, which enhanced the aircraft's maneuverability, particularly at low level.

Above: The F-86F was the ultimate day-fighter Sabre with an all-moving tailplane and an unslatted "hard" wing. The excellent view from the cockpit can be seen as well. A basic ranging radar was fitted in the intake lip.

Two different proposals, plus the work of wartime German scientists, led to the F-86 Sabre, one of the classic jet fighters. In 1944, North American Aviation, maker of the P-51 Mustang and B-25 Mitchell, began work on a jet fighter for the U.S. Navy. Configured with a straight wing and a nose-mounted intake, this eventually became the FJ-1 Fury, one of the U.S. Navy's first jets. The U.S. Army Air Force took an interest and ordered a similar model as the XP-86, but before it was complete, captured German studies on the superiority of swept wings became available. Using this data, the XP-86 was revised, and emerged with a 35-degree swept wing and tail in 1947, flying in October.

The F-86A reached the USAF in March 1949. It was not immediately dispatched to Korea when fighting broke out in July 1950. When the Mikoyan-Gurevich MiG-15 appeared on the scene in November, Sabres were rushed to bases in the south and were soon engaging enemy jets in what became known as "MiG Alley," around the Yalu River. F-86Es with a "hard" (non-slatted) wing and F-86F fighter-bombers reached U.S. and South African squadrons by the war's end, which saw an official victory-to-loss ratio of 792 to 78 in aerial combat between USAF Sabres and the North Korean Air Force.

PROVING ITS WORTH

The MiG and Sabre were closely matched, with the former having a better climb rate and performance at high altitude, and heavier armament. The Sabre was a more stable gun platform and performed better at lower levels. Crucially, the American pilots were better trained than their North Korean,

Above: "Karen's Kart" was an F-86E assigned to the USAF's 51st Fighter Wing at Suwon Air Base, South Korea. The colored nose stripe denotes that this is the wing commander's aircraft.

Russian and Chinese adversaries. In fact, the Sabre was probably the most successful jet fighter in terms of both aerial victories and foreign sales and production.

Twenty-two users outside of the United States acquired new American-built F-86s, and they were also built under license by Canada, Australia and Japan. Canadian-built Sabres were supplied to several countries, including the United Kingdom, West Germany and South Africa. Some were even sold to the United States. Fifteen countries used the radar-equipped F-86D,

K and L "Sabre Dog" variants. Pakistani and Taiwanese Sabres also saw air combat. In 1958, Taiwan's F-86s made the first use of guided AAMs in combat, destroying several Chinese MiGs with AIM-9s in fighting over disputed islands.

The F-86D "Sabre Dog" was developed for Air Defense Command, with a Hughes radar in a prominent nose radome and "Mighty Mouse" rockets in a retractable tray under the forward fuselage. The F-86K, built mainly for export, had 1.18-in (30-mm) cannon insead. The F-86H, a dedicated strike variant, had a much deeper fuselage and provision for atomic weapons.

MAKING THE SABRE THEIR OWN

Both Australia and Canada developed their own versions of the Sabre. Canadair-built Sabres included the Mk 3, Mk 5 and Mk 6, each with versions of the Canadian-designed Orenda engine. Australia's Commonwealth Aircraft Corporation (CAC) built over 100 "Avon Sabres" in three different versions. To accommodate the Rolls-Royce Avon engine, fuselage depth was increased and the intake widened. Twin 1.18-in (30-mm) ADEN cannon were the standard armament. The Mk 31 and 32 versions could carry AIM-9s. Some were later supplied to Malaysia and Indonesia.

Above: The Sabre's cockpit was somewhat cluttered. The large instrument above the control column is the engine temperature gauge.

Mikoyan-Gurevich MiG-17 "Fresco"

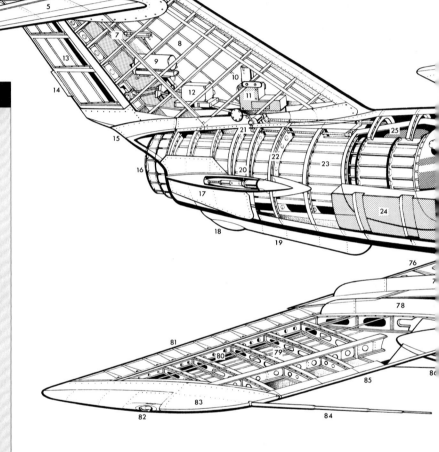

MIG-17F "FRESCO-C" SPECIFICATION

Dimensions

Wingspan: 31 ft 7 in (9.628 m)
Wing area: 243.27 sq ft (22.60 m²)
Length: 36 ft 11½ in (11.264 m)
Height: 12 ft 5½ in (3.80 m)
Wheel track: 12 ft 7½ in (3.849 m)
Wheel base: 11 ft ½ in (3.368 m)

Power plant

One Klimov VK-1F turbojet rated at 5,732 lb st
(29.50 kN) dry and 7,451 lb st (33.14 kN) with
afterburning

Weights

Empty equipped: 8,664 lb (3930 kg)
Maximum takeoff: 13,380 lb (6069 kg)

Fuel and load

Internal fuel: 2,579 lb (1170 kg)
External fuel: up to 1,444 lb (655 kg) in two 106- or
63-gal (400- or 240-liter) drop tanks
Maximum ordnance: 1,102 lb (500 kg)

Performance

Limiting Mach number: 1.03
Maximum level speed "clean" at 9,845 ft (3000 m):
594 kt (684 mph; 1100 km/h)
Maximum level speed "clean" at 32,810 ft (10,000 m):
578 kt (666 mph; 1071 km/h)
Speed limit with drop tanks: 486 kt (559 mph;
900 km/h)
Ferry range: 1,091 nm (1,255 miles; 2020 km) with
drop tanks
Combat radius: 378 nm (435 miles; 700 km) on a
hi-lo-hi attack mission with two 551-lb (250-kg) bombs
and two drop tanks
Maximum rate of climb at sea level: 12,795 ft
(3900 m) per minute
Service ceiling: 49,215 ft (15,000 m) at dry thrust and
54,460 ft (16,600 m) at afterburning thrust
Takeoff run: 1,936 ft (590 m) at normal takeoff weight
Landing run: 2,789 ft (850 m) at normal landing weight

**Mikoyan-Gurevich's second MiG jet was only slightly
more sophisticated than its predecessor, but nevertheless
it gave the United States a run for its money in Vietnam,
and saw action in many Middle East and African
conflicts from the 1960s onwards.**

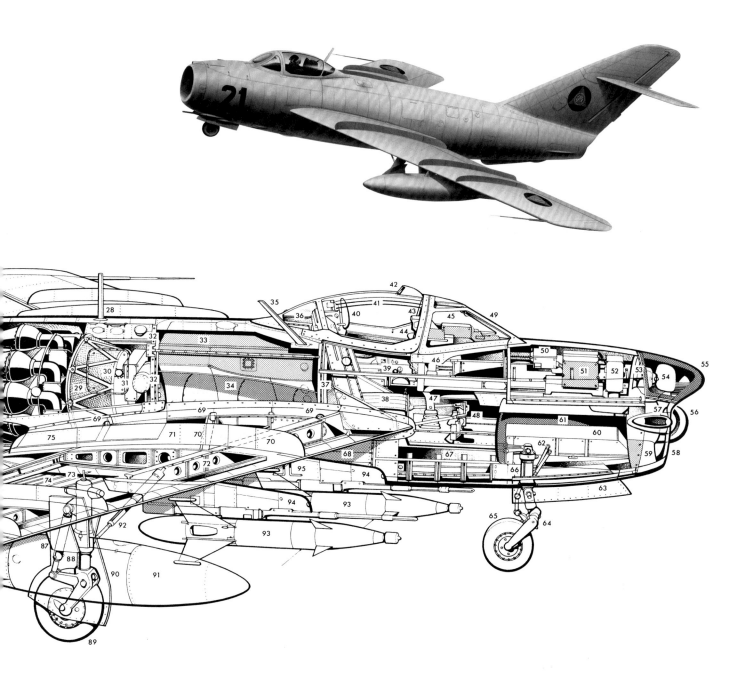

Cutaway Key

1 Rudder upper hinge/balance
2 Rudder (upper section)
3 Passive tail-warning radar unit
4 Rear navigation light
5 Fixed incidence tailplane
6 Elevator control linkage
7 Control lines
8 Tailfin construction
9 Transformer
10 Gyro compass
11 Magnetic amplifier for gyro
12 Tail-warning master unit
13 Rudder (lower section)
14 Rudder trim tab
15 Tailpipe shield
16 Afterburner nozzle
17 Starboard airbrake
18 Tail skid
19 Ventral strake
20 Airbrake hydraulic activator
21 Control linkage assembly
22 Rear fuselage structure
23 Afterburner pipe
24 Aft fuselage fuel tank
25 Afterburner outer casing
26 Klimov VK-1F turbojet
27 Inspection panel
28 IFF antenna
29 Engine intake grille
30 Inspection panel
31 Engine auxiliaries
32 Aft/forward fuselage breakpoint
33 Main fuselage fuel tank
34 Intake trunking
35 VHF antenna
36 Canopy track
37 Bulkhead
38 Ejector seat
39 Port control console (throttle quadrant)
40 Pilot's headrest
41 Canopy heating web
42 Rear-view mirror
43 Rocket sight
44 Radar-scope shield
45 Enlarged cockpit quarterlight
46 Instrument panel
47 Control column
48 Rudder pedals
49 Windshield
50 RDF ranging unit
51 VHF transmitter/receiver
52 Accumulator
53 Radar ranging unit
54 Radar scanner
55 Extended upper intake lip
56 AI scanner in central intake bullet
57 Combat camera housing
58 Bifurcated intake
59 Intake center-body
60 Center-section
61 Intake trunking
62 Nosewheel retraction radii
63 Nosewheel doors
64 Nosewheel fork
65 Forward-retracting nosewheel
66 Nosewheel strut
67 Forward fuselage members
68 Inboard-section wing leading edge
69 Three wing/fuselage attachment points
70 Y-section inner main spar
71 Inboard wing fence
72 Forward main spar
73 Undercarriage nosewheel well
74 Inner wing skinning
75 Split landing flap (inner section)
76 Split landing flap structure (outer section)
77 Center wing fence
78 Outboard wing fence
79 Wing construction
80 Rear spar
81 Aileron construction
82 Starboard navigation light
83 Wingtip
84 Starboard pitot head
85 Outboard-section wing leading edge
86 Auxiliary-tank fin
   indicator spigot
87 Triple-strut auxiliary-tank bracing
88 Mainwheel leg
89 Starboard mainwheel
90 Mainwheel door
91 Auxiliary tank (106-gal/400-liter capacity)
92 Mainwheel retraction rod
93 AA-1 "Alkali"-type beam-riding air-to-air missiles
94 Weapon pylons
95 Altimeter radio dipole (port outboard/starboard inboard)
   assembly

"No matter how good the F-4 is in air-to-air combat, it is no match for the MiG-17 if you fight the way they do – and that's World War II-style dog-fighting."
– Colonel Robin Olds, USAF Wing Commander, Vietnam War

FACTS

- The MiG-17 is slightly longer than the MiG-15, but with a shorter wingspan.

- The majority of MiG-17s were built outside of the USSR, in places such as Poland, Czechoslovakia and China.

- The MiG-17P became Russia's first operational radar-equipped single-seat fighter.

Above: A MiG-17F built in Poland in 1957 and restored by Bill Reesman in 1994. This example served with the Polish Air Force for 25 years during the height of the Cold War, when Poland was part of the Soviet Bloc.

MIG-17F – VARIANTS & OPERATORS

VARIANTS

I-300: Prototype.

MiG-17 ("Fresco-A"): Basic fighter version powered by VK-1 engine ("aircraft SI").

MiG-17A: Fighter version powered by VK-1A engine with longer lifespan.

MiG-17AS: Multirole conversion, fitted to carry unguided rockets and K-13 air-to-air missiles.

MiG-17P ("Fresco-B"): All-weather fighter equipped with Izumrud radar ("aircraft SP").

MiG-17F ("Fresco-C"): Basic fighter powered by VK-1F engine with afterburner ("aircraft SF").

MiG-17PF ("Fresco-D"): All-weather fighter version equipped with Izumrud radar and VK-1F engine ("aircraft SP-7F").

MiG-17PM/PFU ("Fresco-E"): Fighter version equipped with radar and K-5 (NATO: AA-1 "Alkali") air-to-air missiles ("aircraft SP-9").

MiG-17R: Reconnaissance aircraft with VK-1F engine and camera ("aircraft SR-2s").

MiG-17SN: Unproduced experimental variant with twin side intakes, no central intake, and nose redesigned to allow cannons to pivot, to engage ground targets.

Shenyang J-5: Some withdrawn aircraft were converted to remotely controlled targets.

OPERATORS

Air Forces
Afghanistan
Albania
Algeria
Angola
Bangladesh
Bulgaria
Burkina Faso
Cambodia
China
Congo
Cuba
Czechoslovakia
East Germany
Egypt
Ethiopia
Guinea
Guinea-Bissau
Indonesia
Iraq

Hungary
Libya
Madagascar
Mali
Mongolia
Morocco
Mozambique
Nigeria
North Korea
Pakistan
Poland
Romania
Somalia
Somaliland
Soviet Union
Sri Lanka
Sudan
Syria
Tanzania
Uganda
Vietnam
Yemen
Zimbabwe

Navies
China
Soviet Union

Anti-Aircraft Defense
Soviet Union

MIKOYAN-GUREVICH MIG-17F "FRESCO"

Indonesia began a re-equipment program in the late 1950s, obtaining a large amount of Soviet-made equipment, including about 30 MiG-17F "Fresco-Cs," later supplemented with a dozen Shenyang F-6s (Chinese-built versions of the MiG-19 "Farmer"), supplied by Communist China. This MiG-17F belonged to No. 11 Squadron of the Indonesian Air Force (Tentara Nasional Indonesia – Angkatan Udara, or TNI-AU), which operated an aerobatic team at one time.

Indonesia held back its MiG-17s and MiG-21s for the defense of Jakarta during the "Confrontation" with the United Kingdom and its allies over Borneo in 1962–64. RAF fighters including Gloster Javelins and English Electric Lightnings never tangled with the MiGs, although they did intercept Tu-16 bombers, C-130 transports and other TNI-AU aircraft.

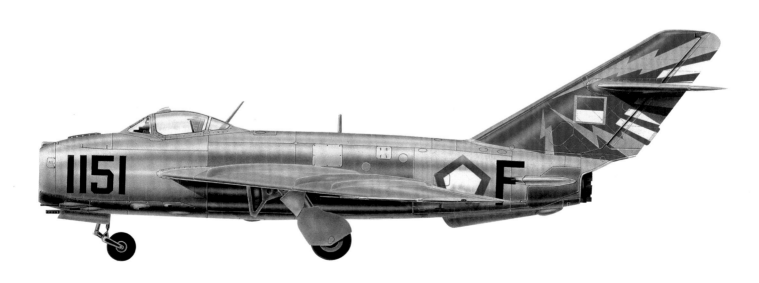

Even before the MiG-15 had entered service, an improved follow-up design was being developed. The MiG-17 prototype first flew under the designation SI-1 in January 1950 and, although it crashed on an early test flight, was adopted for production in September 1951.

In side view, the MiG-17 was very similar in appearance to its predecessor, although it had an enlarged tail fin, different-shaped airbrakes and a ventral fin under the lower fuselage. In plan view, the differences were more marked. An all-new wing, sometimes described as being of "scimitar"

configuration, was fitted. It was swept at 49 degrees in the inboard section and 45.5 degrees outboard. Three prominent wing fences were fitted.

ADDITIONAL WEAPONRY

The engine fitted to the new version of the MiG was the Klimov VK-1A turbojet, replaced soon after the MiG-17's introduction by the VK-1F with afterburner. The afterburner-equipped aircraft were designated MiG-17F by the Soviet Union and "Fresco-C" by Western powers. The MiG-17's gun armament was the same as the MiG-15's: three nose-mounted cannon. Additionally, however, the "Fresco" could carry bombs or rocket pods for ground-attack missions.

Above: Egypt operated nearly 500 MiG-17s over the years. These examples wear the roundel in use by the Egyptian Air Force up to 1958. Many "Frescos" were destroyed on the ground in 1967, as the result of an attack by the Israeli Air Force during the Six-Day War.

Above: In a spin, the MiG-17 pilot began recovery by aligning the joystick with the white stripe running down the center of the instrument panel.

VARIATIONS ON A THEME

In a similar way to how the North American F-86 Sabre spawned the F-86D derivative with an air interception radar and afterburner, the basic MiG-17 begat the MiG-17PF with a nose-mounted radar. The Izumrud RP-1 radar was in two parts – a search radar in the upper intake lip and a fire control set for weapons aiming in a cone set within the intake. This allowed the aircraft a limited night and bad-weather capability, but had to be used in conjunction with ground-based radar and direction by operators on the ground to get the MiG anywhere near the target. MiG-17PFs were designated "Fresco-D" and usually had three 0.91-in (23-mm) cannon. The later MiG-21PFU dispensed with the cannon and instead had in its possession up to four AA-1 "Alkali" radar-guided air-to-air missiles.

Like the MiG-15, the MiG-17 was built by factories in the Warsaw Pact countries such as Poland and exported to China, which also built large numbers, initially under license, and then without one when Sino–Soviet relations soured in 1960. Chengdu-built Chinese MiG-17s were designated J-5 (MiG-17F), J-5A (MiG-17PF) and the two-seat JJ-5. China's J-5s fought a number of air battles with Taiwanese aircraft from the late 1950s onwards, in various skirmishes over the Straits of Taiwan.

CLOSE-COMBAT ADVANTAGE

Vietnam saw the most prominent use of the MiG-17, however. Despite their lack of sophistication and gun-only armament, North Vietnamese Frescos often managed to get the better of both U.S. Air Force and U.S. Navy aircraft, whose pilots were unable to use their long-range missiles due to rules of engagement requiring that they visually identify their targets before firing. This drew them into close combats where the MiGs had superior turning advantage. Although the final tally favored the Americans, the top ace of the Vietnam War was again a MiG pilot, Nguyen van Bay, who as a pilot with the North Vietnamese Air Force is credited with seven kills in the MiG-17F, and who also damaged a U.S. Navy cruiser, USS *Oklahoma City*, in a rare North Vietnamese bombing attack.

MiG-17s and their Chinese counterparts continue to serve with a few nations such as Syria, North Korea and Ethiopia. JJ-5 (export designation FT-5) trainers are used as trainers by nations that have retired their single-seaters.

Republic F-84 Thunderjet and Thunderstreak

Republic's F-84 was one of the most important early Cold War jets. In Korea, Thunderjets undertook the brunt of the U.S. Air Force's ground-attack duties. In Europe, the Thunderstreak formed the backbone of many NATO air forces.

F-84F THUNDERSTREAK SPECIFICATION

Dimensions

Length: 43 ft 4 in (13.23 m)
Wingspan: 33 ft 7 in (10.27 m)
Height: 14 ft 4½ in (4.39 m)
Wing area: 324.70 sq ft (98.90 m²)

Power plant

One Wright J65-W-3 turbojet delivering 7,220 lb
(32.50 kN) of thrust

Weights

Empty: 13,380 lb (6273 kg)
Maximum takeoff: 28,000 lb (12,700 kg)

Performance

Maximum speed at 20,000 ft (6095 m): 658 mph
(1059 km/h)
Maximum speed at sea level: 695 mph (1118 km/h)
Initial climb rate: 8,200 ft (2500 m) per minute
Service ceiling: 46,000 ft (14,020 m)
Combat radius (high with two drop tanks): 810 miles
(1304 km)

Armament

Six 0.5-in (12.7-mm) Browning M3 machine guns and
up to 6,000 lb (2722 kg) of external stores, originally
including U.S. tactical nuclear weapons

Cutaway Key

1 Engine air intake
2 Gun tracking radar antenna
3 Machine-gun muzzles
4 Pitot tube
5 Nose undercarriage hydraulic retraction jack
6 Leg compression link
7 Nosewheel leg strut
8 Nosewheel
9 Mudguard
10 Steering jack
11 Taxiing lamp
12 Nose undercarriage leg rear strut
13 Nosewheel doors

14 Intake duct framing
15 Nose compartment 0.5-in (12.7-mm) 50 Colt-Browning M3 machine guns (four)
16 Radar electronics equipment
17 Ammunition tanks, total of 1,800 rounds
18 Forward avionics bay, including LABS bombing computer
19 Static ports
20 Battery
21 Intake ducting
22 Cockpit front pressure bulkhead

23 Rudder pedals
24 Instrument panel shield
25 Windshield panels
26 A-4 radar gunsight
27 Standby compass
28 Instrument panel
29 Ejection seat footrests
30 Aileron hydraulic booster
31 Intake suction relief door
32 Duct screen clearance access panel
33 Wing root machine-gun muzzle
34 Intake duct screen

35 Port side console panel
36 Engine throttle
37 External canopy release handle
38 Pilot's ejection seat
39 Safety harness
40 Headrest
41 Ejection seat guide rails
42 Cockpit canopy cover
43 Starboard automatic leading-edge slat, open
44 Slat guide rails
45 Starboard navigation light
46 Wingtip fairing

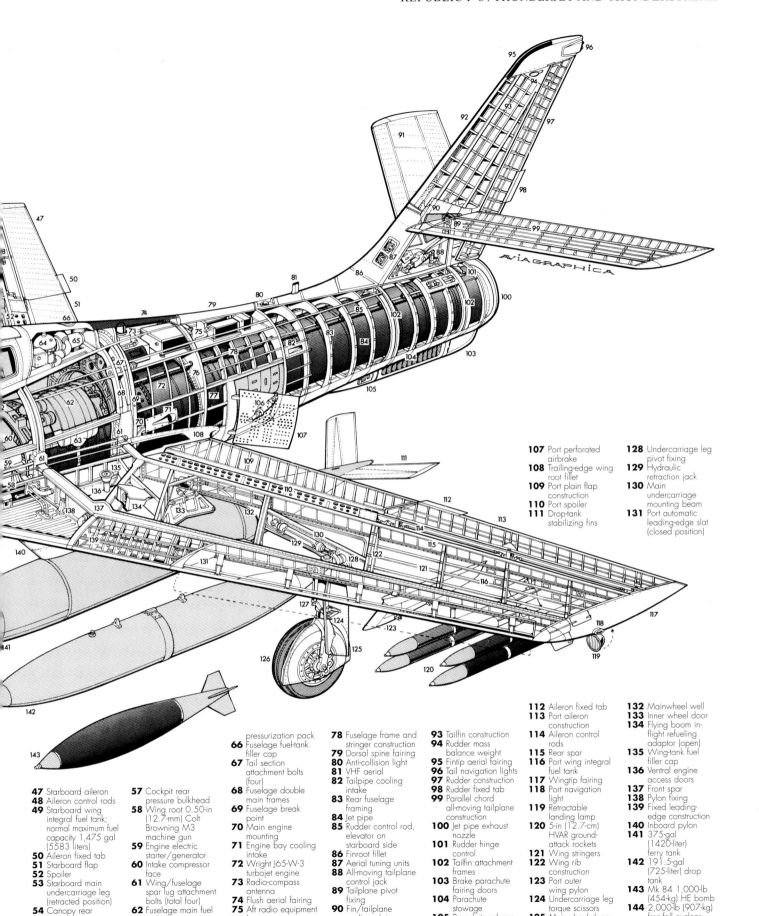

AVIAGRAPHICA

107 Port perforated airbrake
108 Trailing-edge wing root fillet
109 Port plain flap construction
110 Port spoiler
111 Drop-tank stabilizing fins

128 Undercarriage leg pivot fixing
129 Hydraulic retraction jack
130 Main undercarriage mounting beam
131 Port automatic leading-edge slat (closed position)

112 Aileron fixed tab
113 Port aileron construction
114 Aileron control rods
115 Rear spar
116 Port wing integral fuel tank
117 Wingtip fairing
118 Port navigation light
119 Retractable landing lamp
120 5-in (12.7-cm) HVAR ground-attack rockets
121 Wing stringers
122 Wing rib construction
123 Port outer wing pylon
124 Undercarriage leg torque scissors
125 Mainwheel doors
126 Port mainwheel
127 Main undercarriage leg strut

132 Mainwheel well
133 Inner wheel door
134 Flying boom in-flight refueling adaptor (open)
135 Wing-tank fuel filler cap
136 Ventral engine access doors
137 Front spar
138 Pylon fixing
139 Fixed leading-edge construction
140 Inboard pylon
141 375-gal (1420-liter) ferry tank
142 191.5-gal (725-liter) drop tank
143 Mk 84 1,000-lb (454-kg) HE bomb
144 2,000-lb (907-kg) free-fall nuclear weapon

47 Starboard aileron
48 Aileron control rods
49 Starboard wing integral fuel tank; normal maximum fuel capacity 1,475 gal (5583 liters)
50 Aileron fixed tab
51 Starboard flap
52 Spoiler
53 Starboard main undercarriage leg (retracted position)
54 Canopy rear hinge arm
55 Cockpit aft glazing
56 Ammunition feed chute

57 Cockpit rear pressure bulkhead
58 Wing root 0.50-in (12.7-mm) Colt Browning M3 machine gun
59 Engine electric starter/generator
60 Intake compressor face
61 Wing/fuselage spar lug attachment bolts (total four)
62 Fuselage main fuel tanks
63 Engine oil tank
64 Oxygen bottle
65 Air-conditioning and pressurization pack
66 Fuselage fuel-tank filler cap
67 Tail section attachment bolts (four)
68 Fuselage double main frames
69 Fuselage break point
70 Main engine mounting
71 Engine bay cooling intake
72 Wright J65-W-3 turbojet engine
73 Radio-compass antenna
74 Flush aerial fairing
75 Aft radio equipment bay
76 Engine firewall
77 Engine turbine section

78 Fuselage frame and stringer construction
79 Dorsal spine fairing
80 Anti-collision light
81 VHF aerial
82 Tailpipe cooling intake
83 Rear fuselage framing
84 Jet pipe
85 Rudder control rod, elevator on starboard side
86 Finroot fillet
87 Aerial tuning units
88 All-moving tailplane control jack
89 Tailplane pivot fixing
90 Fin/tailplane sealing plates
91 Starboard all-moving tailplane
92 Fin leading edge

93 Tailfin construction
94 Rudder mass balance weight
95 Fintip aerial fairing
96 Tail navigation lights
97 Rudder construction
98 Rudder fixed tab
99 Parallel chord all-moving tailplane construction
100 Jet pipe exhaust nozzle
101 Rudder hinge control
102 Tailfin attachment frames
103 Brake parachute fairing doors
104 Parachute stowage
105 Parachute release link
106 Airbrake hydraulic jack

"Let's admit it – the MiG is all right. The F-84 is all right, too. But if we were flying the MiG and they were flying the '84, I think we would be murdering them."
– Captain William Slaughter,
F-84 pilot, Korea 1951

Above: The U.S. Air Force's "Thunderbirds" aerial demonstration team flew the Republic F-84F in 1955 and 1956.

REPUBLIC F-84F THUNDERSTREAK – VARIANTS AND OPERATORS

VARIANTS

YF-84F: Two swept-wing prototypes of the F-84F, initially designated YF-96.

F-84F Thunderstreak: Swept-wing version with Wright J65 engine. Tactical Air Command aircraft were equipped with Low-Altitude Bombing System (LABS) for delivering nuclear bombs. 2,711 built; 1,301 went to NATO under Mutual Defense Assistance Program (MDAP).

GRF-84F: 25 RF-84Fs were converted to be carried and launched from the bomb bay of a GRB-36F bomber as part of the FICON (FIghter CONveyor) project. The aircraft were later redesignated RF-84K.

RF-84F Thunderflash: Reconnaissance version of the F-84F 715 were built.

XF-84H: Two F-84Fs were converted into experimental aircraft. Each was fitted with a Allison XT40-A-1 turboprop engine of 5,850 shaft horsepower (4365 kW) driving a supersonic propeller. Ground crews dubbed the XF-84H the "Thunderscreech" due to its extreme noise level.

YF-84J: Two F-84Fs were converted into YF-84J prototypes with enlarged nose intakes and a deepened fuselages for the General Electric J73 engine. The YF-84J reached Mach 1.09 in level flight on April 7, 1954. The project was cancelled due to the excessive cost of conversion of existing F-84Fs.

OPERATORS

Belgium
Denmark
France
Greece
Iran
Italy
Netherlands
Norway
Portugal
Taiwan
Thailand
Turkey
United States
West Germany
Yugoslavia

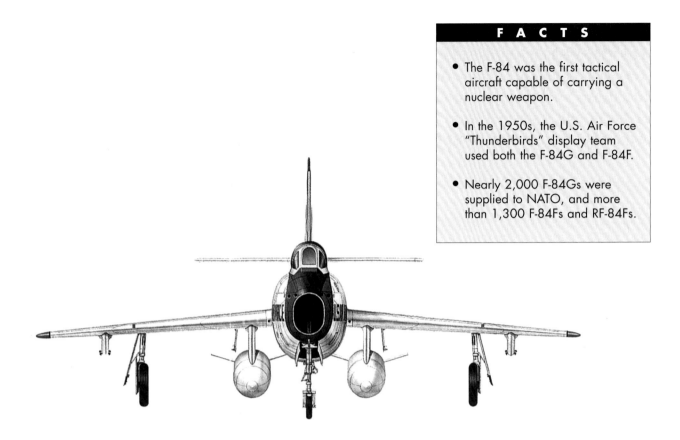

F A C T S

- The F-84 was the first tactical aircraft capable of carrying a nuclear weapon.

- In the 1950s, the U.S. Air Force "Thunderbirds" display team used both the F-84G and F-84F.

- Nearly 2,000 F-84Gs were supplied to NATO, and more than 1,300 F-84Fs and RF-84Fs.

REPUBLIC F-84F THUNDERSTREAK

The 81st Tactical Fighter Wing was based at the airfields of Bentwaters and nearby Woodbridge in Suffolk, England, for many years. In 1958, its equipment was the F-84F Thunderstreak, and this example flew with the 78th Tactical Fighter Squadron. The F-84Fs were used as nuclear-capable fighter-bombers, as illustrated by the 78th TFS's mushroom-cloud emblem. 52-6675, which features a brake parachute housing under the tail as retrofitted to many F-84Fs in service, was later sold to the Luftwaffe, then passed on to Greece. After serving its career almost exclusively outside the United States, it found its way back to Peoria, Arizona, where it is displayed on a pole downtown.

With more than 18,000 delivered, the Republic P-47 Thunderbolt was the most numerous American fighter of all time. It was equally effective as a fighter and a ground-attack platform, and it was renowned for its toughness and ability to withstand battle damage.

An attempt to redesign the P-47 for jet power failed, and Republic went back to the drawing board, producing an all-new design. Its new proposal was offered with six 0.50-in (12.7 mm) machine guns (two fewer than the P-47) or four 0.60-in (15.2-mm) machine guns. The USAAF awarded Republic a contract for a jet fighter-bomber in 1944, and increased the order before the prototype XP-84A flew in February 1946.

NEWLY INDEPENDENT ROLE

The U.S. Air Force was created as an independent arm of the military in 1937. The same year, P for "Pursuit" was replaced with F for "Fighter" in the Pentagon's designation system. The P-84 therefore entered service in December

Above: As on most fighters at the time, the instrument panel of the F-84 was crowded with dials, which occupied every inch of available space.

Above: Large external fuel tanks were needed to give the F-84F a reasonable radius of action.

Above: An F-84F fires an AGM-12 Bullpup missile during tests at Edwards Air Force Base, California. In service, the Thunderstreak almost exclusively used unguided bombs, rockets and guns.

1947 as the F-84B Thunderjet. A fairly conventional-looking machine, it had an unswept wing and a "straight-through" intake in the nose leading to an Allison J35 axial-flow turbojet. A bubble canopy gave the pilot a good all-around view.

Early Thunderjets had a number of structural and performance issues. The F-84B, C and D all came and went fairly quickly, before the much improved F-84E arrived in 1949, followed by the definitive F-84G. By now the bubble canopy had gone, replaced by a heavily framed reinforced unit. Provision for both boom and probe-and-drogue refueling was fitted, and a Mk 7 nuclear weapon could be carried.

TACTICAL ATTACK

In Korea, the F-84 followed the traditions of its predecessor the P-47, becoming the primary tactical-attack aircraft. Although technically outclassed by the Mikoyan-Gurevich MiG-15, Thunderjets brought down eight MiGs during the conflict.

Nearly 4,500 straight-wing F-84s were built. As well as the U.S. Air Force, it was operated by 15 foreign nations, including Portugal, Taiwan, West Germany and Iran. The F-84F Thunderstreak was intended to be a swept-wing

version with few other differences. In reality, it was almost totally new by the time the first production aircraft flew in November 1952. The fuselage was deeper, with an oval cross section, and contained a Wright J65 engine. The canopy was faired into the spine and opened upwards and to the rear. Six machine guns were fitted. The F-84F served with Tactical Air Command from 1954, but had been mostly passed to Air National Guard service by the late 1950s.

COLD WAR TENSIONS

The regular USAF reintroduced the F-84F during tensions over Berlin in the early1960s. A mass deployment of more than 200 US F-84Fs was made to Europe, to bolster defenses against a possible Soviet attack in 1961.

The Thunderstreak spawned the RF-84F Thunderflash with a camera nose and side-mounted intakes. As with the F-84G, the swept-wing models were supplied in large numbers to NATO and other U.S. allies. French F-84Fs claimed at least one Egyptian aircraft during the 1956 Suez crisis. More than 450 served with the newly reformed Luftwaffe. The last F-84s in service were RF-84Fs retired by Greece in 1991.

Dassault Mystère and Super Mystère

Dassault's Mystère and Super Mystère helped to get the French aviation industry back on its feet after World War II and were the workhorses of three air forces through the 1960s and early 1970s.

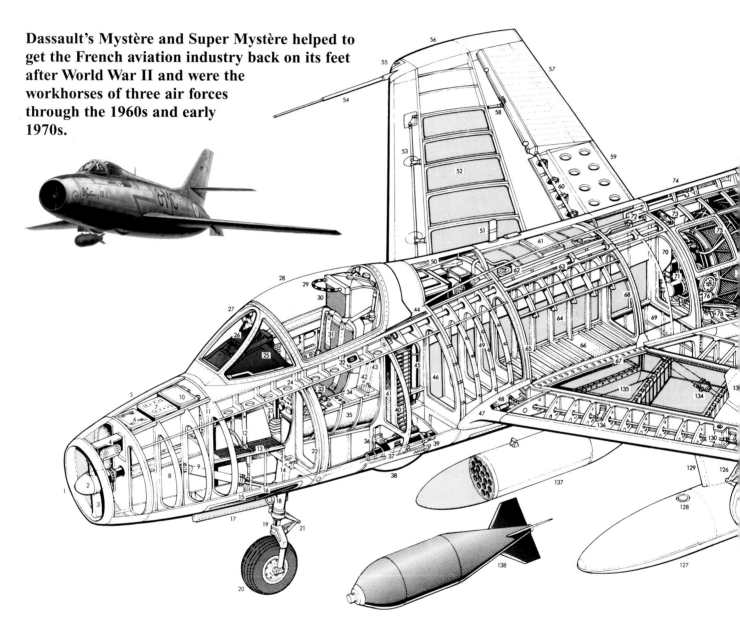

Cutaway Key

1 Engine air intake
2 Radar range finder antenna
3 Intake divider
4 Gun camera
5 Nose electronics compartment access door
6 Radar transmitter
7 Radar receiver
8 Nose undercarriage wheel bay
9 Hydraulic retraction jack
10 Battery
11 Cockpit front pressure bulkhead
12 Rudder pedals
13 Cockpit floor level
14 Nose undercarriage pivot fixing
15 Cannon blast trough
16 Cannon muzzle
17 Nosewheel leg door
18 Landing/taxiing lamp
19 Nose undercarriage leg strut
20 Nosewheel
21 Torque scissor links
22 Bifurcated intake duct framing
23 Control column
24 Cockpit coaming
25 Instrument panel shield
26 Gyro gunsight
27 Windshield panels
28 Cockpit canopy cover
29 Ejection-seat face blind firing handle
30 Headrest
31 Pilot's ejection seat
32 Canopy emergency release lever
33 Engine throttle lever
34 Port side console panel
35 Cockpit pressurized enclosure
36 Cannon mounting
37 DEFA 1.18-in (30-mm) cannon
38 Spent cartridge case collector box
39 Gun bay access panel
40 Ammunition feed chute
41 Ammunition box (150 rounds per gun)
42 Control rod runs
43 Cockpit armored rear pressure bulkhead
44 Sliding canopy rail
45 Oxygen bottle
46 Forward fuselage fuel tank (total internal capacity 476 gal/ 1800 liters)
47 Wing root fillet
48 Aileron hydraulic booster
49 Intake duct framing
50 Radio and electronics equipment bay
51 UHF aerial
52 Starboard wing fuel cells
53 Aileron push-pull control rods
54 Pitot tube
55 Starboard navigation light
56 Wingtip fairing
57 Starboard aileron
58 Aileron hinge control
59 Split trailing-edge flap
60 Flap torque shaft actuator

SUPER MYSTÈRE B2 SPECIFICATION

Dimensions

Length: 46 ft 4¼ in (14.13 m)
Height: 14 ft 11 in (4.55 m)
Wingspan: 34 ft 6 in (10.52 m)
Wing area: 376.75 sq ft (35.00 m²)
Wheel base: 14 ft 11½ in (4.56 m)

Power plant

One SNECMA Atar 101-G-2/-3 turbojet rated at 9,833 lb (43.76 kN) thrust with afterburning

Weights

Empty equipped: 15,282 lb (6932 kg)
Maximum takeoff: 22,046 lb (10,000 kg)

Performance

Maximum speed: 646 mph (1040 km/h) at sea level and 743 mph (1195 km/h) at 39,370 ft (12,000 m)
Initial climb rate: 17,505 ft (5335 m) per minute
Service ceiling: 55,775 ft (17,000 m)
Normal range: 540 miles (870 km)

Armament

Two 1.18-in (30-mm) DEFA 551 cannon plus 35 2.68-in (68-mm) SNEB rockets in retractable pack; plus up to 2,205 lb (1000 kg) of stores on four underwing hard points, including bombs up to 1,102 lb (500 kg); some aircraft later upgraded to carry AIM-9 Sidewinder or Shafrir AAMs

61 Fuel tank access door
62 Fuel filler cap
63 Control rod duct
64 Center fuselage fuel tank
65 Wing front spar/fuselage main frame
66 Wing center-section carry-through
67 Wing skin bolted root joint
68 Rear spar/fuselage main frame
69 Main undercarriage wheel bay
70 Hydraulic reservoir
71 Engine accessory compartment
72 Fuel system piping
73 Control rod runs
74 Dorsal spine fairing
75 Engine bay access door
76 Generator
77 Compressor intake filter screens
78 Intake plenum chamber
79 Main engine mounting
80 Hispano-Suiza Verdon 350 centrifugal-flow turbojet
81 Rear fuselage break point (engine removal)
82 Engine flame cans
83 Fin-root fillet
84 Engine turbine section
85 Tailplane control rods
86 Trimming tailplane electric screwjack
87 Tailplane sealing plate
88 Elevator control linkage
89 Rudder push-pull control rod
90 Starboard tailplane
91 Starboard elevator
92 IFF aerial
93 Tailfin construction
94 VHF aerial
95 Fin-tip aerial fairing
96 Rudder construction
97 Tail navigation light
98 Port elevator construction
99 All-moving tailplane construction
100 Engine exhaust nozzle
101 Jet pipe
102 Jet pipe heat shield
103 Airbrake housing
104 Hydraulic jack
105 Port airbrake, open
106 Wing root trailing-edge fillet
107 Port split trailing-edge flap
108 Main undercarriage leg pivot fixing
109 Flap shield ribs
110 Port aileron tab
111 Aileron mass balance weights
112 Aileron hinge control
113 Port aileron construction
114 Wingtip fairing
115 Port navigation light
116 Wing rib construction
117 Rear spar
118 Port wing fuel-tank bays
119 Drop-tank stabilizing fins
120 Front spar
121 Leading-edge nose ribs
122 500-lb (227-kg) bomb
123 Outboard stores pylon
124 Port mainwheel
125 Mainwheel hydraulic brake unit
126 Torque scissor links
127 Drop tank (127-gal/480-liter capacity)
128 Fuel filler cap
129 Fuel tank pylon
130 Inboard pylon fixing
131 Corrugated wing skin sandwich panel
132 Main undercarriage leg strut
133 Wing skin panelling
134 Main undercarriage hydraulic retraction jack
135 Inboard fuel cells
136 Aileron push-pull control rod
137 18 x 2.68-in (68-mm) rocket launcher
138 1,000-lb (454-kg) HE bomb

"The [Improved Super Mystère] had the advantage of speed. It was a lot faster than the [Douglas] A-4, even though it had the same engine, but the French aircraft was slicker."
– Shlomo Shapira, Israeli Air Force pilot

FACTS

- The Mystère series had a radar-ranging gunsight but no air-intercept radar, except on some experimental models.

- The Dassault Ouragan and Mystère IV were both used by the Patrouille de France aerobatic team.

- The Israelis named the Super Mystère B2 or SMB2 the "Sambad."

DASSAULT MYSTÈRE – VARIANTS

MD 450 Ouragan: Original design on which the Mystère series is based.

MD 452 Mystère I: Initial prototype model designation; total of three examples produced; fitted with Rolls-Royce Tay turbojet engine.

Mystère IIA: Prototype model; two examples produced.

Mystère IIB: Prototype mode; four examples produced.

Mystère IIC: Pre-production model designation fitted with SNECMA Atar 101 6,614-lb (3000-kg) turbojet engine.

Mystère IV: Production prototype model designation. Modified tail, refined aerodynamic features, longer fuselage, Tay power plant.

Mystère IVA: Pre-production and production models, of which nine examples were produced. Production run led to 480 fighters fitted with Tay and Hispano-Suiza power plants.

Mystère IVB: Further development of IVA fitted with Rolls-Royce Avon turbojet. Revised fuselage.

Super Mystère B1: Production prototype model of the IVB with an afterburning turbojet.

Super Mystère B2: Production model designation of the B1; 185 were produced. It was fitted with SNECMA Atar 101G-2/3 afterburning turbojet engines.

Above: A Mystère pilot illustrates the relatively basic flying equipment supplied to the first generation "jet jockeys."

DASSAULT MYSTÈRE IVA

Mystère IVA No. 83 belonged to the last unit of the Armée de l'Air to operate the type. Escadron de Chasse 1/8 "Saintonge" at Cazaux, southwest of Borde, flew the Mystère IVA from 1964 until 1982, when it re-equipped with the Dassault/Dornier Alphajet. Its role was as an advanced trainer for pilots destined to fly higher performance fighters. Part of 8 Escadre de Transformation (ET 8), EC 1/8 was further divided into two *escadrilles* (flights), which used the insignia of historic units. The winged arrow was that of 3C2. On the reverse side was a leaping lion, the insignia of 4C1. This Mystère was donated to the Newark Air Museum in England in 1978 and has been displayed there ever since.

In 1945, the French aviation industry was in ruins and years behind those of the United Kingdom, United States and Soviet Union. The Armée de l'Air was forced to continue producing Focke-Wulf 190s and other German designs in the factories that had been taken over for Luftwaffe production during the war.

Pre-war designer Marcel Bloch returned from Nazi captivity, changed his name to Dassault and drew up a design for a simple Rolls-Royce Nene–powered jet fighter. This was accepted for production as the Ouragan (Hurricane), and a prototype was flown in February 1949.

OPTING FOR SWEPT WINGS

By this time Dassault was already working on a swept-wing successor. The Mystère (Mystery) with a 30-degree wing sweep and a Rolls-Royce Tay engine flew in early 1951. The Mystère IIC was the production version, with a SNECMA Atar 101C turbojet.

Above: The Mystère IVN was a one-off attempt to produce a two-seat radar-equipped night-fighter variant with cannon armament.

Although similar in appearance, the Mystère IV was an all-new design with a 41-degree wing sweep, a new tail and an oval fuselage section and intake. It first flew in September 1952. Mystère IVs were fitted with either a Rolls-Royce Tay or a license-built Hispano-Suiza version called the Verdon 350. The

Above: A Mystère IV shows off the range of bombs, rockets, fuel tanks and cannon ammunition that it could carry.

Mystère IVA was a rather conventional aircraft with a thin wing that lacked any fancy high-lift devices. Underneath were four pylons, two of which usually carried fuel tanks, while the others sported either a bomb or a rocket pod. The main armament was a pair of 1.18-in (30-mm) DEFA cannon.

In French service, the Mystère IVA was initially used as an interceptor, before reassignment as a ground-attack fighter as the Mirage III entered service.

COMBAT TESTED

The Mystére IV was exported to Israel and India. With India it saw action in both the 1965 and 1971 wars with Pakistan. In an engagement in the former war, a Mystère IV was damaged by a Lockheed F-104, but succeeded in shooting it down before it crashed itself. Israel's Mystères saw combat against Egyptian Mikoyan-Gurevich MiG-15s in 1956, scoring seven victories with cannon. They were again used in 1967, by which time Shafrir missiles were in limited use.

The Super Mystère B1 with an Avon engine flew in 1955, but production B2 models had afterburning Atar 101 engines. The Super Mystère had a 45-degree sweep and became the first fighter in Western Europe to exceed Mach 1 in level flight. Again, Israel was the main user.

Israeli Super Mystères saw the most action in the ground-attack role, fighting in the Six-Day War of 1967 and Yom Kippur War of 1973. To get more from the aircraft, which was becoming obsolescent by the early 1970s, Israel re-engined a number with the Pratt & Whitney J52 engine, as used in the Douglas A-4 Skyhawk. This version was the Improved Super Mystère, or in Hebrew the *Sa'ar* (Tempest), and it was faster than the heavier A-4. Again, it was used mainly for ground-attack missions in 1973. Some upgraded Super Mystères were supplied to Honduras, which used them as late as the 1990s.

A CONTINUED ROLE IN TRAINING

The Armée de l'Air continued to use the Mystère IVA in the advanced training role until the early 1980s, by the 8th Fighter Wing at Cazaux in southwest France. Many of the Mystères were paid for by the United States under the Mutual Defense Assistance Program (MDAP), and survivors on display in museums today are technically on loan from the National Museum of the U.S. Air Force.

Above: A flight of some of the last Mystère IVs, used in the fighter conversion training role into the 1980s by the Armée de l'Air.

Chance Vought F-8 Crusader

The Crusader was regarded as a real fighter pilot's aircraft, with great maneuverability compared to its contemporaries. It had the best victory-to-loss rate of any U.S. fighter in the Vietnam War, where it served from land and sea throughout the conflict.

F-8E CRUSADER SPECIFICATION

Dimensions

Length: 54 ft 6 in (16.61 m)
Height: 15 ft 9 in (4.80 m)
Wingspan: 35 ft 2 in (10.72 m)
Wing area: 350 sq ft (35.52 m²)

Power plant

One Pratt & Whitney J57-P-20A turbojet rated at 10,700 lb (48.15 kN) static thrust or 18,000 lb st (81 kN) with afterburner

Weights

Empty: 17,541 lb (7957 kg)
Gross weight: 28,765 lb (13,048 kg)
Combat weight: 25,098 lb (11,304 kg)
Maximum takeoff: 34,000 lb (15,422 kg)

Performance

Maximum level speed at sea level: 764 mph (1230 km/h)
Maximum level speed at 40,000 ft (12,192 m): 1,120 mph (1802 km/h)
Cruising speed: 570 mph (917 km/h)
Stalling speed: 162 mph (261 km/h)
Rate of climb in one minute: 31,950 ft (9738 m)
Service ceiling: 58,000 ft (17,678 m)
Combat ceiling: 53,400 ft (16,276 m)

Range

Range: 453 miles (729 km)
Maximum range: 1,737 miles (2795 km)

Armament

Four Colt-Browning (0.79-in (20-mm)) Mk 12 cannon with 144 rounds per gun; plus up to four AIM-9 Sidewinder AAMs; 12 250-lb (113-kg) bombs; or eight 500-lb (227-kg) bombs; or eight Zuni rockets; or two AGM-12A or AGM-12B Bullpup A AGMs

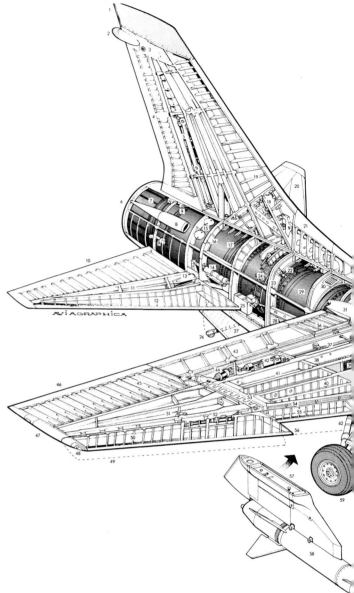

Cutaway Key

1 Fintip VHF aerial fairing
2 Tail warning radar
3 Tail navigation light
4 Rudder construction
5 Rudder hydraulic jack
6 Engine exhaust nozzle
7 Variable-area nozzle flaps
8 Afterburner cooling air duct
9 Nozzle control jacks
10 Starboard all-moving tailplane construction
11 Tailplane spar box
12 Leading-edge ribs
13 Tailplane pivot fixing
14 Tailplane hydraulic control jack
15 Tailpipe cooling air vents
16 Fin attachment main frame
17 Afterburner duct
18 Rudder control linkages
19 Fin leading-edge construction
20 Port all-moving tailplane
21 Fin-root fillet construction
22 Rear engine mounting
23 Fuselage break point double frame (engine removal)
24 Afterburner fuel spray manifold
25 Tailplane autopilot control system
26 Deck arrestor hook
27 Starboard ventral fin
28 Rear fuselage fuel tank
29 Pratt & Whitney J57-P-20A afterburning turbojet
30 Engine-bay cooling air louvers
31 Wing root trailing-edge fillet
32 Bleed air system piping
33 Engine oil tank (85 gal/322 liters)
34 Wing spar pivot fixing
35 Hydraulic flap jack
36 Starboard flap
37 Control rod linkages
38 Rear spar
39 Engine accessory gearbox compartment
40 Inboard wing panel multi-spar construction
41 Starboard wing integral fuel tank, total fuel system capacity 1,348 gal (5103 liters)
42 Aileron power control unit
43 Starboard drooping aileron construction
44 Wing-fold hydraulic jack
45 Trailing-edge ribs
46 Fixed portion of trailing edge
47 Wingtip fairing
48 Starboard navigation light
49 Leading-edge flap, lowered position

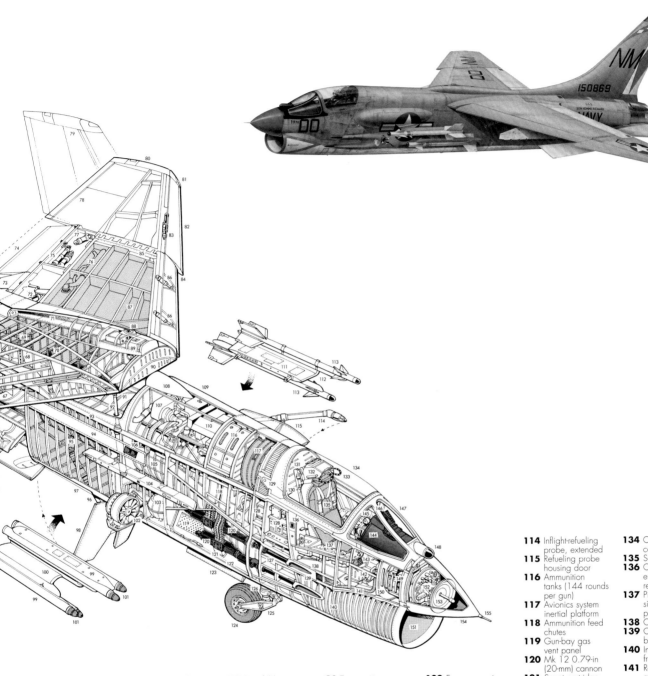

50 Leading-edge flap rib construction
51 Outer wing panel spar construction
52 Leading-edge flap hydraulic jack
53 Wingfold hinge
54 Front spar
55 Leading-edge flap inboard section
56 Leading-edge dogtooth
57 Wing pylon
58 AGM-12B Bullpup A air-to-ground missile
59 Starboard mainwheel
60 Main undercarriage leg strut
61 Shock absorber strut
62 Hydraulic retraction jack
63 Landing lamp

64 Wheel bay doors
65 Main undercarriage pivot fixing
66 Wing spar/front engine mounting main bulkhead
67 Engine compressor intake
68 Wing root rib
69 Center-section fuel tank
70 Wing spar carry-through structure
71 Dorsal fairing
72 Port flap jack
73 Port plain flap, lowered position
74 Port drooped aileron, lowered position
75 Aileron power control unit
76 Fuel system piping

77 Wing-fold hydraulic jack
78 Fixed portion of trailing edge
79 Port wing folded position
80 Wingtip fairing
81 Port navigation light
82 Port outboard leading-edge flap, lowered
83 Outboard flap hydraulic jack
84 Leading-edge dogtooth
85 Wing-fold hinge
86 Inboard leading-edge flap hydraulic jacks
87 Port wing integral fuel tank
88 Anti-collision light
89 Missile system avionics

90 Two-position variable-incidence wing, raised position
91 Intake trunking
92 Wing incidence hydraulic jack
93 Fuselage upper longeron
94 Air system exhaust heat shield
95 Main fuselage fuel tank
96 Airbrake hydraulic jack
97 Airbrake housing
98 Ventral airbrake, lowered
99 Rocket launch tubes
100 Rocket launcher pylon adaptor
101 Zuni folding-fin ground attack rockets (8)

102 Emergency air-driven generator
103 Liquid oxygen bottle (LOX)
104 Fuselage stores pylon
105 Intake duct
106 Heat exchanger air exhaust
107 Air-conditioning plant
108 Dorsal fairing
109 Upper fuselage access panels
110 Electronics bay and electrical power system
111 Fuselage pylon adaptor
112 Missile launch rails
113 AIM-9 Sidewinder air-to-air missiles (4)

114 Inflight-refueling probe, extended
115 Refueling probe housing door
116 Ammunition tanks (144 rounds per gun)
117 Avionics system inertial platform
118 Ammunition feed chutes
119 Gun-bay gas vent panel
120 Mk 12 0.79-in (20-mm) cannon
121 Spent cartridge case/link collector chutes
122 Gun compartment access panel
123 Nosewheel doors
124 Nosewheel
125 Pivoted axle beam
126 Nose undercarriage leg strut
127 Cannon barrels
128 Radio and electronics equipment bays
129 Canopy hinge point
130 Cockpit rear pressure bulkhead
131 Ejection seat rails
132 Pilot's Martin-Baker ejection seat
133 Face-blind firing handle

134 Cockpit canopy cover
135 Safety harness
136 Canopy emergency release
137 Pilot's starboard-side console panel
138 Cockpit floor level
139 Cannon muzzle blast troughs
140 Intake duct framing
141 Radar cooling air piping
142 Rudder pedals
143 Control column
144 Instrument panel shield
145 Engine throttle control
146 Radar gunsight
147 Bullet-proof windshield
148 Infrared seeker head
149 Radar electronics package
150 Cockpit front pressure bulkhead
151 Engine air intake
152 Radar scanner tracking mechanism
153 Radar antenna
154 Fiberglass radome
155 Pitot tube

"When you are out of F-8s,
you are out of fighters."
– Crusader pilots' slogan

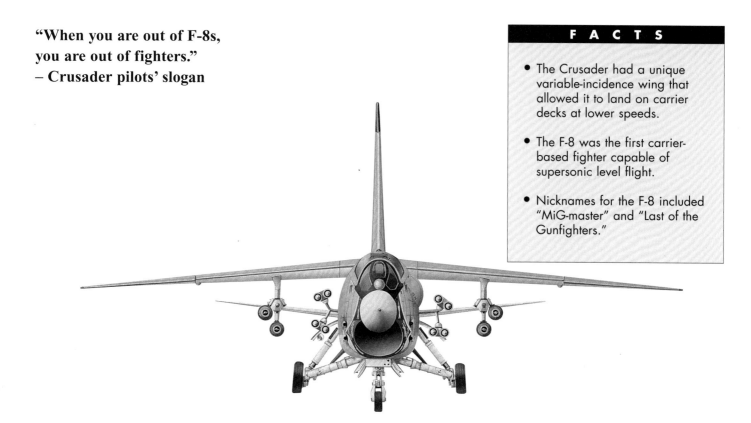

VOUGHT F-8 CRUSADER – VARIANTS

XF8U-1 (XF-8A): The two original unarmed prototypes – V-383.

F8U-1 (F-8A): First production version. J57-P-12 engine replaced with more powerful J57-P-4A, starting with 31st production aircraft. 318 built.

YF8U-1 (YF-8A): One F8U-1 fighter used for development testing.

YF8U-1E (YF-8B): One F8U-1 converted to serve as an F8U-1E prototype.

F8U-1E (F-8B): Added a limited all-weather capability, thanks to the AN/APS-67 radar. First flight: September 3, 1958. 130 built.

XF8U-1T: One XF8U-2NE used for evaluation as a two-seat trainer.

F8U-2 (F-8C): J57-P-16 engine with 16,900 lbf (75 kN) of afterburning thrust. First flight August 20, 1957. 187 built. This variant was sometimes referred to as Crusader II.

F8U-2N (F-8D): All-weather version, unguided rocket pack replaced with an additional fuel tank, J57-P-20 engine with 18,000 lbf (80 kN) of afterburning thrust. First flight February 16, 1960. 152 built.

YF8U-2N (YF-8D): One aircraft used in the development of the F8U-2N.

YF8U-2NE: One F8U-1 converted to serve as an F8U-2NE prototype.

F8U-2NE (F-8E): J57-P-20A engine, AN/APQ-94 radar in a larger nose cone. First flight June 30, 1961. 286 built.

F-8E(FN): Air-superiority fighter version for the French Navy (Aéronavale), significantly increased wing lift due to greater slat and flap deflection,

and the addition of a boundary-layer control system, enlarged stabilators. 42 built.

F-8H: Upgraded F-8D with strengthened airframe and landing gear.

F-8J: Upgraded F-8E, similar to F-8D but with wing modifications. 136 rebuilt.

F-8K: Upgraded F-8C with Bullpup capability and J57-P-20A engines.

F-8L: F-8B upgraded with underwing hard points. 61 rebuilt.

F-8P: 17 F-8E(FN) of the Aéronavale underwent a significant overhaul at the end of the 1980s, to stretch their service life another ten years. They were retired in 1999.

F8U-1D (DF-8A): Retired F-8A modified to controller aircraft for testing of the SSM-N-8 Regulus cruise missile.

DF-8F: Retired F-8A modified for target-tug duty.

F8U-1KU (QF-8A): Retired F-8A modified into remote-controlled target drones.

YF8U-1P (YRF-8A): Prototypes used in the development of the F8U-1P photo-reconnaissance aircraft – V-392.

RF-8G: Modernized RF-8As.

XF8U-3 Crusader III: New design loosely based on the earlier F-8 variants, created to compete against the F-4 Phantom II.

CHANCE VOUGHT F-8 CRUSADER

Although not designed with much thought given to ground-attack missions, the F-8 became an effective bomber in Vietnam, mainly with the U.S. Marine Corps. All-weather Marine fighter squadron VMF(AW)-235 with its colorful F-8Es was based at Da Nang, South Vietnam, in 1968. At that time, it was called on to support the besieged Marines at Khe Sanh, in danger of being overrun by the North Vietnamese. This F-8 is shown armed with eight Mk 82 500-lb (227-kg) bombs and eight 5-in (127-mm) Zuni rockets. The rockets are mounted on the so-called "Y" launchers that were developed during the Crusader's service to allow carriage of four AIM-9s.

The Crusader's origins were in a 1952 U.S. Navy requirement for a supersonic carrier-based fighter. In March 1955, the XF8U-1 prototype made its first flight and exceeded the speed of sound. The designation arose from the pre-1962 U.S. Navy system, in which it was the eighth fighter design from Chance Vought (which was assigned "U" as its company designation letter). From October 1962, the system was rationalized and F8Us became F-8s. Testing and evaluation were swift and the F8U-1, soon named "Crusader," was in service two years after first flying. This was in contrast to some other aircraft of the period (including Vought's own F7U Cutlass) that spent longer in development than they did in the fleet.

Above: Commander Dick Bellinger was one of the more colorful F-8 pilots of the Vietnam era. In October 1966, he became the first U.S. Navy pilot to shoot down a MiG-21.

The Crusader had a long fuselage and a short undercarriage. The variable-incidence wing was raised for takeoffs and landings to give a higher angle of attack and thus more lift, while keeping the fuselage level. This prevented the jetpipe from scraping the deck and gave the pilot a better forward view. The engine was the Pratt & Whitney J57 turbojet, one of the most successful U.S. jet engines, used in different forms on everything from the North American F-100 Super Sabre to the Boeing B-52 bomber and 707 airliner.

The F-8 was armed with four 0.79-in (20-mm) cannon in the forward fuselage. Early models also had a 16-shot rocket pack mounted in the speed brake. Two or four Sidewinders became standard air-to-air armament, and bombs and air-to-ground rockets were widely used in

Vietnam, particularly by the U.S. Marines. The AGM-12 Bullpup air-to-ground missile could be carried, but appears to have been rarely used in action.

RECORD-WINNING SPEED

Even before its service entry in December 1956, the Crusader was used to set speed records, both for measured circuits and cross-country point-to-point flights. Crusaders made the first official U.S. flights over 1,000 mph (1609 km/h), flew from carriers off the West Coast to carriers off the East Coast, and flew from Los Angeles to New York in under three and a half hours among other milestones.

The Crusader could fly from the smaller "Essex"-class carriers, unlike the Phantom, although safety margins were

Above: The all-weather F8U-2N Crusader first flew in 1960. Under the post-1962 designation system it became the F-8D.

Above: A photo-reconnaissance RF-8 Crusader makes a touch-and-go landing on an angled deck carrier. The variable-incidence wing that allowed operations from smaller ships can be seen.

small and there were many accidents. In Vietnam, F-8s provided air defense and fighter escort for these carriers and were flown by Marine Corps squadrons from land bases. Photo-reconnaissance RF-8 versions provided targeting information and post-strike battle damage assessment.

SUCCESS IN COMBAT
In air combat, the Crusader acquitted itself well, shooting down 19 North Vietnamese MiGs, four of them with cannon, against the loss of four F-8s in dogfights.

France became the only customer for new-build Crusaders, ordering the first of 42 in 1962. These F-8E(FN)s

had a higher wing incidence, larger tailplanes and boundary layer control, a method of blowing engine bleed air over the flaps to give extra takeoff lift. These modifications helped them to fly from the small French carriers *Clemenceau* and *Foch*. From the late 1980s, they were modified as F-8Ps ("P" standing for *prolonge*, or prolonged), and the last squadron kept flying them until 1999.

The Philippines bought 25 F-8Hs (which they also designated F-8Ps) for use from land bases in 1977. Humid conditions were hard on the aircraft, which suffered from poor reliability, and by 1991 the last one had been withdrawn from service.

Mikoyan-Gurevich MiG-21F "Fishbed"

The MiG-21 is the most numerous jet fighter ever, with more than 10,000 built in several countries. Hard to spot and nimble, in the hands of a good pilot it was a match for much more sophisticated Western fighters.

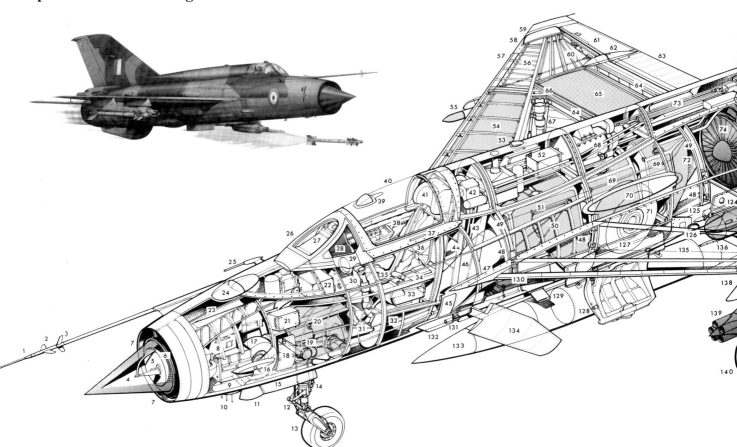

Cutaway Key

1 Pitot static boom
2 Pitch vanes
3 Yaw vanes
4 Conical three-position intake center-body
5 "Spin Scan" search-and-track radar antenna
6 Boundary layer slot
7 Engine air intake
8 "Spin Scan" radar
9 Lower boundary layer exit
10 IFF antennas
11 Nosewheel doors
12 Nosewheel leg and shock absorbers
13 Castoring nosewheel
14 Anti-shimmy damper
15 Avionics bay access

16 Attitude sensor
17 Nosewheel well
18 Spill door
19 Nosewheel retraction pivot
20 Bifurcated intake trunking
21 Avionics bay
22 Electronics equipment
23 Intake trunking
24 Upper boundary layer exit
25 Dynamic pressure probe for Q feel
26 Semi-elliptical armor glass windshield
27 Gunsight mounting
28 Fixed quarterlight
29 Radar scope
30 Control column (with tailplane trim

switch and two firing buttons)
31 Rudder pedals
32 Underfloor control runs
33 KM-1 two-position zero-level ejection seat
34 Port instrument console
35 Undercarriage handle
36 Seat harness
37 Canopy release/lock
38 Starboard wall switch pane
39 Rear-view mirror fairing
40 Starboard hinged canopy
41 Ejection seat

headrest
42 Avionics bay
43 Control rods
44 Air-conditioning plant
45 Suction relief door
46 Intake trunking
47 Wing root attachment fairing
48 Wing/fuselage spar-lug attachment points (four)
49 Fuselage ring frames
50 Intermediary frames
51 Main fuselage fuel tank
52 RSIU radio bay
53 Auxiliary intake
54 Leading-edge integral fuel tank
55 Starboard outer

weapons pylon
56 Outboard wing construction
57 Starboard navigation light
58 Leading-edge suppressed aerial
59 Starboard aileron
60 Aileron control jack
61 Starboard aileron
62 Flap actuator fairing
63 Starboard blown flap SPS (*sduva pogranichnovo slova*)
64 Multi-spar wing structure
65 Main integral wing fuel tank
66 Undercarriage

mounting/pivot point
67 Starboard mainwheel leg
68 Auxiliaries compartment
69 Fuselage fuel tanks Nos 2 and 3
70 Mainwheel well external fairing
71 Main wheel (retracted)
72 Trunking contours
73 Control rods in dorsal spine
74 Compressor face
75 Oil tank
76 Avionics pack
77 Engine accessories
78 Tumanskii R-13 turbojet
79 Fuselage break/

transport joint
80 Intake
81 Tail surface control linkage
82 Artificial feel unit
83 Tailplane jack
84 Hydraulic accumulator
85 Tailplane trim motor
86 Fin spar attachment plate
87 Rudder jack
88 Rudder control linkage
89 Fin structure
90 Leading-edge panel
91 Radio cable access
92 Magnetic detector
93 Fin mainspar
94 RSIU (*radio-stantsiya istrebitelnaya*)

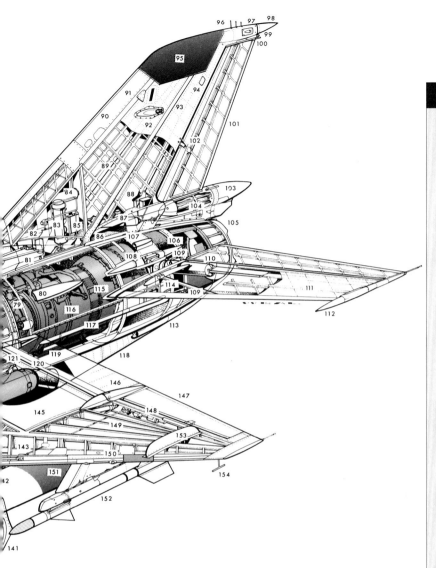

MIG-21MF "FISHBED-J" SPECIFICATION

Dimensions

Length with probe: 51 ft 8½ in (15.76 m)
Length excluding probe: 40 ft 4 in (12.29 m)
Height: 13 ft 6 in (4.13 m)
Span: 23 ft 6 in (7.15 m)
Wing area: 247.5 sq ft (23 m²)
Wing aspect ratio: 2.23
Wheel track: 9 ft 1¾ in (2.79 m)
Wheel base: 15 ft 5½ in (4.71 m)

Power plant

One MNPK "Soyuz" (Tumanskii/Gavrilov) R-13-300
turbojet rated at 8,972 lb st (39.92 kN) dry and
14,037 lb st (63.66 kN) with afterburning

Weights

Empty: 11,795 lb (5350 kg)
Normal takeoff with four AAMs and three 129-gal (490-
liter) drop tanks: 17,967 lb (8150 kg)
Maximum takeoff: 20,723 lb (9400 kg)

Fuel and load

Internal fuel: 687 gal (2600 liters)
External fuel: up to 387 gal (1470 liters) in three drop
tanks
Maximum ordnance: 4,409 lb (2000 kg)

Performance

Maximum rate of climb at sea level: 23,622 ft
(7200 m) per minute
Service ceiling: 59,711 ft (18,200 m)
Takeoff run: 2,625 ft (800 m)

Range

Ferry range: 971 nm (1,118 miles; 1800 km) with
three drop tanks
Combat radius: 200 nm (230 miles; 370 km) on a
hi-lo-hi attack mission with four 551-lb (250-kg) bombs,
or 400 nm (460 miles; 740 km) on a hi-lo-hi mission
with two 551-lb (250-kg) bombs and drop tanks

Armament

Standard gun is the GSh-23L, which has a caliber of
0.91-in (23 mm) and can fire AP or HE ammunition,
with 420 rounds being carried. The only guided
missiles normally carried are for air-to-air use. The MF
is capable of firing the K-13A (AA-2 "Atoll") and the
AA-2-2 Advanced "Atoll." As with other MiG-21s, up
to eight R-60 (AA-8 "Aphid") infrared missiles can also
be carried. There is provision for various FABs (free-fall
general-purpose bombs), up to 1,102 lb (500 kg) in
weight. A wide range of fragmentation, chemical,
cluster bombs and rocket-boosted penetrators for use
against concrete can be carried, as well as 2.24-in
(57-mm) or 9.45-in (240-mm) caliber rockets.

*ultrakorotkykh
vol'n* – very short-
wave fighter radio)
antenna plate
95 VHF/UHF aerials
96 IFF antennas
97 Formation light
98 Tail warning radar
99 Rear navigation
light
100 Fuel vent
101 Rudder
construction
102 Rudder hinge
103 Braking parachute
hinged bullet
fairing
104 Braking parachute
stowage
105 Tailpipe
(variable
convergent
nozzle)
106 Afterburner
installation
107 Afterburner bay
cooling intake
108 Tail plane linkage
fairing

109 Nozzle actuating
cylinders
110 Tailplane
torque tube
111 All-moving
tailplane
112 Anti-flutter
weight
113 Intake
114 Afterburner
mounting
115 Fixed tailplane
root fairing
116 Longitudinal
lap joint
117 External duct
(nozzle hydraulics)
118 Ventral fin
119 Engine guide rail
120 ATO assembly
canted nozzle
121 ATO assembly
thrust plate forks
(rear-mounting)
122 ATO assembly
pack
123 Ventral airbrake
(retracted)
124 Trestle point

125 ATO assembly-
release solenoid
(front-mounting)
126 Underwing
landing light
127 Ventral stores
pylon
128 Mainwheel
inboard door
129 Splayed link chute
130 0.91-in (23-mm)
GSh-23 cannon
installation
131 Cannon muzzle
fairing
132 Debris deflector
plate
133 Auxiliary ventral
drop tank
134 Port forward air
brake (extended)
135 Leading-edge
integral fuel tank
136 Undercarriage
retraction strut
137 Aileron control rods
in leading edge
138 Port inboard
weapons pylon

139 UV-16-57 rocket
pod
140 Port mainwheel
141 Mainwheel
outboard
door section
142 Mainwheel leg
143 Aileron control
linkage
144 Mainwheel leg
pivot point
145 Main integral
wing fuel tank
146 Flap actuator
fairing
147 Port aileron
148 Aileron control
jack
149 Outboard wing
construction
150 Port navigation
light
151 Port outboard
weapons pylon
152 Advanced "Atoll"
IR-homing AAM
153 Wing fence
154 Radio altimeter
antenna

"Perhaps the most important lesson on fighting the MiG-21 was that it was very maneuverable and that it was better to take care of it before you got into a tussle with it."
– Bob Sheffield, U.S. Air Force fighter pilot

MIKOYAN-GUREVICH MIG-21 "FISHBED" – MAJOR VARIANTS

Generation Zero (1954–56)
Ye-1: Swept-wing prototype.

Ye-2A/MiG-23: Ye-2 design modified for RD-11 turbojet.

Ye-4: First delta-wing MiG-21.

Ye-50: Swept-wing experimental high-altitude interceptor.

Ye-50A/MiG-23U: A refinement of the Ye-50.

Ye-5: Delta-wing research prototype powered by Mikulin AM-11 turbojet.

MiG-21: The first series of fighters, production version of Ye-5.

Generation One (1957–76)
Ye-6: Three pre-production versions of MiG-21F.

Ye-50P: Rocket-boosted high-altitude interceptor project.

MiG-21F: Single-seat day-fighter aircraft. It was the first production aircraft, with 93 machines being made.

MiG-21P-13: Two MiG-21s were converted to use the K-13 missile system.

MiG-21F-13: Existing MiG-21Fs using K-13 missiles.

Generation Two (1961–66)
MiG-21PF/FL: Production versions of all-weather interceptors. PF was the Warsaw Pact export version; FL the developing nations export version.

MiG-21PFS: Identical to PF variant, but with blown flaps.

MiG-21PFM: A PF model with uprated radar and avionics.

MiG-21R: Combat-capable reconnaissance aircraft.

MiG-21S: Tactical fighter. Delivered only to the Soviet Air Force.

MiG-21N: Variant of the 21S. Capable of delivering the RN-25 tactical nuclear weapon.

Generation Three (1968–72)
MiG-21M: Export variant of MiG-21S.

MiG-21SM: Upgrade of the MiG-21S.

MiG-21MF: Export version of the MiG-21SM.

MiG-21MT: MiG-21MF with increased fuel capacity.

MiG-21SMT: A development of the MiG-21SM with increased fuel capacity. Easily spotted from its larger spine.

MiG-21ST: Rebuilt versions of the unpopular MiG-21SMT with smaller saddle tanks of the MiG-21bis.

MiG-21bis: Ultimate development of the MiG-21. Fitted with a Turmansky R25-300 turbojet and many other advances.

MiG-21bis-D: 2003 upgrade for the Croatian Air Force. Modernized for NATO interoperability.

MIKOYAN-GUREVICH MIG-21 "FISHBED"

The Romanian Air Force (Fortele Aeriene Române) is one of the last in Europe to use the MiG-21. In the 1990s, faced with the need but not the finances for new fighters, Romania chose to upgrade its existing fleets of MiG-21s and MiG-29s. The "Fulcrum" upgrade was eventually abandoned, but Aerostar planned to turn MiG-21Ms, MFs and UMs into the modernized Lancer with the help of Israeli firm Elbit. The Lancer A (shown) was optimized for ground attack. New weapons (depicted) include the Opher IR-guided bomb, which resembles a laser-guided bomb, but homes in on infrared emissions such as those from a vehicle engine, and the Python III short-range air-to-air missiles. The Lancer B was the two-seat trainer and the Lancer C a dedicated interceptor version.

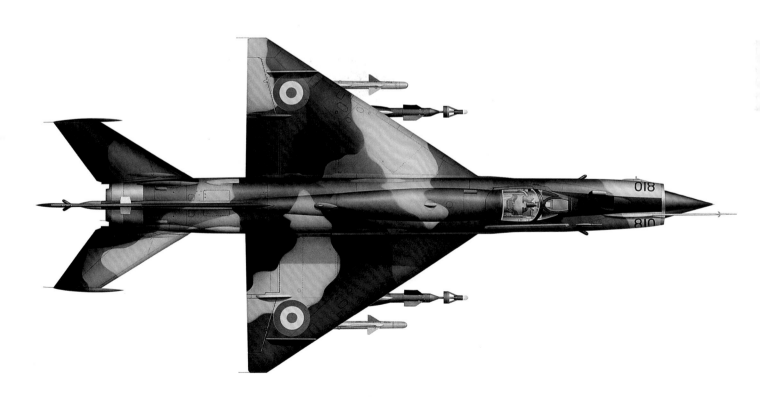

Above: The Slovak Air Force inherited MiG-21s from the Czech Republic in the 1993 "Velvet Divorce," or dissolution of Czechoslovakia. It retained some, including the MiG-21US trainer, until 2000.

In an effort to develop a lightweight Mach 2 interceptor to replace the MiG-19, Mikoyan-Gurevich started with a clean slate. There was debate as to whether swept or delta wings were the most efficient. The Ye-1 prototype of 1955 had a slender fuselage and highly swept wings, while the Ye-4 used a delta wing. Several further prototypes were ordered in each configuration; the delta-winged Ye-5 was judged marginally superior and chosen as the basis for the MiG-21.

The initial MiG-21 "Fishbed-A" was built in relatively small numbers, but the MiG-21F-13 "Fishbed-C" that entered production in 1960 was produced in the thousands. Like the prototypes, it had a bubble canopy that hinged at the front to provide wind blast protection during an ejection and had its

radar in a shock cone within the engine inlet. Aerodynamic "fences" on the wing were reduced to two rather than six.

Armament was two R-3S (AA-2 "Atoll") guided missiles, which were copied from the U.S. AIM-9B Sidewinder, and a 0.91-in (23-mm) cannon. "Fishbed-Cs" were exported to India, Romania, Finland and China.

IN CHINESE HANDS

In China, the MiG-21F-13 was built by Chengdu as the F-7 and entered service around 1965. Even today nearly 400 are believed to remain in service. The Chinese improved the MiG-21 and offered the F-7M Airguard for export. This had a rearward-opening canopy, a pair of cannon and provision for four air-to-air missiles. A considerable amount of Western equipment was included, including Martin Baker ejection seats. F-7Ms were sold to Iran, Zimbabwe and Pakistan. Older F-7Ps and F-7Ms are the most numerous aircraft in Pakistan's inventory, with nearly 150 in service.

CONTINUED DEVELOPMENT

In the Soviet Union, development continued with the MiG-21S fighter, R reconnaissance aircraft and M and MF fighter-bombers. The latter had enlarged spines containing extra fuel and/or avionics. All these second-generation MiG-21s had smaller canopies that hinged to the side. The next step was the MiG-21bis, which could carry R-60 (AA-8 "Aphid") missiles, plus a wide range of conventional or nuclear air-to-ground weapons. It was exported to over a dozen nations.

Initially employed as an interceptor with very limited endurance, the MiG-21 evolved into the fighter-bomber of choice (limited though that might have been) for the Communist nations of the world.

WIDELY BATTLE-TESTED

MiG-21s and their Chinese derivatives have been involved in almost every area of conflict since the mid-1960s, with an exception being the Falklands War. In several cases, including Iran–Iraq and the Balkans conflicts of the 1990s, MiG-21s or F-7s were used by both sides. Most air-to-air action was seen in the Middle East by Syrian and Egyptian "Fishbeds" against Israel and by the North Vietnamese Air Force against the United States.

Although wealthier countries have been able to replace their "Fishbeds" with MiG-29 "Fulcrums" or Lockheed Martin F-16 Fighting Falcons (although usually not on a one-for-one basis), retaining and upgrading MiG-21s remains the

Above: The radar scope was given priority over forward vision in the busy cockpit of the MiG-21.

only option for many air forces. Upgrade programs have included RAC MiG's own MiG-21-93, and Romania's Lancer. The MiG-21-93 formed the basis of India's Bison upgrade, which was applied to more than 100 aircraft. Likewise, around 50 Lancers were modified from MiG-21M, MF and UM airframes.

Above: India acquired around 900 MiG-21s over the years. About 125 of them are being upgraded to remain competitive in the modern era.

McDonnell Douglas F-4 Phantom II

The Phantom was the most potent combat aircraft in service through the 1960s and early 1970s. Although superseded in most air arms by more modern types, considerable numbers remain in service.

Cutaway Key

1 Pitot head
2 Radome
3 Radar scanner dish
4 Radar dish tracking mechanism
5 Texas Instruments AN/APQ-99 forward-looking radar unit
6 Nose compartment construction
7 No. 1 camera station
8 KS-87 forward oblique camera
9 Forward radar warning antennas, port and starboard
10 Camera bay access hatches
11 Ventral camera aperture
12 KA-57 low-altitude panoramic camera
13 Lateral camera aperture (alternative KS-87 installation)
14 No. 2 camera station
15 ADF sense aerial

16 Windshield rain-dispersal air duct
17 Camera viewfinder periscope
18 Nose undercarriage emergency air bottles
19 Recording unit
20 No. 3 camera station
21 KA-91 high-altitude panoramic camera
22 Air-conditioning ram air intake
23 Landing/taxiing lamp (2)
24 Lower UHF/VHF aerial
25 Nosewheel leg door
26 Torque scissor links
27 Twin nosewheels, aft retracting
28 Nosewheel steering mechanism
29 AN/AVQ-26 "Pave Tack" laser designator pod
30 Swivelling optical package

31 Fuselage centerline pylon adaptor
32 Sideways-looking radar antenna (SLAR)
33 Electroluminescent formation lighting strip
34 Canopy emergency-release handle
35 Air-conditioning plant, port and starboard
36 Cockpit floor level
37 Front pressure bulkhead
38 Rudder pedals
39 Control column
40 Instrument panel
41 Radar display
42 Instrument panel shield
43 LA-313A optical viewfinder
44 Windshield panels
45 Forward cockpit canopy cover
46 Face-blind seat firing handle
47 Pilot's Martin-Baker Mk.H7 ejection seat

48 External canopy latches
49 Engine throttle levers
50 Side console panel
51 Intake boundary layer splitter plate
52 APQ-102R/T SLAR equipment
53 AAS-18A infrared reconnaissance package
54 Intake front ramp
55 Port engine air intake
56 Intake ramp bleed air holes
57 Rear canopy external latches
58 Rear instrument console
59 Canopy center arch
60 Starboard engine air intake
61 Starboard external fuel tank, capacity 370 gal (1400 liters)
62 Rearview mirrors
63 Rear cockpit canopy cover

64 Navigator/sensor operator's Martin-Baker ejection seat
65 Intake ramp bleed air spill louvers
66 Avionics equipment racks
67 Rear pressure bulkhead
68 Liquid oxygen converter
69 Variable intake ramp jack
70 Intake rear ramp door
71 Fuselage centerline external fuel tank, capacity 600 gal (2271 liters)
72 Position of pressure refueling connection on starboard side
73 ASQ-90B data annotation system equipment
74 Cockpit voice recorder
75 Pneumatic system air bottle
76 Bleed air ducting
77 Fuselage No. 1 fuel

cell, capacity 215 gal (814 liters)
78 Intake duct framing
79 Boundary layer spill duct
80 Control cable runs
81 Aft avionics equipment bay
82 IFF aerial
83 Upper fuselage light
84 Fuselage No. 2 fuel cell, capacity 185 gal (700 liters)
85 Center fuselage frame construction
86 Electroluminescent formation lighting strip
87 Engine intake center-body fairing
88 Intake duct rotary spill valve
89 Wing spar attachment fuselage main frames
90 Control cable ducting
91 In-flight refueling receptacle, open

92 Starboard main undercarriage leg pivot fixing
93 Starboard wing integral fuel tank, capacity 315 gal (1192 liters)
94 Wing pylon mounting
95 Boundary layer control air duct
96 Leading-edge flap hydraulic actuator
97 Inboard leading-edge flap segment, down position
98 Leading-edge dogtooth
99 Outboard wing panel attachment joint
100 Boundary layer control air ducting
101 Hydraulic flap actuator
102 Outboard leading-edge flap
103 Starboard navigation light
104 Electroluminescent formation light

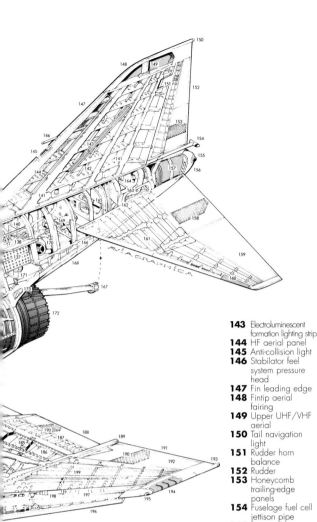

F-4E PHANTOM II SPECIFICATION

Dimensions

Wingspan: 38 ft 7½ in (11.77 m)
Wingspan (folded): 27 ft 7 in (8.41 m)
Wing aspect ratio: 2.82
Wing area: 530 sq ft (49.2 m²)
Length: 63 ft (19.20 m)
Wheel track: 17 ft 10½ in (5.45 m)
Height: 16 ft 5½ in (5.02 m)

Power plant

Two General Electric J79-GE-17A turbojets, each rated at 17,900 lb (80 kN) thrust with afterburning

Weights

Empty: 30,328 lb (13,757 kg)
Operating empty: 31,853 lb (14,448 kg)
Combat takeoff: 41,487 lb (18,818 kg)
Maximum takeoff: 61,795 lb (28,030 kg)

Fuel and load

Internal fuel capacity: 1,855 gal (7022 liters)
Provision for one 600-gal (2271-liter) tank on centerline and two 370-gal (1400-liter) tanks under the wings
Maximum weapon load: 16,000 lb (7250 kg)

Performance

Maximum speed: approximately Mach 2.2
Maximum rate of climb: 61,400 ft (18,715 m) per minute
Service ceiling: 62,250 ft (18,975 m)
Takeoff run at maximum takeoff weight: 4,390 ft (1338 m)
Landing run at maximum landing weight: 3,780 ft (1152 m)

Range

Ferry range: 1,978 miles (3184 km)
Area intercept combat radius: 786 miles (1266 km)
Defensive counter-air combat radius: 494 miles (795 km)
Interdiction combat radius: 712 miles (1145 km)

Armament

Fixed internal M61A1 Vulcan 0.79-in (20-mm) six-barrelled cannon; standard intercept load of four AIM-7 Sparrow missiles in fuselage recesses and four AIM-9 Sidewinders on wing pylon shoulder stations; four wing pylons and one centerline station available for carriage of wide range of air-to-ground ordnance, including M117 and Mk 80 series bombs, cluster weapons, laser-guided bombs, gun pods, napalm, fuel-air explosives and rocket pods; nuclear weapon options included B28, B43, B57 and B61; various ECM pods, training targets and laser designator pods available; air-to-surface missiles included AGM-12 Bullpup, AGM-45 Shrike, AGM-65 Maverick and AGM-78 Standard

143 Electroluminescent formation lighting strip
144 HF aerial panel
145 Anti-collision light
146 Stabilator feel system pressure head
147 Fin leading edge
148 Fintip aerial fairing
149 Upper UHF/VHF aerial
150 Tail navigation light
151 Rudder horn balance
152 Rudder
153 Honeycomb trailing-edge panels
154 Fuselage fuel cell jettison pipe
155 Rear radar warning antennas
156 Tailcone/brake parachute hinged door
157 Brake parachute housing
158 Honeycomb trailing-edge panel
159 Port all-moving tailplane/stabilator
160 Stabilator mass balance weight
161 Stabilator multi-spar construction
162 Pivot sealing plate
163 All-moving tailplane hinge mounting
164 Rudder hydraulic actuator
165 Tailplane hydraulic actuator
166 Heat-resistant tailcone skinning
167 Arrestor hook, lowered
168 Arrestor hook stowage
169 Stabilator feel system balance mechanism
170 Artificial feel system pneumatic bellows
171 Arrestor hook jack and shock absorber
172 Variable-area afterburner exhaust nozzle
173 Engine bay cooling exit louvers
174 Afterburner duct
175 Exhaust nozzle
176 Hinged engine cowling panels actuators
177 Port blown flap, down position
178 Boundary layer control air blowing slot
179 Lateral autopilot servo
180 Airbrake jack
181 Flap hydraulic jack
182 Rear spar
183 Port spoiler hydraulic jack
184 Aileron hydraulic actuator
185 Aileron flutter damper
186 Port spoiler housing
187 Aileron rib construction
188 Port drooping aileron, down position
189 Wing fuel-tank jettison pipe
190 Honeycomb trailing-edge panels
191 Port dihedral outer wing panel
192 Fixed portion of trailing edge
193 Rearward identification light
194 Electroluminescent formation light
195 Port navigation light
196 Outboard leading-edge flap, lowered
197 Boundary layer control air blowing slot
198 Leading-edge flap actuator
199 Outer wing panel multi-spar construction
200 Outer wing panel attachment joint
201 Leading-edge dogtooth
202 Port mainwheel
203 Mainwheel multi-plate disc brake
204 Mainwheel leg door
205 Outboard wing pylon
206 Inner wing panel outboard leading-edge flap, down position
207 Leading-edge flap rib construction
208 Wing pylon mounting
209 Main undercarriage leg pivot fixing
210 Hydraulic retraction jack
211 Undercarriage uplock
212 Port ventral airbrake panel, open
213 Main undercarriage wheel bay
214 Hydraulic reservoir
215 Hydraulic system accumulator
216 Port wing integral fuel tank, capacity 315 gal (1192 liters)
217 Two-spar torsion box fuel-tank construction
218 Wing skin support posts
219 Leading-edge

105 Rearward identification light
106 Starboard dihedral outboard wing panel
107 Wing fuel-tank vent pipe
108 Starboard drooping aileron, down position
109 Aileron flutter damper
110 Starboard spoilers, open
111 Spoiler hydraulic actuators
112 Fuel jettison and vent valves
113 Aileron hydraulic actuator
114 Starboard ventral airbrake panel
115 Starboard blown flap, down position
116 TACAN aerial
117 Fuel system piping
118 No. 3 fuselage fuel cell, capacity 150 gal (566 liters)
119 Engine intake compressor face
120 General Electric J79 GE-15 afterburning turbojet engine
121 Ventral engine accessory equipment gearbox
122 Wing rear spar attachment joint
123 Engine and afterburner control equipment
124 Emergency ram air turbine
125 Ram air turbine housing
126 Turbine doors, open
127 Turbine actuating link
128 Port engine bay frame construction
129 No. 4 fuselage fuel cell, capacity 200 gal (759 liters)
130 Jet pipe heat shield
131 No. 5 fuselage fuel cell, capacity 180 gal (681 liters)
132 Fuel feed and vent system piping
133 LORAN aerial
134 Dorsal access panels
135 Fuel pumps
136 No. 6 fuselage fuel cell, capacity 213 gal (806 liters)
137 Photographic flare dispenser, port and starboard
138 Flare compartment doors, open
139 Ram air intake, tailcone venting
140 Tailcone attachment bulkhead
141 Three-spar fin torsion box construction
142 Fin rib construction

220 Bleed air blowing slot
221 Outboard flap actuator
222 Inboard leading-edge flap, lowered
223 Hydraulic flap actuator
224 Inboard wing pylon
225 AN/ALQ-101 ECM pod
226 Port external fuel tank, capacity 370 gal (1400 liters)

boundary layer control air duct

"It was really fun to fly the F-4. It was a big, powerful, stable airplane that would bite an inexperienced guy in a heartbeat."
– Colonel Ron "Gunman" Moore, U.S. Air Force

MCDONNELL DOUGLAS F-4 PHANTOM II – VARIANTS

XF4H-1: Two prototypes for the U.S. Navy, first flown 1958.

F4H-1F (F-4A): Two-seat all-weather carrier-based fighter for the U.S. Navy. Named Phantom II in 1959 and redesignated F-4A in 1962; 45 built.

F4H-1 (F-4B): Two-seat all-weather carrier-based fighter and ground-attack aircraft for the U.S. Navy and Marine Corps. Redesignated F-4B in 1962.

F-110A Spectre: The original U.S. Air Force designation for the F-4C.

F-4C: Two-seat all-weather tactical fighter, ground-attack version for the U.S. Air Force. The aircraft exceeded Mach 2 during its first flight on May 27, 1963. 583 built.

EF-4C Wild Weasel IV: F-4Cs converted into Wild Weasel ECM aircraft.

F-4D: F-4C with updated avionics. First flight June 1965. 825 built.

EF-4D Wild Weasel IV: F-4Ds converted into Wild Weasel ECM aircraft.

F-4E: U.S. Air Force version with an integral

M61 Vulcan cannon in the elongated RF-4C nose. First flight August 7, 1965. The most numerous Phantom variant; 1,389 built.

F-4E Kurnass 2000: Modernized Israeli F-4Es.

F-4E Peace Icarus 2000: Greek Air Force modernized F-4Es.

F-4 Terminator 2020: The latest in a long line of F-4 variants, the Terminators are Turkish AF F-4Es, modernized by Israel.

F-4EJ: Two-seat all-weather air-defense fighter version of F-4E. 140 built, 138 of them under license in Japan.

F-4EJ Kai: Upgraded version of the F-4EJ with improved avionics.

F-4F: F-4E for German Luftwaffe with simplified equipment.

F-4F ICE: Upgraded F-4F.

F-4G: U.S. Navy version; 12 F-4Bs were fitted with the AN/ASW-21 data-link digital communications system for automatic carrier landings.

F-4G Wild Weasel V: F-4E converted to SEAD aircraft for the U.S. Air Force.

F-4J: Improved F-4B version for U.S. Navy and Marine Corps.

F-4J(UK): Designation of 15 low airtime F-4J aircraft purchased by the Royal Air Force from the U.S. Navy in 1984, upgraded to F-4S standard with some British equipment.

F-4K: F-4J version for Fleet Air Arm of the Royal Navy. Operated as the Phantom FG1 (Fighter/Ground attack).

F-4M: Tactical fighter, ground-attack and reconnaissance aircraft developed from F-4K for the Royal Air Force; RAF designation Phantom FGR Mk 2.

F-4N: F-4B modernized under project Bee Line, the same aerodynamic improvements as F-4J, smokeless engines.

F-4S: F-4J modernized with smokeless engines, reinforced airframe, leading-edge slats for improved maneuverability. 302 converted.

MCDONNELL DOUGLAS F-4 PHANTOM II

From 1973, Japan acquired 140 F-4EJ and RF-4EJ Phantoms, all but two built under license by Mitsubishi. Operated for many years as interceptors, a number were reassigned in the late 1990s to the fighter support role with ground-attack and anti-shipping capabilities. This F-4EJ Kai of the Japan Air Self-Defense Force's 8 Hikotai, 3 Kokudan, at Misawa carries a pair of indigenously designed turbojet-powered ASM-2 anti-shipping missiles. The F-4EJ Kai upgrade program saw the installation of APG-66J radar, a HUD, new radar warning equipment and a structural life extension program. Phantoms in the fighter support role are slowly being replaced with the Mitsubishi F-2, derived from the Lockheed Martin F-16.

Above: High above Europe, a Luftwaffe F-4F prepares to receive fuel in its dorsal receptacle. Empty Sidewinder rails can be seen under the wings.

The McDonnell Aircraft Company produced only one aircraft, the XP-67 Bat, in World War II. Its first jets were the FH-1 Phantom and F2H Banshee, the latter seeing considerable action in the ground-attack role in Korea. The F3H Demon was the company's first swept wing and supersonic aircraft, but its inadequate and unreliable Westinghouse engines led to it being regarded as something of a failure.

Several company proposals for a twin-engined fighter-bomber development of the Demon eventually morphed into a larger, all-new two-seat design with the designation F3H-G. The U.S. Navy liked the design, but wanted all-missile armament rather than four 0.79-in (20-mm) cannon. With guns deleted and other changes, the XF4H was ordered and a prototype first flew in May 1958, soon being named Phantom II.

ENTERING SERVICE
After extensive testing and several speed and climb records were taken by F4H (later F-4A) test aircraft, the U.S. Navy ordered a large batch of F-4Bs with a larger nose, improved

Above: This F-4 cockpit features a head-up display, a feature added to most upgraded Phantoms.

Above: The F-4D had no built-in gun, but this U.S. Air Force example is carrying a 0.79-in (20-mm) Vulcan in an SUU-23 pod under the centerline. It was less accurate than the internal gun on the F-4E.

radar and a larger rear canopy for the Radar Intercept Officer (RIO). In what was then a very unusual move, the U.S. Air Force ordered its own version, which was initially called the F-110A, and later the F-4C.

The Phantom was characterized by the upturn (dihedral) of its outer wing panels and downturn (anhedral) of its all-moving tailplanes, or stabilators. The former corrected roll instability and the latter kept the tail surfaces in clear air at high angles of attack. Under the belly were recesses for four AIM-7 Sparrow missiles, while wing pylons could carry two more, or four AIM-9 Sidewinders, or a combination of fuel tanks and missiles.

DIFFERING ROLES

The U.S. Air Force regarded the Phantom as a fighter-bomber, while the U.S. Navy operated it primarily as a fleet defense interceptor from its larger carriers. In Vietnam, where the F-4 was the workhorse of both forces, USAF Phantoms proved the most successful MiG-killers and the Navy's were often employed as bombers. Vietnam showed up the foolishness of dispensing with guns, as restrictive rules of engagement and poor missile reliability meant that many North Vietnamese

enemy MiGs escaped. A centerline gun pod was a partial answer, but a crash program saw development of the F-4E with a built-in M61 Vulcan cannon under a slimmer nose. It arrived too late to much affect the kill–loss ratio in Vietnam, but became the version of choice for export customers.

EXPORT SUCCESS

The Phantom sold to Israel, West Germany, Greece, Turkey, Iran, Egypt and South Korea. Japan built nearly 140 under license. The United Kingdom ordered versions powered by the Rolls-Royce Spey turbofan rather than the General Electric J79 turbojet. The F-4Ks (or FG 1s) flew off the Royal Navy's last big deck carrier, HMS *Ark Royal*, joining the Royal Air Force's F-4Ms (FGR 2s) when the "Ark" was retired.

Israel's F-4Es saw the most combat action, scoring 116 victories from 1970 onwards. Iran's saw extensive combat with Iraq in the 1980s and Turkey's have been used in the ground-attack role against Kurdish factions.

A number of upgrades, such as Turkey's Terminator 2020, have kept the Phantom viable into the twenty-first century, by allowing use of weapons such as the AIM-120 AMRAAM and adding a head-up display and modern multimode radar.

Saab J 35 Draken

Sweden's Saab company has become famous for its innovative fighter designs. One of the most unusual was the Draken (Dragon), which was also the first Saab fighter to be exported in reasonable numbers.

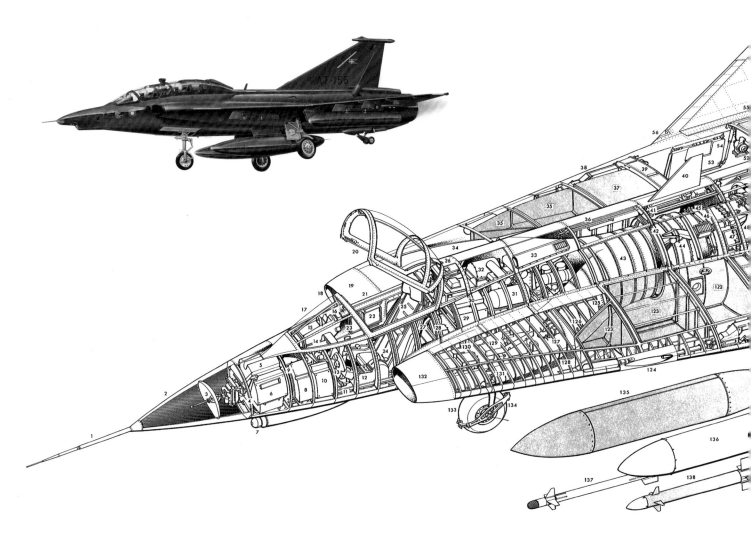

Cutaway Key

1 Nose probe
2 Fiberglass nose cone
3 Radar scanner
4 Scanner mounting frame
5 Radar pack
6 Saab S7-collision-course fire control
7 L.M. Ericsson (Hughes license) infrared seeker
8 Electronics pack
9 Front pressure bulkhead
10 Data-handling unit
11 Rudder pedal assembly
12 Port instrument console

13 Side panel
14 Instrument panel/radar scope shield
15 Windshield frame
16 Weapons sight
17 Windshield
18 Starboard intake
19 Fiberglass intake lip
20 Aft-hinged cockpit canopy
21 Cockpit sill
22 Control panel
23 Control column
24 Throttle quadrant
25 Pilots Saab RS 35 ejection seat
26 Canopy hinge mechanism
27 Seat support frame

28 Rear pressure bulkhead
29 Navigation computer
30 Forward avionics equipment bay
31 Gyro unit
32 TACAN transmitter-receiver
33 Auxiliary air intake
34 Starboard intake trunk
35 Starboard fuel tanks
36 Dorsal spine
37 Starboard forward bag-type fuel tank
38 1.18-in (30-mm) ADEN cannon
39 Ammunition magazine

(100 rounds)
40 Dorsal antenna
41 Electrical wiring
42 Mid-fuselage production break line
43 Intake trunking
44 Oil-cooler air intake
45 Volvo Flygmotor RM6C (Rolls-Royce Avon 300 series) turbojet
46 Louvers
47 Access panels
48 Fuselage frames
49 Engine firewall
50 Cooling air inlet scoop
51 Fin-root fairing
52 Fuel transfer

53 Starboard mainwheel door
54 Door actuating rod
55 Inner/outer wing joint strap
56 Starboard navigation light
57 Wing skinning
58 Starboard outer elevon
59 Hinge point
60 Actuating jack access
61 Control hinge
62 Access panels
63 Starboard aft integral fuel tank
64 Starboard aft bag-type fuel tanks (3)
65 Intake grille

66 Jet pipe
67 Engine aft mounting ring
68 Access
69 Tailfin main spar attachment
70 Control stick angle indicator unit
71 Computer amplifier
72 Synchronizer pack
73 Tailfin structure
74 Pitot tube
75 Rudder mass balance
76 Rudder structure
77 Rudder post
78 Tailfin rear spar
79 Rudder servo mechanism and actuator

80 Attachment point
81 Speed brake
82 Fuselage structure
83 Detachable tail cone (engine removal)
84 Access panel
85 Brake parachute housing
86 Aft fairing
87 Afterburner assembly
88 Exhaust
89 Air intake (afterburner housing)
90 Control surface blunt trailing edge
91 Port inner elevon
92 Hinge points
93 Elevon actuator

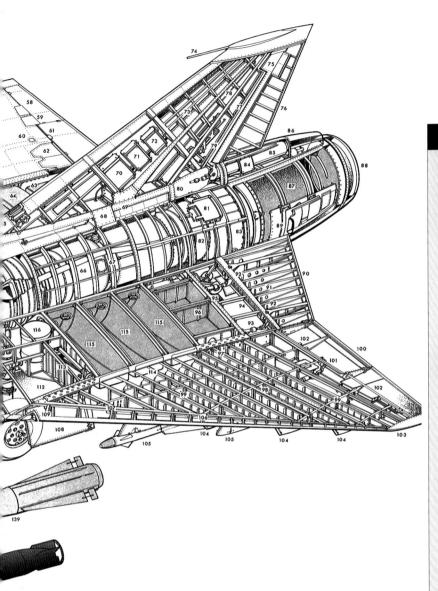

J 35J DRAKEN SPECIFICATION

Dimensions

Length: 50 ft 4 in (15.35 m)
Wingspan: 30 ft 10 in (9.40 m)
Height: 12 ft 9 in (3.89 m)
Wing area: 529.60 sq ft (49.20 m²)
Wing aspect ratio: 1.77
Wheel track: 8 ft 10¹/₂ in (2.70 m)

Power plant

One 12,790-lb st (56.89-kN) dry or 17,650-lb st
(78.5-kN) with afterburning Volvo Flygmotor RM6C
turbojet (license-built Rolls-Royce Avon Series 300
turbojet fitted with a Swedish-designed afterburner)

Weights

Empty: 18,188 lb (8250 kg)
Normal takeoff: 25,132 lb (11,400 kg)
Maximum takeoff: 27,050 lb (12,270 kg) for
  interceptor mission or 33,069 lb (17,650 kg) for
  attack mission

Fuel

Internal fuel: 1,057 gal (4000 liters)
External fuel: provision for up to 1,321 gal (5000 liters)
  in external drop tanks

Performance

Maximum level speed "clean" at 36,000 ft (10,975 m):
  more than 1,147 kt (1,317 mph; 2119 km/h)
Maximum speed at 300 ft (90 m): 793 kt (910 mph;
  1465 km/h)
Maximum climb rate at sea level: 34,450 ft (10,500 m)
  per minute with afterburning
Service ceiling: 65,600 ft (19,995 m)
Takeoff run: 2,133 ft (650 m) at normal takeoff weight
Takeoff distance to 50 ft (15 m): 3,150 ft (960 m) at
  normal takeoff weight

Range

Ferry range: 1,533 nm (1,763 miles; 2837 km)
Combat radius: 304 nm (350 miles; 564 km) on a
  hi-lo-hi attack mission with internal fuel only

Armament

Usual air-to-air armament of two AIM-9J Sidewinder
air-to-air missiles on center-section pylons, two Hughes
Falcon air-to-air missiles on wing pylons and one
1.18-in (30-mm) ADEN cannon with 90 rounds in
starboard wing. Maximum ordnance of 6,393 lb
(2900 kg).

---

94 Rear spar
95 Twin (retractable) tailwheels
96 Port aft
97 Inner/outer wing joint
98 Wing outer structure
99 Rib stations
100 Port outer elevon
101 Elevon actuator
102 Hinge points
103 Port wingtip
104 Anti-buffet underwing fences (6)
105 Stores pylons (maximum 8)
106 Nose ribs
107 Forward spar
108 Wheel door
109 Port navigation light

110 Port main wheel
111 Door inboard section
112 Port main wheel well
113 Fuel transfer
114 Wing joint strap
115 Port aft bag-type fuel tanks (3)
116 Fuel collector
117 Mainwheel retraction mechanism
118 Mainwheel oleo leg mounting
119 Engine accessory gearbox
120 Port cannon ammunition magazine
121 Port 1.18-in (30-mm) ADEN cannon

(Saab 35F has
starboard gun only,
earlier intercept and
export 35X versions
retaining port gun
as illustrated)
122 Port forward bag-type fuel tank
123 Port forward integral fuel tanks
124 Cannon port
125 Inner wing/fuselage integral structure
126 Angled frame member
127 Emergency ventral ram-air turbine
128 Trunking formers
129 Gyro amplifiers
130 Intake trunking
131 Nosewheel leg
132 Fiberglass

intake lip
133 Forward retracting nosewheel
134 Steering mechanism
135 Possible stores (including jettisonable tanks)
136 Pod containing 19 x 3-in (75-mm) rockets
137 Rb 28 (Sidewinder) IR-homing missile
138 5.3-in (13.5-cm) rocket
139 Rb 27 (Falcon) radar-homing missile
140 1,102-lb (500-kg) bomb

"The Draken was the first aircraft that combined low speed and short take-off and landing ability with Mach 2 performance." – Per Pellesberg, Saab test pilot

SAAB J 35 DRAKEN – VARIANTS

J 35A: Fighter version. The J 35As were delivered from 1959–61. The tail section was lengthened. This forced the installation of a retractable tail wheel. The two versions were nicknamed "Adam kort" (Adam short) and "Adam lång" (Adam long). Total production: 90.

J 35B: Fighter version. Built and delivered from 1962–63. This variant had improved radar and gunsights and was also fully integrated into the Swedish STRIL 60 system (a combat guidance and air surveillance system). Total production: 73.

SK 35C: 25 J 35As with short tail sections rebuilt into a twin-seat trainer version. The minor modification meant that the aircraft could easily be converted back to a J 35A standard if necessary.

J 35D: Fighter version. Delivered from 1963–64. The aircraft had a new and more powerful Rolls-Royce Avon 300 (RM 6C), which could deliver 17,386 lb (77.3 kN) thrust when using its afterburner. This was also the fastest Draken version, capable of accelerating until out of fuel. It was also the last Draken to carry two cannons. Total production: 120.

S 35E: Reconnaissance version. The aircraft was unarmed, but was fitted with a countermeasure system to increase its survivability. A total of 28 aircraft were rebuilt J 35Ds. Total production: 60.

J 35F: Fighter version. Delivered from 1965–72. Improved electronics and avionics (integrated radar, aim and missile systems).

J 35F2: A J 35F produced with a Hughes Aircraft Company N71 infrared sensor, a so-called IR seeker.

J 35J: In 1985, the Swedish government decided to modify 54 J 35F2s to J 35J standard. In 1987, 12 more modifications were ordered. Between 1987 and 1991, the aircraft were given a longer lifespan, more modern electronics, a modernized cannon, an additional two Sidewinder pylons under the air intakes and increased fuel capacity. The final operative J 35J flew for the last time in 1999.

Saab 35H: Proposed export version for the Swiss Air Force.

Saab 35XD: Danish export versions. F-35 single-seat Strike Aircraft, TF-35 two-seat trainer and RF-35 reconnaissance aircraft. The type was heavily modified to make it into a strike aircraft in comparison to the Swedish versions.

Saab 35XS: Fighter version for the Finnish Air Force; built by Saab and assembled under license by Valmet in Finland.

Saab 35BS: Used J 35Bs sold to Finland.

Saab 35FS: Used J 35F1s sold to Finland.

Saab 35CS: Used SK 35Cs sold to Finland.

Saab 35Ö: In the mid-1980s, Saab purchased back 24 J 35D aircraft from the Swedish Air Force and converted them into the J 35Ö version (also called J 35OE in English literature). These examples were later exported to Austria.

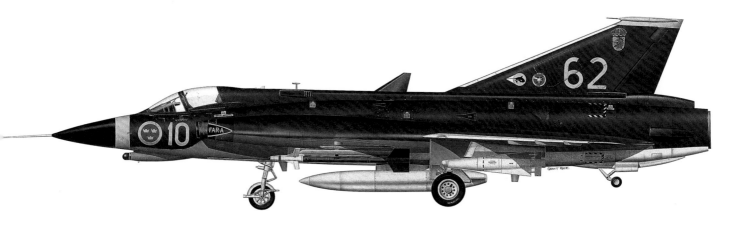

SAAB J 35 DRAKEN

The J 35J Draken was an upgraded version of the J 35F for the Swedish Air Force. The program was undertaken to keep two squadrons of Drakens operational during a period of delays with Saab's JAS 39 Gripen. To create the J 35J, the nose and cockpit were removed and rebuilt by Saab, while FFV refurbished the rest of the airframe. External changes included an infrared search-and-track sensor unit under the nose and two extra fuselage pylons, shown here carrying AIM-9J Sidewinders. The wing pylons have Rb28 (AIM-4C Falcon) missiles. The modified J 35Js re-entered service between 1987 and 1991. This particular aircraft served with F 10 Wing at Ängelholm in southern Sweden until 1999.

Above: Finland's Drakens operated in all kinds of weather from 1974 until 2000. Austria and Denmark were the other export customers.

The Draken (Dragon) was Saab's first supersonic fighter. The company made a leap ahead in just a few years from the first-generation J 29 Tunnan, equivalent to the North American F-86, and the Hunter-like J 32 Lansen, to a tailless delta capable of Mach 2. The specification that led to the Draken was issued in 1949, when supersonic flight and delta wings were both novelties. As well as high performance and onboard radar, the specification called for the ability to operate from straight stretches of highway as part of Sweden's measures to avoid its fighters being destroyed on the ground in the first hours of war.

The Draken was designed as a "double delta," with its swept wing having different sweep on its inboard and outboard sections. This contrasted with "pure" deltas such as the

Convair F-102 and Dassault Mirage III. To test the unique configuration, Saab built a scale testbed called the "Lill Draken," or "Little Dragon," which first flew in 1952. This was about 70 percent the size of the proposed fighter, but the Armstrong Siddeley Adder engine was proportionally much smaller than the one intended for the Draken, and the Lill Draken's performance was very low. Nonetheless, it validated the wing design and proved the need for a longer nose to improve airflow into the intakes.

MATCHING POWER TO PERFORMANCE

The full-size J 35 Draken flew in October 1955, powered by a license-built Rolls-Royce Avon engine. Production Drakens had the Volvo RM6B, a version of the Avon with a Swedish-designed afterburner. Standard armament was a pair of 1.18-in (30-mm) Aden cannon and two AIM-9B Sidewinder missiles (locally designated Rb24). Later models could carry the Hughes AIM-4 Falcon (Rb27 and Rb28), and export versions could use later versions of the Sidewinder.

78

Several improved versions followed the initial J 35A, among them the J 35D (which was the first to be capable of Mach 2 speeds), the S 35E reconnaissance model and the J 35F with Falcon missile capability. Swedish policy at the time prevented sales of weapons to most nations likely ever to use them, but NATO member Denmark became the first export customer in 1968, taking just over 50 fighters, reconnaissance aircraft and trainers. Finland bought a similar number, all single-seaters. Austria acquired 24 in the 1980s, finally retiring them in 2005.

CRUCIAL INNOVATION

One of the less visible but most important features of the Draken was its connection with the Swedish data-link system, one of the first to be used anywhere. The STRIL 60 ground-control network used early digital computer technology and could guide the Draken pilot to a firing solution by presenting him with guidance on his cockpit instruments. It was resistant to electronic jamming.

The unusual shape of the Draken caused one unfortunate flight characteristic – a tendency to "super-stall," when the nose pitched up quickly and the aircraft fell out of control if

Above: The two-seat Draken featured a periscope to give the instructor a forward view for landings.

mishandled. Particular attention was needed to avoid this condition during air combat maneuvers. Several Drakens were lost in super-stall accidents in training.

The Draken never saw combat, although the user nations frequently intercepted intruding aircraft with them. The first good photographs of many new Soviet aircraft were captured by Draken pilots over the Baltic in the 1970s and 1980s.

Above: A pair of early Flygvapnet (Swedish Air Force) J 35As of F13 Wing show off the Rb 24, the Swedish-produced version of the AIM-9B Sidewinder.

Modern Jets 1960–Present

As the Vietnam War came to its conclusion, the fighter rule book was being torn up. Air forces and designers stopped referring to fighters as missile platforms or as the manned component of a weapons system.

Above: The Saab 37 Viggen typified the 1970s approach of different versions for different roles, as illustrated by this AJ 37 of the Swedish Air Force's F 7 Såtenäs, loaded with Mk 81 general-purpose bombs.

Emphasis was placed on air combat again, with agility favored over pure performance. Features such as bubble canopies returned, the head-up display (HUD) and hands-on-throttle-and-stick (HOTAS) allowed the pilot to concentrate on the target without taking his eyes off it, and there were multifunction displays (MFDs) to manage weapons, sensors and systems in a single-seat cockpit.

Miniaturization and advances in electronics permitted a comparatively tiny fighter such as the Lockheed Martin F-16 to be far more effective than a monster such as the Republic F-105, although turn performance and climb rate were achieved at the expense of range and straight-line speed. For some roles such as fleet defense and long-range interception, a two-man crew was usually deemed necessary.

THE ADVENT OF FLY-BY-WIRE

The most significant advance in the fourth generation was "fly-by-wire." Direct or hydraulically boosted connection between the pilot's hands and feet and the control surfaces was replaced by electrical connections routed through computers. This allowed almost any input, no matter how violent, with the computers (there were usually at least three) regulating the control movement to produce the maximum effect without fear of overstressing the airframe. This meant instantaneous changes of direction and sustained turn rates that put the stress on the pilot. Whereas most third-generation aircraft were stressed to 7 g (acceleration of gravity), their successors were usually rated up to 12. Turns of 9 g became common, and the threat of GLOC, or g-induced loss of consciousness, became a concern and was cited as the cause of many accidents. Pilots were more strictly screened for g tolerance, given improved g-suits and trained to deal with high forces by straining to prevent blood flow away from the upper body under high g.

The first fourth-generation fighter was the F-16 Fighting Falcon. In its initial F-16A form as delivered to the U.S. Air Force in 1978, it was little more than an agile day fighter

Right: The Eurofighter Typhoon lacks obvious stealth features, but it is the top-of-the-line fighter in production and on the market in the early 2010s.

Above: The MiG-29 has remained viable through upgrade programs, including those that make them compatible with NATO systems and procedures.

with a basic ground-attack capability with "dumb" bombs. More than 30 years later, the F-16 remains in production, but under the skin is virtually a new aircraft, offering advanced electronic warfare and self-protection capabilities, as well as an enormous range of precision weapons from numerous U.S. and foreign manufacturers.

ADVANCING A HALF GENERATION

Conformal fuel tanks have boosted the F-16 range, and new radars and sensors are offered to suit the needs of the customer. Not, however, the U.S. Air Force, which long ago accepted its last Fighting Falcon. For the first time, export users (notably Israel and the United Arab Emirates) are fielding a fighter considerably more advanced than the versions in use by the domestic customer. These later F-16s, plus the newer block Super Hornets, the Saab JAS 39C/D Gripen, Eurofighter Typhoon, Dassault Rafale and Sukhoi Su-30/-35 are sometimes

called "4.5 generation fighters," having a network-enabled capability allowing them to share data from their radars and other sensors (which can be presented on the one display in a process called "sensor fusion") via secure data links.

Today, as in 1945, only five countries have an indigenous jet fighter in production: the United States, Russia, Sweden, France and China, although there are others collaborating on projects such as the Typhoon.

THE FIFTH GENERATION … OR NOT?

The U.S. Air Force has moved directly on to the fifth generation, fielding (after a long development) the Lockheed Martin/Boeing F-22 Raptor, and progressing with the Lockheed Martin F-35 Lightning II. Each of these embodies stealth technology and unparalleled electronic self-defense systems. The colossal cost of the F-22 (nearing $140 million apiece) and restrictions on technology transfer mean that no

Above: France's Rafale is the only one of the "Eurocanard" fighters built in both land-based (rear) and carrier-capable versions.

Above: The Lockheed Martin/Boeing F-22 Raptor, with its stealth technology, is the only true fifth-generation fighter in service, but rivals from Russia and China can be expected in the next decade.

more than 187 will likely ever be built, all of them for U.S. Air Force use only. The F-35 was conceived as a lower-cost complement to the F-22, with a primary ground-attack role and significant international contribution from risk-sharing partner nations. The program is highly dependent, however, on sales to the U.S. forces, partner countries and beyond of 4,500–6,000 aircraft. At least one independent analysis of the market suggests that because of delays and cost hikes, and a trend to not replace older fighters at all in some regions, fewer F-35s will be purchased than anticipated and the real figure may be closer to 2,500.

MOVING TOWARD THE FUTURE

In the United States, purchases of increased numbers of 4.5-generation aircraft such as the Boeing F/A-18E/F Super Hornet and the proposed Boeing F-15SE Silent Eagle with some stealth characteristics may be needed to close the U.S. Air Force's and U.S. Navy's "fighter gap" between retiring aircraft and the F-35. In January 2010, Sukhoi finally flew the prototype T-50, the mysterious fifth-generation stealth fighter that had spawned the concept of fighter generations two decades before.

Whereas most third-generation aircraft were stressed to 7 g, their successors were usually rated up to 12. Turns of 9 g became common, and the threat of GLOC, or g-induced loss of consciousness, became a concern and was cited as the cause of many accidents.

Mikoyan-Gurevich MiG-23 "Flogger"

Powerful and fast, the MiG-23 was the backbone of the Soviet Union's air-defense squadrons through the 1970s and 1980s, but was fairly soon outmoded by fly-by-wire Western fighters. A wide number of subvariants were supplied to Soviet allies and client states, but it has become increasingly rare in the 2000s.

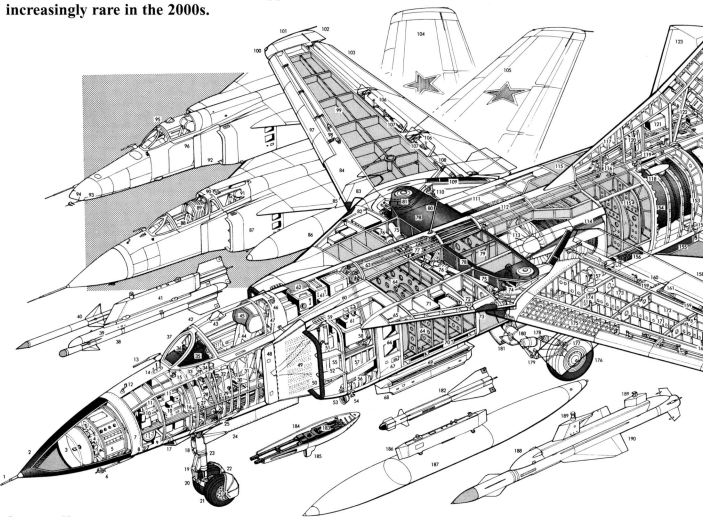

Cutaway Key

1 Pitot tube
2 Radome
3 Flat dish radar scanner
4 Scanner tracking mechanism
5 "High Lark" J-band pulse-Doppler radar module
6 "Swift-Rod" ILS aerial
7 Radar-mounting bulkhead
8 Cooling air scoop
9 Ventral doppler navigation aerial
10 Weapons system avionics equipment
11 Nose compartment access doors

12 Yaw vane
13 Dynamic pressure probe (Q-Feel)
14 SRO-2 "Odd-Rods" IFF antenna
15 Temperature probe
16 Cockpit front pressure bulkhead
17 Ventral laser range finder
18 Nosewheel steering control
19 Torque scissor links
20 Pivoted axle beam
21 Twin aft-retracting nosewheels
22 Nosewheel spray/debris guards

23 Shock-absorber strut
24 Nosewheel doors
25 Hydraulic retraction jack
26 Angle-of-attack transmitter
27 Rudder pedals
28 Control column
29 L-position wing sweep control lever
30 Engine throttle lever
31 Cockpit section framing
32 Ejection-seat firing handles
33 Radar "head-down" display
34 Instrument panel

35 Instrument panel shield
36 Weapons sighting unit "head-up" display
37 Armored-glass windshield panel
38 AA-2 "Atoll" K-13A infrared homing air-to-air missile
39 Missile launch rail
40 AA-2-2 Advanced "Atoll" radar homing air-to-air missile
41 Wing glove pylon
42 Cockpit canopy cover, upward-hinging

43 Electrically heated rear-view mirror
44 Pilot's "zero-zero" ejection seat
45 Ejection-seat headrest/drogue parachute container
46 Canopy hinge point
47 Canopy hydraulic jack
48 Boundary layer splitter plate
49 Boundary layer ramp bleed air holes
50 Port engine air intake
51 Adjustable intake ramp screw jack control

52 Intake internal flow fences
53 Retractable landing/taxiing lamp, port and starboard
54 Pressure sensor, automatic intake control system
55 Variable-area intake ramp doors
56 Intake duct framing
57 Ventral cannon ammunition magazine
58 Control rod linkages
59 Intake ramp bleed air ejector

60 Boundary layer spill duct
61 Avionics equipment
62 ADF sense aerial
63 Tailplane control rods
64 Forward fuselage fuel tanks
65 Wing glove fairing
66 Intake duct suction relief doors
67 Ground power and intercom sockets
68 Twin missile carrier/launch unit
69 Port fuselage stores pylon

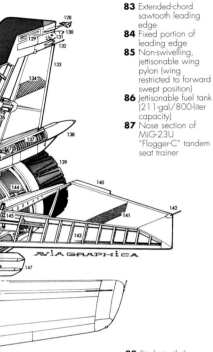

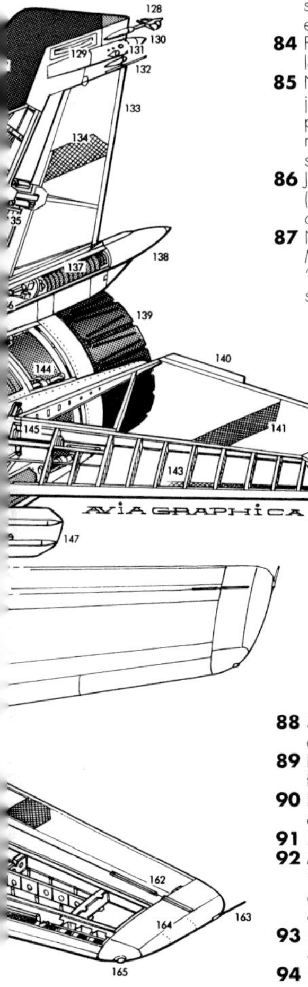

AVIAGRAPHICA

83 Extended-chord sawtooth leading edge
84 Fixed portion of leading edge
85 Non-swivelling, jettisonable wing pylon (wing restricted to forward swept position)
86 Jettisonable fuel tank (211-gal/800-liter capacity)
87 Nose section of MiG-23U "Flogger-C" tandem seat trainer
88 Student pilot's cockpit
89 Folding blind flying hood
90 Rear-seat periscope, extended
91 Instructor's cockpit
92 MiG-23BN "Flogger-F" dedicated ground-attack variant
93 Radar-ranging antenna
94 Laser-ranging nose fairing
95 Raised cockpit canopy
96 Armored fuselage side panels
97 Starboard wing leading-edge flap (lowered)
98 Leading-edge flap hydraulic actuator
99 Starboard wing integral fuel tank (total fuel capacity 1,519 gal/ 5750 liters)
100 Starboard navigation light
101 Wing fully forward (16° sweep) position
102 Static discharger
103 Full-span 3-segment plain flap (lowered)
104 Starboard wing intermediate (45° sweep) position
105 Starboard wing full (72° sweep) position
106 Two-segment spoilers/lift dumpers (open)

107 Spoiler hydraulic actuators
108 Flap hydraulic jack
109 Wing glove flexible seal
110 Flap mechanical interconnection and disengage mechanism
111 Wing root housing
112 Dorsal spine fairing
113 Engine intake compressor face
114 Wing root housing sealing plate
115 Rear-fuselage fuel tanks
116 Tailplane control linkages
117 Fin-root fillet
118 Afterburner duct cooling air scoop
119 Artificial feel control units
120 Control system hydraulic accumulator
121 Artificial feel and autopilot controls
122 Tailplane trim controls
123 Starboard all-moving tailplane
124 Fin leading edge
125 Tailfin construction
126 Short-wave ground-control communications aerial
127 Fintip UHF aerial fairing
128 ILS aerial
129 ECM aerial
130 "Sirena-3" tail warning radar
131 Tail navigation light
132 Static discharger
133 Rudder
134 Honeycomb core construction
135 Rudder hydraulic actuators, port and starboard
136 Parachute release links
137 Brake parachute housing
138 Split conic fairing parachute doors
139 Variable-area afterburner nozzle
140 Fixed tailplane tab
141 Honeycomb core trailing-edge panel
142 Static discharger
143 Port all-moving tailplane construction
144 Afterburner nozzle control jacks (6)
145 Tailplane pivot bearing
146 Tailplane actuator
147 Airbrakes (4), upper and lower surfaces
148 Airbrake hydraulic jacks

149 Afterburner duct heat shield
150 Ventral fin, folded (undercarriage down) position
151 Ventral fin down position
152 Screw jack fin actuator
153 Fin attachment fuselage main frame
154 Tumanskii R-29B afterburning turbojet engine
155 Lower UHF aerial
156 Engine accessory equipment compartment
157 Air-conditioning system equipment
158 Port plain flap
159 Spoiler actuators
160 Port spoilers/lift dumpers
161 Flap guide rails
162 Fixed spoiler strips
163 Static discharger
164 Wingtip fairing
165 Port navigation light
166 Port leading-edge flap
167 Leading-edge flap control linkage
168 Front spar
169 Wing rib construction
170 Rear spar
171 Auxiliary center spar
172 Wing skin support struts
173 Port wing integral fuel tank
174 Wing pylon attachment fitting
175 Leading-edge rib construction
176 Port mainwheel
177 Mainwheel door/ debris guard
178 Shock-absorber strut
179 Pivoted axle beam
180 Articulated mainwheel leg strut
181 Mainwheel leg doors
182 AA-8 "Aphid" (R-60) short-range air-to-air missile
183 GSh-23L twin-barrel 0.91-in (23-mm) cannon
184 Ventral cannon pack
185 Gun gas venting air scoop
186 Fuselage centerline pylon
187 Ventral fuel tank (211-gal/800-liter capacity)
188 "Apex" missile launch rail
189 Launch rail attachment hard points
190 AA-7 "Apex" (R-23) long-range air-to-air missile

70 Weapons system electronic control units
71 Electronic countermeasures equipment
72 Wing glove pylon attachment fitting
73 SO-69 "Sirena-3" radar warning and suppression aerials
74 Wing sweep control horn
75 Screw jack wing sweep rotary actuator
76 Twin hydraulic motors
77 Central combining gearbox
78 Wing pivot box carry-through unit (welded steel construction)
79 Pivot box integral fuel tank
80 VHF aerial
81 Wing pivot bearing
82 Starboard "Sirena-3" radar warning and suppression aerials

MIG-27 "FLOGGER-D" SPECIFICATION

Dimensions

Wingspan (spread): 45 ft 9⅘ in (13.97 m)
Wingspan (swept): 25 ft 6¼ in (7.78 m)
Wing aspect ratio (spread): 5.22
Wing aspect ratio (swept): 1.77
Tailplane span: 18 ft 10¼ in (5.75 m)
Wing area (spread): 402.05 sq ft (37.35 m²)
Wing area (swept): 367.71 sq ft (34.16 m²)
Length (including probe): 56 ft ¼ in (17.08 m)
Wheel track: 8 ft 8¾ in (2.66 m)
Wheel base: 18 ft 11¼ in (5.77 m)
Height: 16 ft 5 in (5.00 m)

Power plant

One Soyuz/Khachaturov R-29B-300 turbojet rated at 17,625 lb st (78.40 kN) dry and 25,335 lb st (112.77 kN) with afterburning

Weights

Empty equipped: 26,252 lb (11,908 kg)
Normal takeoff: 39,903 lb (18,100 kg)
Maximum takeoff: 44,753 lb (20,300 kg)

Fuel and load

Internal fuel: 10,053 lb (4560 kg), or 1,427 gal (5400 liters)
External fuel: Up to three 209-gal (790-liter) drop tanks
Maximum weapon load: 8,818 lb (4000 kg)

Performance

Maximum level speed "clean" at 26,245 ft (8000 m): 1,170 mph (1885 km/h)
Maximum level speed "clean" at sea level: 839 mph (1350 km/h)
Maximum rate of climb at sea level: 39,370 ft (12,000 m) per minute
Service ceiling: 45,930 ft (14,000 m)
Takeoff run at maximum takeoff weight: 3,117 ft (950 m)
Landing run at normal landing weight (without brake parachute): 4,265 ft (1300 m)
Landing run at normal landing weight (with brake parachute): 2,953 ft (900 m)

Range

Combat radius: 335 miles (540 km) on a lo-lo-lo attack mission with two Kh-29 ASMs and three drop tanks, or 140 miles (225 km) with two Kh-29 ASMs

Armament

One 0.91-in (23-mm) GSh-23L twin-barrelled cannon in underfuselage pack; two bomb or JATO hard points either side of rear fuselage, plus five additional hard points for the carriage of tactical nuclear bombs; Kh-23 (AS-7 "Kerry") and Kh-29 (AS-14 "Kedge") ASMs; 9½-in (240-mm) S-24 rockets, 2¼-in (57-mm) UB-32 or UB-16 rocket packs; 22 110-lb (50-kg) or 220-lb (100-kg) bombs, or nine 551-lb (250-kg) bombs, or eight 1,102-lb (500-kg) bombs; napalm containers or R-3S/K-13T (AA-2D "Atoll-D") and R-13M AAMs

Iraq's MiG-23s had some success against Iran's Northrop F-5s, McDonnell Douglas F-4 Phantoms and even F-14s.

MIKOYAN-GUREVICH MIG-23 "FLOGGER" – VARIANTS

FIRST GENERATION

MiG-23 ("Flogger-A"): The pre-production model. This model marked the divergence of the MiG-23/-27 and Sukhoi Su-24 from their common ancestor.

MiG-23S ("Flogger-A"): The initial production variant.

MiG-23SM ("Flogger-A"): The second pre-production variant, which was also known as the MiG-23 Type 1971. It was considerably modified compared to the MiG-23S.

MiG-23M ("Flogger-B"): The first truly mass-produced version of the MiG-23, and the first Soviet Air Force (VVS) fighter to feature look-down/shoot-down capabilities. This variant first flew on June 1972.

MiG-23MF ("Flogger-B"): An export derivative of the MiG-23M to Warsaw Pact countries and other allies and clients. Some 1,300 MiG-23Ms were produced for the Soviet Air Force (VVS) and Soviet Air Defense Forces (PVO Strany) between 1972 and 1978. It was the most important Soviet fighter type from the mid- to late 1970s.

MiG-23U ("Flogger-C"): A twin-seat training variant.

MiG-23UB ("Flogger-C"): Very similar to MiG-23U except that the R-29 turbojet engine replaced the older R-27 installed in the MiG-23U.

MiG-23MP ("Flogger-E"): Similar to the MiG-23MS, but produced in much fewer numbers and never exported.

MiG-23MS ("Flogger-E"): An export variant, as the 1970s MiG-23M was considered too advanced to be exported to developing countries.

SECOND GENERATION

MiG-23P ("Flogger-G"): A specialized air-defense interceptor variant with the same airframe and power plant as the MiG-23ML, but with a cutback fin-root fillet instead of the original extended one on other models. Not exported.

MiG-23bis ("Flogger-G"): Similar to the MiG-23P.

MiG-23ML: A considerable redesign of the airframe with refined aerodynamics, maneuverability, new engine and thrust-to-weight ratio.

MiG-23MLA ("Flogger-G"): The later production variant of the "ML." Cooperative group search operations were now possible because the radars would not jam each other.

MiG-23MLD ("Flogger-K"): The ultimate fighter variant of the MiG-23 with improved maneuverability.

GROUND-ATTACK VARIANTS

MiG-23BM ("Flogger-D"): A MiG-23BK upgrade, with a digital computer replacing the original analog one.

MiG-23BM: The MiG-23BM experimental aircraft served as a predecessor to the MiG-27.

MiG-23B ("Flogger-F"): The MiG-23 appeared suitable for conversion to fit the new requirement for a late 1960s fighter-bomber.

MiG-23BK ("Flogger-H"): Exported to Warsaw Pact countries.

MiG-23BN ("Flogger-H"): The MiG-23BN was the definitive fighter-bomber variant. Extensively exported.

MiG-27: A simplified ground-attack version with simple pitot air intakes, no radar and a simplified engine with two-position afterburner nozzle.

UPGRADES

MiG-23K: A carrier-borne fighter variant based on the MiG-23ML.

MiG-23A: A multirole variant based on the "K."

MiG-23-9: A late 1990s upgrade.

MiG-23-98-2: An export upgrade including the Saphir radar fitted to their MiG-23MLs.

MiG-23LL (flying laboratory): MiG-23s and MiG-25s were used as the first jet-fighter platforms to test a new in-cockpit warning system with a pre-recorded female voice designed to inform pilots about various flight parameters.

FACTS

- The Mikoyan-Gurevich MiG-23 was the Soviet Union's first variable-geometry fighter.

- Unlike most other "swing-wing" aircraft, the MiG-23 possessed a wing that swept into one of three angles, rather than being fully variable.

- A ventral fin under the rear fuselage was needed for inflight stability, but could be swung out of the way for landing.

Above: A "Flogger" pilot and a mechanic discuss a technical point before a mission is undertaken.

MIKOYAN-GUREVICH MIG-23 "FLOGGER"

Libyan air power is organized along Soviet lines, with interceptors, surface-to-air missiles and radars assigned to Libyan Arab Air Defense Command, and transports, helicopters and fighter-bombers to the Libyan Arab Air Force. The country acquired 54 MiG-23MF and MS fighters in the mid-1970s, and later added a similar number of MiG-23BNs. In January 1989, Libya's "Floggers" repeated the mistake of its Sukhoi Su-22s and tangled with two U.S. Navy Grumman F-14 Tomcats over the Gulf of Sirte. Two MiG-23s were brought down, one by an AIM-9 and one by an AIM-7. Unable for many years to buy Western equipment due to embargoes, Libya has retained its MiG-23s into the 2010s. An Air Defense Command MiG-23MS is illustrated, armed with four AA-2 "Atoll" missiles.

The MiG-23 began as an attempt to replace the MiG-21 with an aircraft that had higher flight performance, but shorter takeoff and landing distances and better handling at low speeds than were possible with the MiG-21's delta wing. Mikoyan-Gurevich first tried two lift jet engines in an enlarged delta-winged airframe, but this aircraft, designated the 23-01, was unsuccessful.

The aircraft regarded as the true MiG-23 prototype flew in June 1967. The 23-11 had variable-geometry wings with three sweep angles and a single Tumansky R-27 turbojet engine. It was soon chosen as the basis for the MiG-23 fighter, which would become known in the West by the NATO reporting name "Flogger."

WORKING TOWARD SUCCESS

The original MiG-23S "Flogger-A" was built in relatively small numbers and issued only to the VVS (Voenno-Vozdushnye Sily – Soviet Air Force), and never achieved full operational status. The MiG-23M "Flogger-B" was the first truly successful model. It had "High Lark" pulse-Doppler radar and an infrared search and track (IRST) system for passive detection of enemy aircraft. This version was used by the VVS and the PVO (Soviet Air Defense Forces).

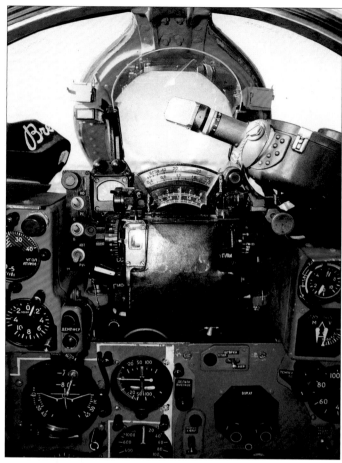

Above: A close-up of the instruments and HUD of the front cockpit of a Czech Air Force MiG-23 two-seater.

Above: The MiG-23-98 was an upgrade program offered for export customers. Among other improvements, it enabled the use of R-73 (AA-11 "Archer") and RVV-AE (AA-12 "Adder") missiles.

Above: Although it has retired its MiG-23s, India remains a big user of the MiG-27 "Flogger-M," which it calls "Bahadur" (Valiant).

Downgraded MiG-23MS "Flogger-E" export models went to Algeria, Libya and Syria. They had a simplified radar and no beyond-visual-range missile capability. Syrian "Floggers" were destroyed in large numbers by the Israeli Air Force, mainly during the invasion of Lebanon in 1982. Libya lost two in an engagement with U.S. Navy Grumman F-14s in 1989.

WIDESPREAD EXPORT

The MiG-23 was supplied to all of the Warsaw Pact air forces, plus many communist nations and non-aligned India. In Europe, Bulgaria, Romania, Czechoslovakia, East Germany, Hungary and Poland were MiG-23 users. Since the end of the Cold War, former Soviet republics including Belarus, Ukraine and Kazakhstan have also operated the MiG-23, but the "Flogger" is now gone from Europe and the former Soviet Union. In East Asia, Vietnam and North Korea are the only users, but China did receive several Egyptian MiG-23s in the late 1970s, with a view to reverse-engineering.

Many of Iraq's MiG-23s were lost in the 1991 Gulf War, and two dozen fled to Iran, where they were incorporated into that nation's air force. Ironically, in the Iran-Iraq War (1980–88), Iraq's MiG-23s had some success against Iran's Northrop F-5s, McDonnell Douglas F-4 Phantoms and even F-14s. PVO MiG-23s destroyed several Iranian helicopters that crossed the Soviet Union's borders in the 1980s.

MiG-23s also saw combat in conflicts between South Africa and Angola, Afghanistan and Pakistan, Ethiopia and Eritrea, and in other hotspots around the world. While effective as a ground-attacker, the "Flogger" increasingly lost out when faced by more modern aircraft such as the McDonnell Douglas F-15 and Lockheed Martin F-16.

INTERIM MODEL

MiG-23s, usually regarded as fighters, overlap with dedicated ground-attack MiG-27s. The MiG-23BN "Flogger-F" had a derated engine and improved navigation/attack system. Its radar was replaced by a "duck-bill" nose containing a laser range finder and an optical bombsight. Widely exported, the Mig-23BN saw combat in Indian skirmishes with Pakistan. Regarded as an interim type by the Soviets, it evolved into the MiG-27 "Flogger H," used mainly within the Soviet Union and by Cuba, India and Sri Lanka, where they still serve.

Grumman F-14 Tomcat

Grumman's F-14 was the most powerful and heavily armed naval fighter ever built. In the 1990s, precision attack was added to its repertoire, extending its career by a decade.

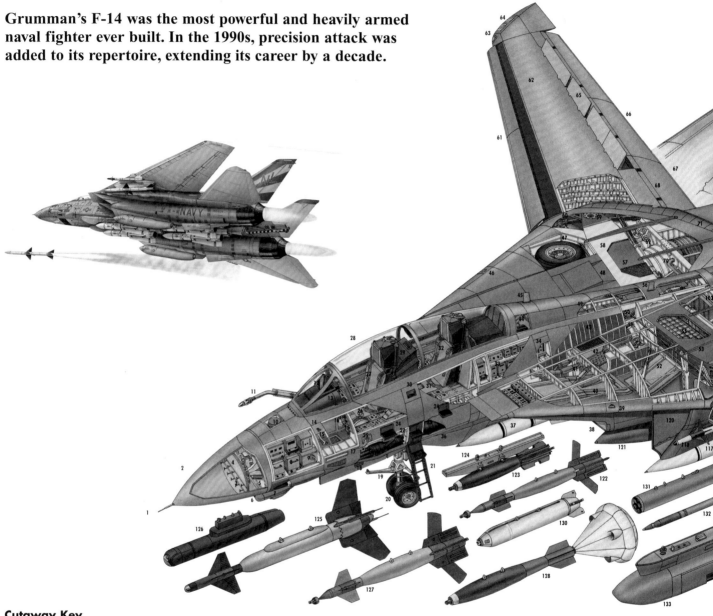

Cutaway Key

1 Pitot head
2 Fiberglass radome
3 IFF aerial array
4 AN/APG-71 flat plate radar scanner
5 Scanner tracking mechanism
6 Infrared search and track sensor (IRST) and television camera housing
7 Cannon port
8 Weapons system avionics equipment bay
9 Angle-of-attack transmitter
10 ADF aerial
11 Flight refueling probe
12 Pilot's head-up display
13 Instrument panel shield
14 Temperature probe
15 Rudder pedals
16 Control column
17 Electroluminescent formation lighting strip
18 Nosewheel doors
19 Catapult strop link
20 Twin nosewheels, forward-retracting
21 Boarding ladder, extended
22 M61A1 Vulcan cannon
23 Ammunition drum
24 Pull-out steps
25 Pitot static head
26 Engine throttle levers
27 Pilot's Martin-Baker Mk 14 Navy Aircrew Common

Ejection Seat (NACES)
28 Upward-hinged cockpit canopy cover
29 Naval flight officer's instrument console
30 Kick-in step
31 Tactical information display hand controller
32 NFO's ejection seat
33 Rear avionics equipment bay
34 Air data computer
35 Electrical system relays
36 Fuselage missile pallet
37 AIM-54A Phoenix air-to-air missile
38 Port engine air intake

39 Port navigation light
40 Variable-area intake control ramps
41 Intake ramp hydraulic actuators
42 Air-conditioning pack
43 Forward fuselage fuel tanks
44 Canopy hinge point
45 UHF/TACAN aerial
46 Starboard navigation light
47 Mainwheel stowed position
48 Starboard intake duct spill door
49 Dorsal control and cable duct
50 Central flap and slat drive hydraulic motor
51 Emergency hydraulic generator

52 Intake bypass door
53 Electron-beam welded titanium wing pivot box
54 Port wing pivot bearing
55 Pivot box beam integral fuel tank
56 UHF datalink/IFF aerial
57 Honeycomb skin panels
58 Wing glove stiffeners
59 Starboard wing pivot bearing
60 Flap and slat drive shaft and gearbox
61 Starboard leading-edge slat
62 Wing panel fully forward position
63 Navigation light

64 Wingtip formation light
65 Roll control spoilers
66 Outboard maneuver flaps
67 Inboard high-lift flap
68 Flap sealing vane
69 Mainwheel leg hinge fitting
70 Variable wing-sweep screw jack
71 Wing glove sealing plates
72 Wing glove pneumatic seal
73 Starboard wing fully swept position
74 Starboard all-moving tailplane
75 Fintip aerial fairing
76 Tail navigation light

77 Starboard rudder
78 Rudder hydraulic actuator
79 Variable-area afterburner nozzle control jack
80 Dorsal airbrake (split ventral surfaces)
81 Chaff/flare dispensers
82 Fuel jettison
83 ECM antenna
84 Aluminium honeycomb fin skin panels
85 Anti-collision light
86 Formation lighting strip
87 ECM aerial
88 Port rudder
89 Variable-area afterburner nozzle

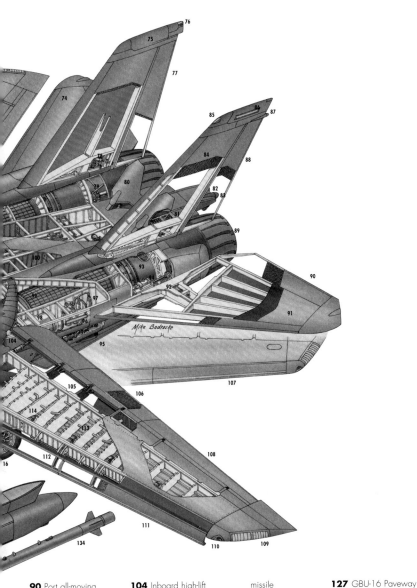

F-14A TOMCAT SPECIFICATION

Dimensions

Fuselage length (including probe): 62 ft 8 in (19.10 m)
Wing span: (unswept) 64 ft 1½ in (19.54 m);
   (swept) 38 ft 2½ in (11.65 m);
   (overswept) 33 ft 3½ in (10.15 m)
Wing aspect ratio: 7.28
Tailplane span: 32 ft 8½ in (9.97 m)
Overall height: 16 ft (4.88 m)
Wheel track: 16 ft 5 in (5.00 m)
Wheel base: 23 ft 0½ in (7.02 m)

Power plant

Two Pratt & Whitney TF30-P-412A/414A turbofans
  rated at 20,900 lb st (92.97 kN) with afterburning

Weights

Empty operating: 40,104 lb (18,191 kg)
Maximum takeoff: 72,000 lb (32,659 kg)

Fuel load

Total internal fuel: 2385 gal (9030 liters) [approx
  16,200 lb/ 7348 kg] in six main tanks, comprising:
  forward fuselage tank 691 gal (2616 liters); rear
  fuselage tank 648 gal (2453 liters); combined left and
  right feed tanks 456 gal (1727 liters); wing tanks 295
  gal (1117 liters) each
External fuel: two 267-gal (1011-liter) under-intake fuel
  tanks

Performance

Maximum level speed at altitude: 1,342 kt
  (1,544 mph; 2485 km/h)
Maximum level speed at low level: 792 kt
  (912 mph; 1468 km/h)
Limiting Mach numbers: 2.38 at altitude; 2.4 attained,
  but initially limited to 2.25 in service; 1.2 at low level
Maximum cruising speed: 550 kt (633 mph; 1019 km/h)
Maximum rate of climb at sea level: 30,000 ft
  (9140 m) per minute
Absolute ceiling: 56,000 ft (17,069 m)
Service ceiling: 50,000 ft (15,240 m) (F-14A);
  53,000 ft (16,154 m) (F-14B/D)

Range

Combat air patrol endurance: (with four AIM-54s, two
  AIM-7, two AIM-9s and external fuel) 90 minutes at
  150 nm (173 miles; 278 km); one hour at 253 nm
  (292 miles; 470 km)
Radius: (deck-launched intercept with four AIM-54s,
  two AIM-7s, two AIM-9s and external fuel) 171 nm
  (197 miles; 317 km) at Mach 1.3; 134 nm
  (154 miles; 248 km) at Mach 1.5
Ferry range: (F-14A with two tanks) 1,730 nm
  (2,000 miles; 3200 km); (F-14B with two tanks)
  2,050 nm (2,369 miles; 3799 km)

Armament

One 0.787 in (20 mm) M61 Vulcan Gatling Gun, with
  675 rounds
Ten hard points with a capacity of 14,500 lb (6,600
  kg) of ordnance and fuel tanks including AIM-54
  Phoenix, AIM-7 Sparrow, AIM-9 Sidewinder

90 Port all-moving tailplane
91 Tailplane boron-fiber skin panels
92 Tailplane pivot bearing
93 Afterburner ducting
94 Tailplane hydraulic actuator
95 Ventral fin
96 Formation lighting strip
97 Hydraulic equipment bay
98 Hydraulic reservoir
99 General Electric F110-GE-400 afterburning turbofan engine
100 Rear fuselage fuel-tank bays
101 Flight control system linkages
102 Engine bleed air ducting
103 Port wing-sweep crew jack

104 Inboard high-lift flap hydraulic jack
105 Flap hinge links
106 Flap honeycomb construction
107 Port wing fully swept position
108 Port maneuver flaps
109 Wingtip formation light
110 Navigation light
111 Port leading-edge slat
112 Slat guide rails
113 Wing integral fuel tank
114 Machined wing rib construction
115 Main undercarriage leg strut
116 Port mainwheel, forward-retracting
117 Wing glove mounted AIM-54A Phoenix air-to-air

missile
118 AIM-9L Sidewinder air-to-air missile
119 Wing glove pylon
120 Mainwheel door
121 External fuel tank
122 GBU-12D/B Paveway II 500-lb (227-kg) laser-guided bomb
123 Mk 82 Snakeye 500-lb (227-kg) retarded bomb
124 Phoenix pallet weapons adapter
125 GBU-24A/B Paveway III 2,000-lb (907-kg) laser-guided bomb
126 AN/AAQ-14 LANTIRN navigation and targeting pod, carried on starboard glove pylon

127 GBU-16 Paveway II 1,000-lb (454-kg) laser-guided bomb
128 Mk 83 AIR, 1,000-lb (454-kg) retarded bomb
129 Mk 83 AIR inflated ballute
130 Mk 7 submunition dispenser
131 LAU-97 four-round rocket launcher
132 5-in (11.06-in (27-mm)) Zuni FFAR (folding-fin air rocket)
133 TARPS reconnaissance pod, carried in centerline tunnel
134 ALQ-167 countermeasures pod, carried on forward fuselage Phoenix pallet station

"It's a beautiful airplane. It's powerful.
It has presence, and it just looks like the
ultimate fighter."
– Captain William Sizemore,
Commander, Carrier Air Wing 8,
U.S. Navy

GRUMMAN F-14 TOMCAT – VARIANTS & OPERATORS

F-14A: Initial two-seat all-weather interceptor fighter variant. The U.S. Navy received 478 F-14A aircraft. 79 were received by Iran.

F-14+ (F-14B): Upgraded engine and new radar. Redesignated F-14B in May 1991. Arrived in time to participate in Desert Storm.

F-14B Upgrade: In the late 1990s, 67 F-14Bs were upgraded to extend airframe life and improve offensive and defensive avionics systems.

F-14D: Final variant of the F-14 was the F-14D Super Tomcat. New engine and new avionics.

F-14D(R): Some F-14Ds received the ROVER III upgrade from 2005.

F-14C: A projected variant of the initial F-14B (F401-powered) with advanced multimission avionics.

UNITED STATES OPERATORS
United States Navy (USN) squadrons
Pacific Fleet
NFWS Navy Fighter Weapons School (TOPGUN). Merged with Strike U to form Naval Strike and Air Warfare Center (NSAWC), 1996.
VF-1 "Wolfpack" (disestablished 1993)

VF-2 "Bounty Hunters" (redesignated VFA-2 with F/A-18F 2003)
VF-21 "Freelancers" (disestablished 1996)
VF-24 "Fighting Renegades" (disestablished 1996)
VF-51 "Screaming Eagles" (disestablished 1995)
VF-111 "Sundowners" (disestablished 1995; re-established as VFC-111 with F-5F 2006)
VF-114 "Aardvarks" (disestablished 1993)
VF-154 "Black Knights" (redesignated VFA-154 with F/A-18F 2003)
VF-191 "Satan's Kittens" (disestablished 1988)
VF-194 "Red Lightnings" (disestablished 1988)

Atlantic Fleet
VF-11 "Red Rippers" (redesignated to VFA-11 with F/A-18F in 2005)
VF-14 "Tophatters" (redesignated VFA-14 with F/A-18E 2001)
VF-31 "Tomcatters" (redesignated VFA-31 with F/A-18E 2006)
VF-32 "Swordsmen" (redesignated VFA-32 with F/A-18F 2005)
VF-33 "Starfighters" (disestablished 1993)
VF-41 "Black Aces" (redesignated VFA-41 with F/A-18F, 2001)
VF-74 "Bedevilers" (disestablished 1994)
VF-84 "Jolly Rogers" (disestablished 1995)
VF-102 "Diamondbacks" (redesignated VFA-102 with F/A-18F, 2002)

VF-103 "Sluggers"/"Jolly Rogers" (redesignated VFA-103 with F/A-18F, 2005)
VF-142 "Ghostriders" (disestablished 1995)
VF-143 "Pukin' Dogs" (redesignated VFA-143 with F/A-18E in 2005)
VF-211 "Fighting Checkmates" (redesignated VFA-211 with F/A-18F, 2004)
VF-213 "Black Lions" (redesignated VFA-213 with F/A-18F 2006)

Fleet Replacement Squadrons
VF-101 "Grim Reapers" (disestablished 2005)
VF-124 "Gunfighters" (disestablished 1994)

Naval Air Reserve Force Squadrons
VF-201 "Hunters" (redesignated VFA-201 with F/A-18A 1999, disestablished 2007)
VF-202 "Superheats" (disestablished 1999)
VF-301 "Devil's Disciples" (disestablished 1994)
VF-302 "Stallions" (disestablished 1994)

Squadron Augmentation Units
VF-1285 "Fighting Fubijars" (disestablished 1994) augmented VF-301 and VF-302
VF-1485 "Americans" (disestablished 1994) augmented VF-124
VF-1486 "Fighting Hobos" (disestablished 2005) augmented VF-101

GRUMMAN F-14 TOMCAT

The first U.S. Navy fleet squadron to receive the F-14 was VF-1 "Wolfpack," in July 1973. A VF-1 F-41A is seen in the early markings when assigned to the USS *Enterprise*, which represent the last period of widespread color use on the U.S. Navy's carrier-based aircraft. The standard paint scheme of gull grey over white gave way to a mix of muted greys from the late 1970s. Color was then mostly restricted to the air wing commander's assigned aircraft in each squadron. This F-14A is depicted "clean" without external weapons or fuel. A VF-1 Tomcat scored the only F-14 kill of the 1991 Gulf War when it destroyed an Iraqi Mi-8 "Hip" helicopter.

Above: The radar intercept officer (RIO) managed the F-14's complex weapons system from the rear seat. Here, an airman checks the functioning of the RIO's "office" before an evening launch from an aircraft carrier.

The F-14 arose out of a 1968 competition to find a new fleet defense fighter for the U.S. Navy following the failure of the General Dynamics F-111B program. Although the U.S. Air Force F-111 went on to be a fine strike aircraft, the U.S. Navy's B model proved too heavy and generally unsuitable for a carrier aircraft, and it was cancelled in 1968. The F-111B's Phoenix missiles and AWG-9 radar were deemed worthy of further development for use in a new fighter.

Grumman won the contest in 1969 with a two-seat twin-tailed swing-wing design it called the "Tomcat" and the Pentagon designated F-14. The prototype F-14 first flew in December 1970, but was lost on its second flight due to hydraulic failure. This did not delay the test program greatly, and deliveries to training squadrons began in October 1972. The F-14 made its first operational cruise in September 1974.

The F-14's role was to defend a carrier battle group at long range against missile-carrying bombers such as the Tupolev Tu-22M "Backfire." Using the radar in combination with that aboard the Grumman E-2 Hawkeye to detect and track intruders, the Tomcat could engage them first with the AIM-54 at a range of up to 115 miles (184 km), then deal with any survivors with the AIM-7, AIM-9 and finally the cannon. The F-14 could carry a maximum of six AIM-54s, but in practice would be too heavy to land back aboard a carrier without firing or dumping some of the expensive missiles, which cost $1 million apiece even in the early 1970s.

A FAMILIAR POWER PLANT

As well as the F-111B's radar and missiles, the F-14 used the same Pratt & Whitney TF 30 turbofans. These gave a lot of trouble in the Tomcat's early years, leading to numerous accidents, and handling restrictions were introduced to prevent compressor stalls.

The F-14 had widely spaced engine trunks, and the space between them was used to mount four of the AIM-54s on pallet mounts. These were adapted later in the Tomcat's career to carry bombs. A Tactical Airborne Reconnaissance Pod System (TARPS) camera pod could also be carried by some aircraft.

MULTIPLE COMBAT TESTS

Two F-14 squadrons were involved in covering the final U.S. evacuation from Saigon in 1975, but saw no combat. During the 1980s, they twice tangled with Libyan fighters over Mediterranean waters Libya claimed as its own. In 1981, F-14s from the USS *Nimitz* destroyed two Sukhoi Su-22s and, in 1989, Tomcats from USS *John F. Kennedy* brought down a pair of Libyan MiG-23 "Floggers." In the 1991 Gulf War, however, Tomcats saw little air-to-air action.

Iran was the only export customer for the F-14. In 1976, the Shah's air force received the first of 79 F-14As. One aircraft was yet to be delivered when the Islamic revolution took place in 1979, and the supply of U.S. weapons and spares was stopped. When neighboring Iraq attacked in 1980, the F-14 played a major part in Iran's air defense. Despite the lack of spare parts, Iran kept about 30 F-14s operational and claimed around 40 kills against Iraqi aircraft versus 10 claims against them. Five Iranian pilots scored five or more victories, including several with the AIM-54.

EXTENDED USEFULNESS

The F-14A+ (later redesignated F-14B) was an improved version with General Electric F110 engines, followed by the F-14D with digital radar processing and new cockpit

Above: VF-31 "Tomcatters" were the last to fly the F-14. Here, an F-14D "Bombcat" with wings swept back makes a pass nearly at the speed of sound.

displays among other changes. In the 1990s, the F-14 was given a strike role, which helped to extend its career. Using LANTIRN targeting pods, F-14s could drop a variety of laser-guided bombs, later supplemented by JDAM satellite-guided weapons. "Bombcats" saw action over the Balkans, Iraq and Afghanistan, before finally being retired in 2006. Iran continues to operate F-14s, with an estimated 25 still remaining in service in 2010.

Above: The F-14 Tomcat was seen in Iraqi skies from 1991 until 2006, during Operation Desert Storm and Operation Iraqi Freedom. In that time, its role changed from interceptor and escort fighter to that of precision-strike aircraft.

Dassault Mirage F1

The Mirage F1 is a relatively simple fighter and ground-attack aircraft that has seen more action than most of its contemporaries. Upgrade programs will keep the F1 in service for many years.

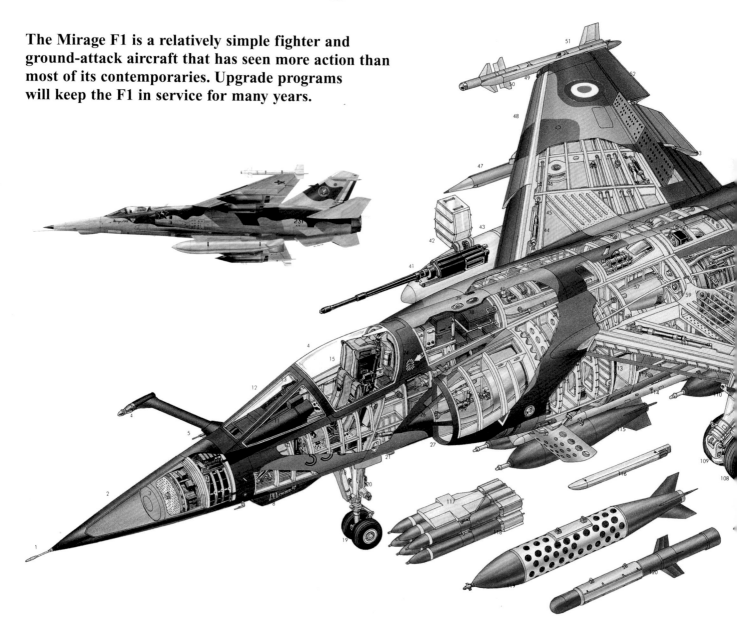

Cutaway Key

1 Pitot head
2 Fiberglass radome
3 Radar scanner housing
4 Inflight refueling probe
5 Dynamic pressure sensor
6 Thomson-CSF Cyrano IVMR radar equipment module
7 Incidence probe
8 TMV 630A laser range finder
9 Rudder pedals
10 Control column
11 Instrument panel shield
12 Windshield panels
13 Thomson VE120 head-up display

14 Upward-hinging cockpit canopy cover
15 Martin-Baker F10M zero-zero ejection seat
16 Engine throttle lever
17 Side console panel
18 Nose undercarriage hydraulic retraction jack
19 Twin nosewheels, aft-retracting
20 Hydraulic steering mechanism
21 TACAN aerial
22 Cockpit sloping rear pressure bulkhead
23 Canopy jack
24 Canopy emergency release

25 Central intake control actuator
26 Movable half-cone intake center-body
27 Port air intake
28 Air-conditioning equipment bay
29 Intake center-body screw jack
30 Intake suction relief door
31 Pressure refueling connection
32 Port airbrake panel
33 Airbrake hydraulic jack
34 Retractable landing lamp
35 Forward fuselage integral fuel tank

36 Boundary layer spill duct
37 Avionics equipment bay
38 Power amplifier
39 Strobe light (white) and anti-collision beacon (red)
40 Fuel system inverted flight accumulator
41 1.18-in (30-mm) DEFA cannon, starboard side only
42 Ammunition magazine, 135 rounds
43 External fuel tank
44 Starboard wing integral fuel tank
45 Forged-steel wing attachment fitting

46 Inboard pylon attachment hard point
47 MATRA-Philips Phimat chaff/flare pod
48 Leading-edge flap
49 Starboard navigation light
50 Wingtip missile launch rail
51 MATRA Magic air-to-air missile
52 Starboard aileron
53 Two-segment double-slotted flaps
54 Spoiler panel (open)
55 Wing panel attachment machined fuselage main frame
56 Fuel system filters

57 Engine intake center-body/ starter housing
58 Wing panel attachment pin joints
59 Engine accessory equipment gearbox
60 SNECMA Atar 9K-50 afterburning engine
61 Engine bleed air pre-cooler
62 Rear spar attachment joint
63 Rear fuselage integral fuel tank
64 Engine turbine section
65 Engine-bay thermal lining

66 Fin spar attachment joint
67 Starboard all-moving tailplane
68 Forward SHERLOC ECM antenna fairing
69 UHF antenna
70 VOR aerial
71 Fintip aerial fairing
72 IFF/VHF 1 aerial
73 Rear navigation light and anti-collision beacon
74 Aft SHERLOC ECM antenna
75 Rudder
76 Rudder hydraulic actuator
77 Rudder trim actuator

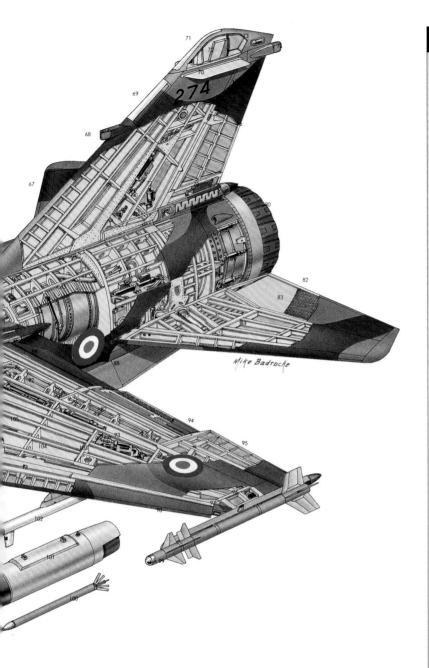

Mike Badrocke

MIRAGE F1C SPECIFICATION

Dimensions

Wingspan without tip stores: 27 ft 6¾ in (8.40 m)
Wingspan with tip-mounted Magic AAMs:
  30 ft 6¾ in (9.32 m)
Wing aspect ratio: 2.82
Wing area: 269.11 sq ft (25.00 m²)
Length: 50 ft 2½ in (15.30 m)
Wheel track: 8 ft 2½ in (2.50 m)
Wheel base: 16 ft 4¾ in (5.00 m)
Height: 14 ft 9 in (4.50 m)

Power plant

One SNECMA Atar 9K-50 turbojet rated at 11,023 lb st
(49.03 kN) dry and 15,785 lb st (70.21 kN) with
afterburning

Weights

Empty: 16,314 lb (7400 kg)
Operating empty (including pilots):
  18,078 lb (8200 kg)
Normal takeoff: 24,030 lb (10,900 kg);
Maximum takeoff: 35,715 lb (16,200 kg)

Fuel and load

Internal fuel capacity: 1,136 gal (4300 liters)
External fuel capacity: Provision for one 581-gal
  (2200-liter) tank on centerline and two 299-gal
  (1130-liter) tanks under the wings
Maximum weapon load: 13,889 lb (6300 kg)

Performance

Maximum level speed "clean" at 36,090 ft (11,000 m):
  1,453 mph (2338 km/h)
Maximum rate of climb at sea level: 41,930 ft
  (12,780 m) per minute; Mirage F1B (without
  afterburning): 13,780 ft (4200 m) per minute
Service ceiling: 65,615 ft (20,000 m); Mirage F1B
  (stabilized supersonic ceiling): 52,495 ft (16,000 m)
Takeoff run at 25,353 lb (11,500 kg) in weight:
  1,969 ft (600 m)
Landing run at 18,739 lb (8500 kg) in weight:
  2,198 ft (670 m)

Range

Combat radius: 264 miles (425 km) on a hi-lo-hi attack
  mission with 14 551-lb (250-kg) bombs, or 373 miles
  (600 km) on a lo-lo-lo attack mission with six 551-lb
  (250-kg) bombs and two drop tanks, or 863 miles
  (1390 km) on a hi-lo-hi attack mission with two 551-lb
  (250-kg) bombs and three drop tanks
Endurance: 2 hours 15 minutes on a CAP with two
  Super 530 AAMs and one drop tank

Armament

Two fixed internal DEFA 553 1.18-in (30-mm) cannon
with 135 rounds per gun; standard air-to-air load of
two MATRA Magic or AIM-9 Sidewinder missiles on
wingtip rails and either one MATRA R.530 on the
centerline station or two Super 530Fs underwing. A
limited ground-attack capability is available using
various unguided bombs, cluster munitions and rockets.

78 VHF 2 aerial
79 Brake parachute
  housing
80 Variable-area
  afterburner nozzle
81 Nozzle control
  jacks
82 Port all-moving
  tailplane
83 Honeycomb trailing-
  edge panel
84 Multi-spar tailplane
  construction
85 Tailplane pivot
  fitting
86 Tailplane hydraulic
  actuator
87 Autopilot controller
88 Port ventral fin
89 Inboard double-
  slotted flap segment
90 Flap hydraulic jack
91 Spoiler hydraulic

  jack
92 Port spoiler housing
  and actuating
  linkage
93 Port aileron
  hydraulic actuator
94 Outboard double-
  slotted flap segment
95 Port aileron
96 Wingtip missile
  interface unit
97 Port navigation light
98 Leading-edge flap
99 Port MATRA Magic
  air-to-air missile
100 2.68-in (68-mm)
  rocket projectile
101 MATRA 18-round
  rocket launcher
102 Thomson-CSF
  ECM pod
103 Outer pylon
  attachment hard

  point
104 Wing panel multi-
  spar construction
105 Port wing integral
  fuel tank
106 Main
  undercarriage
  hydraulic
  retraction jack
107 Shock absorber
  strut
108 Twin mainwheels
109 Levered
  suspension axle
110 Mainwheel leg
  strut and leg
  rotating linkage
111 Leading-edge flap
  hydraulic jack
112 Main
  undercarriage
  wheel bay
113 Port ammunition

  bay, unused
114 Center fuselage
  weapon pylon
115 881-lb (400-kg)
  HE bombs
116 Underwing
  MATRA-Corral
  conformal chaff/
  flare dispenser
117 Multiple bomb-
  carrier
118 Thomson-Brandt
  BAP-100 runway-
  cratering bomb or
  BAT-120 area
  denial/anti-armor
  munition
119 MATRA Belouga
  submunition
  dispenser
120 MATRA Durandal
  retarded concrete-
  piercing bomb

"The Atar engine gave great sea-level performance. Well-balanced flying controls gave the F1 the same positive feel as experienced in the much-loved Sabre."
– Dick Lord, South African Air Force Mirage F1 pilot

Above: This Mirage F1CR-200 flew with L'Armée de l'Air's Center d'Expériences Aériennes Militaires trials unit in France's Aquitaine region.

DASSAULT MIRAGE F1 – VARIANTS

F1A: Single-seat ground-attack fighter aircraft.

F1AD: Export version of the Mirage F1A for Libya. 16 built.

F1AZ: Export version of the Mirage F1A for South Africa. 32 built.

F1B: A two-seat operational conversion trainer.

1BE: Export version of the Mirage F1B for Spain. Six built.

F1BJ: Export version of the Mirage F1B for Jordan. Two built.

F1BK: Export version of the Mirage F1B for Kuwait. Two built.

F1BK-2: Four sold to Kuwait as part of a follow-up order.

F1BQ: Export version of the Mirage F1B for Iraq.

F1CE: Export version of the Mirage F1C for Spain. 45 built.

F1CG: Export version of the Mirage F1C for Greece. 40 built.

F1CH: Export version of the Mirage F1C for Morocco. 30 built.

F1CJ: Export version of the Mirage F1C for Jordan. 17 built.

F1CK: Export version of the Mirage F1C for Kuwait. 18 built.

F1CK-2: Nine F1Cs sold to Kuwait as part of a follow-on order.

F1CZ: Export fighter version of the F1C for South Africa. 16 built.

F1D: Two-seat training version, based on the Mirage F1E multirole fighter and ground-attack aircraft.

F1E: Single-seat all-weather multirole fighter and ground-attack aircraft.

F1JA: Export version of the Mirage F1E for Ecuador. 16 built.

F1ED: Export version of the Mirage F1E for Libya. 14 built.

F1EE: Export version of the Mirage F1E for Spain. 22 built.

F1EH-200: Moroccan aircraft fitted with an inflight refueling probe.

F1EQ-2: Single-seat air-defense fighter version for Iraq. 16 built.

F1EQ-4: Single-seat multirole fighter, ground-attack and reconnaissance version for Iraq. 28 built.

F1EQ-5: Single-seat anti-shipping version for Iraq. 20 built.

F1EQ-6: Single-seat anti-shipping version for Iraq. Built in small numbers.

F1EDA: Export version of the Mirage F1E for Qatar. 12 built.

F1CT: Tactical ground-attack version of the Mirage F1C-200.

Aerosud Mirage F1 AAD2006: Aerosud equipped a Mirage F1 with a Klimov RD-33 engine, the same engine used in the Mikoyan-Gurevich MiG-29. This development was dubbed the "SuperMirage" F1.

DASSAULT MIRAGE F1

The Mirage F1CE entered Spanish Air Force service in 1975, and over the years the Ejército del Aire has operated more than 90 examples. This example is assigned to 142 Escuadrón of Ala de Caza (Fighter Wing) 14 at Albacete in southeastern Spain. In the 1990s, it was one of 40 upgraded to Mirage F1CM standard with new wide-angle HUDs, HoTaS controls, modernized radar, NVG compatibility and a new navigation system. The 142 Escuadrón has a sabre-toothed tiger in its squadron badge, qualifying it for membership in the NATO Tiger Association, which runs an annual "Tiger Meet" event. Tiger stripes and elaborate color schemes often appear on participating aircraft.

FACTS

- The Mirage F1 is the only member of the Mirage family without a delta wing and with a tailplane.

- As well as France, 12 nations have operated the F1.

- Although F1s fought on both sides in the 1991 Gulf War, they never met in combat.

To meet a requirement for an interceptor to replace the Mirage III, Dassault tested various configurations, including one with eight small lift engines and a variable-geometry version called the G8. Another prototype derived from the G8 but with a fixed, high-mounted wing and a conventional tailplane was tested in 1966. This Mirage F2 was intended as a strike aircraft with two seats. Dassault proposed scaled-down versions, and the multirole Mirage F1 design proved the most attractive to the Armée de l'Air (French Air Force). The F1 prototype flew in December 1966 and was chosen as the basis of a new interceptor in September 1967.

Above: The conventional wing and large flaps gave the F1 good landing performance.

Above: Qatar ordered the Mirage F1EDA in 1979, and 14 were in service by 1984. They flew defensive missions in the 1991 Gulf War.

Above: Although the Mirage F1E began as a private venture for export, it was also ordered by France. Subvariants of the F1E were popular in the Middle East, selling to Jordan, Kuwait and Iraq, among others.

The Mirage F1C interceptor reached initial operational status in 1974 with the Armée de l'Air. During C production an inflight refueling probe was added, as was radar warning equipment on the tailfin. Related versions were the F1B two-seat conversion trainer and the F1CR reconnaissance aircraft.

IMPRESSIVE ARMAMENT

The Mirage F1 had a high wing with leading-edge and trailing-edge flaps, ailerons and spoilers. Under its wings and fuselage were a total of seven stores attachments for fuel tanks, bombs, rockets or missiles, including the large Matra 530 and the smaller Magic air-to-air missiles. A 1.18-in (30-mm) cannon was mounted behind each engine intake. There were airbrakes on the fuselage and twin wheels on all undercarriage legs. In the sharply pointed nose was a Cyrano radar. Some export versions had a simplified Aida ranging radar in a slimmer nose.

Like Dassault's Mirage III, the F1 was widely sold abroad. The F1A export version was the basis of South Africa's F1AZ, Ecuador's F1JA, and Libya's F1AD, among other models. Equipment and weapons options varied, but as well as French air-to-air missiles and bombs, export users fitted their F1s with Exocet anti-ship missiles, Israeli and South African air-to-air missiles and even some Russian air-to-surface missiles.

South Africa's F1s saw combat against Angolan MiG-21s and MiG-23s in the bush wars of the 1980s. Against the former, the F1 could hold its own, but a number of South African Air Force Mirages fell to "Floggers." Iraq's F1s were heavily used in the 1980–88 war with Iran and reportedly shot down several Grumman F-14s, but they were largely engaged as Exocet launch platforms, damaging numerous oil tankers and the U.S. frigate USS *Stark*.

Against U.S. fighters in 1991's Operation Desert Storm F1s fared poorly, with at least six F1s falling to U.S. Air Force McDonnell Douglas F-15 Eagles. Toward the end of the conflict, the majority of survivors escaped to Iran to avoid destruction, and they eventually were integrated into the Islamic Republic's air force.

A CHANGING ROLE

France's F1Cs soon lost the dedicated interceptor mission and were upgraded to F1CT standard, with capability to employ laser-guided bombs and missiles, and improved self-defense measures. The F1CTs and F1CRs have seen operational service over Afghanistan and Chad. A reduced number of F1s remain in French service, but numbers remain in use in Africa and the Middle East. In addition, Spain and Morocco have undertaken upgrade programs in the 2000s.

Mikoyan-Gurevich MiG-25 "Foxbat"/ MiG-31 "Foxhound"

In terms of pure numbers, no operational fighter has been able to beat the performance of the MiG-25 and its successor, the MiG-31. Neither was built for agility, instead using speed and long-range missiles to defeat enemies, without the need for dogfighting.

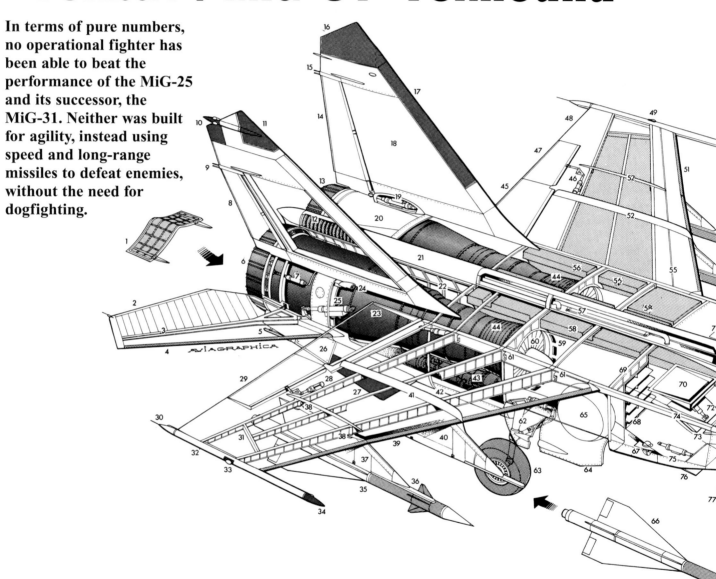

Cutaway Key

1. Ventral airbrake
2. Starboard tailplane (aluminium alloy trailing edge)
3. Steel tailplane spar
4. Titanium leading edge
5. Tail bumper
6. Fully variable engine exhaust nozzle
7. Exhaust nozzle actuator
8. Starboard rudder
9. Static dischargers
10. Sirena 3 tail warning radar and ECM transmitter
11. Transponder aerial
12. Twin brake parachute housing
13. Port engine
14. Port rudder
15. Static dischargers
16. VHF aerial
17. HF leading-edge aerial
18. Port tailfin (steel primary structure)
19. Rudder actuator
20. Titanium rear fuselage skins
21. Dorsal spine fairing
22. Fireproof bulkhead between engine bays
23. Engine afterburner duct
24. Cooling air intake
25. Tailplane hydraulic actuator
26. Starboard ventral fin
27. VHF and ECM

exhaust nozzle
aerial housing
28. Aileron actuator
29. Starboard aileron
30. Static discharger
31. All-steel wing construction
32. Wingtip fairing
33. Sirena 3 radar warning receiver and ECM transmitter
34. Continuous-wave target-illuminating radar
35. AA-6 "Acrid" semi-active radar-guided air-to-air missile
36. Missile-launching rail
37. Outboard missile pylon
38. Pylon attachments
39. Wing titanium leading edge
40. Inboard pylon
41. Wing fence
42. Engine access panels
43. Engine accessory gearbox
44. Tumanskii R-31 single-shaft afterburning turbojet engine
45. Port flap
46. Aileron hydraulic actuator
47. Port aileron
48. Fixed portion of trailing edge
49. Sirena 3 radar warning receiver and ECM transmitter
50. Continuous-wave target-illuminating radar

51. Titanium leading edge
52. Port wing fences
53. AA-6 "Acrid" semi-active radar-guided air-to-air missile
54. Infrared-guided AA-6 "Acrid" missile
55. Stainless-steel wing skins
56. Intake flank fuel tanks
57. Controls and systems ducting
58. Main fuel tanks (welded steel integral construction), total system capacity 31,575 lb (14,322 kg), nitrogen-pressurized
59. Intake bleed air ducts engine bay cooling
60. Engine compressor face
61. Wing spar attachments
62. Main undercarriage leg strut
63. Starboard mainwheel
64. Mainwheel doors
65. Mainwheel stowed position
66. Starboard infrared guided AA-6 "Acrid" missile
67. Retractable landing/taxiing lamp
68. Intake duct control vanes

69. Steel fuselage primary structure
70. Intake bleed air outlet ducts
71. UHF communications aerials
72. Variable-intake ramp doors
73. Ramp jacks
74. Intake water/ methanol injection duct
75. Electric intake tip actuator
76. Variable lower intake lip
77. Nose wheel door/ mudguard
78. Twin nose wheels
79. Nose wheel leg doors

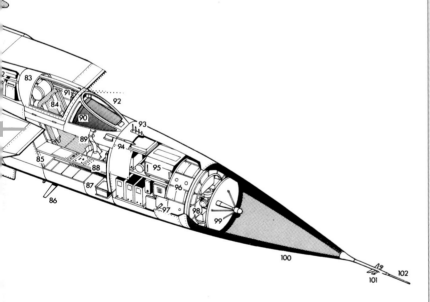

MIG-25PDS "FOXBAT-E" SPECIFICATION

Dimensions

Length: 78 ft 1¾ in (23.82 m)
Length for aircraft modified with IFR capability:
78 ft 11½ in (24.07 m)
Height: 20 ft ¼ in (6.10 m)
Wingspan: 45 ft 11¾ in (14.02 m)
Wing aspect ratio: 3.2
Wing area: 660.93 sq ft (61.40 m²)
Wheel track: 12 ft 7½ in (3.85 m)
Wheel base: 16 ft 10½ in (5.14 m)

Power plant

Two MNPK "Soyuz" (Tumanskii) R-15BD-300 turbojets
each rated at 24,691 lb st (109.83 kN) with
afterburning

Weights

Normal takeoff weight with four R-40s (AA-6s) and
100 percent internal fuel: 80,952 lb (36,720 kg)

Fuel and loads

Internal fuel: 32,121 lb (14,570 kg)
External fuel in an underbelly tank: 9,634 lb (4370 kg)
Maximum ordnance: 8,818 lb (4000 kg)

Performance

Maximum level speed "clean" at 42,650 ft (13,000 m):
Mach 2.8 or 1,619 kt (1,864 mph; 3000 km/h)
Maximum level speed "clean" at sea level: Mach 2.8 or
647 kt (745 mph; 1200 km/h)
Climb to 65,615 ft (20,000 m): 8 minutes 54 seconds
Service ceiling: 67,915 ft (20,700 m)
Takeoff run at normal takeoff weight: 4,101 ft (1250 m)
Landing run at normal landing weight with brake chutes:
2,624 ft (800 m)
g limits: + 4.5 supersonic

Range

With internal fuel at subsonic speed: 933 nm
(1,075 miles; 1730 km)
With internal fuel at supersonic speed: 675 nm
(776 miles; 1730 km)
Endurance: 2 hours 5 minutes

Armament

Standard intercept fit is two or four R-40 (AA-6 "Acrid")
missiles. MiG-25PDS aircraft are armed with two R-40s
and four R-60 (AA-8 "Aphid") AAMs

80 Starboard
navigation light
81 Curved intake
inboard sidewall
82 Rear avionics bay,
communications
and ECM
equipment
83 Cockpit canopy
cover, hinges to
starboard
84 Pilot's ejection seat
85 Cockpit rear
pressure bulkhead
86 UHF
communications
aerial
87 Radar altimeter

88 Pilot's side console
panel
89 Control column
90 Instrument panel
shield
91 Stand-by visual
sighting system for
infrared missiles
92 Windshield panels
93 "Odd Rods"
IFF aerials
94 Pitot tube
95 Forward avionics
compartment, radar
and navigation
equipment
96 "Fox Fire" fire-
control radar system

97 Angle-of-attack
probe
98 Scanner tracking
mechanism
99 Radar scanner dish,
33½-in (85-cm)
diameter
100 Radome
101 "Swift Rod"
ILS antenna
102 Pitot tube
103 MiG-25U
"Foxbat-C" two-
seat operational
training variant
104 Student pilot's
cockpit enclosure
105 Instructor's cockpit

106 MiG-25R
"Foxbat-B"
reconnaissance
variant
107 Reconnaissance
cameras, one
vertical and four
oblique
108 Sideways-looking
airborne radar
(SLAR) aperture
109 Ground mapping
and Doppler
radar antenna
110 "Jay-Bird" forward-
looking radar

"From the height at which we fly, you can see the entire Himalayan range at one go. No aircraft has ever been able to achieve for us what the Foxbat has."
– Wing Commander Sanjeev Taliyan, Indian Air Force

Above: A MiG-25 pulls away from a Western aircraft. The "Foxbat" was virtually immune to interception at its normal operating speeds and heights.

FACTS

- The first close-up view the West had of the "Foxbat" was in 1976, when a Russian pilot defected with one to Japan.

- The MiG-25 was limited to Mach 2.83. If it went faster, the engines were likely to melt.

- For high-altitude flight, "Foxbat" and "Foxhound" pilots are required to wear pressure suits like astronauts.

MIKOYAN-GUREVICH MIG-25 "FOXBAT"/MIG-31 "FOXHOUND" – MAIN VARIANTS & OPERATORS

MAIN VARIANTS

Ye-155-P1: Interceptor fighter prototype.

MiG-25P "Foxbat-A": Single-seat all-weather interceptor fighter aircraft.

MiG-25PU "Foxbat-C": Two-seat trainer aircraft.

MiG-25RB "Foxbat-B": Single-seat reconnaissance-bomber aircraft.

MiG-25RBS "Foxbat-D": Single-seat reconnaissance-bomber aircraft.

MiG-25RBSh: MiG-25RBS Foxbats fitted with new equipment.

MiG-25RBK: Single-seat Elint aircraft, fitted with an airborne radar.

MiG-25RBT: Single-seat Elint aircraft.

MiG-25RBV: Single-seat reconnaissance-bomber aircraft.

MiG-25RU: Two-seat reconnaissance/trainer aircraft.

MiG-25BM "Foxbat-F": Single-seat defense-suppression aircraft.

MiG-25PD "Foxbat-E": Single-seat all-weather interceptor fighter.

MiG-25PDS: Designation applied to all surviving MiG-25P "Foxbat-As."

CURRENT OPERATORS

Algerian Air Force: MiG-25A, PD, PDS, R, RBV, PU, RU.

Armenian Air Force: One MiG-25PD.

Azerbaijan Air Force: MiG-25PD, MiG-25RB and MiG-25 trainers.

Russian Air Force: MiG-25 interceptors and MiG-25RB reconnaissance.

Syrian Air Force: MiG-25PD and MiG-25RB, R and U.

Turkmenistan Air Force: MiG-25PD and MiG-25PU.

FORMER OPERATORS

Bulgarian Air Force: MiG-25RBT, MiG-25RU.

Belarus Air Force: 50 MiG-25s, including 13 MiG-25PD.

Indian Air Force: MiG-25RBK, MiG-25RU.

Iraqi Air Force: Two MiG-25PUs, four MiG-25RBs, five MiG-25RBTs and 11 MiG-25PDs. Seven MiGs were flown over to Iran in 1991, the rest were destroyed in the Gulf War and Operation Southern Watch, or buried during the 2003 invasion of Iraq. A MiG-25 was found buried under the sand at Al Taqaddum Air Base in February 2004.

Libyan Air Force: MiG-25PD, MiG-25RBK, MiG-25PU and MiG-25RU variants.

Soviet Union: The largest operator historically, Soviet aircraft were passed on to its successor states in 1991.

Ukrainian Air Force: Took over 79 aircraft after the breakup of the Soviet Union. They have been withdrawn from service.

MIKOYAN-GUREVICH MIG-25 "FOXBAT"/MIG-31 "FOXHOUND"

The MiG-25BM "Foxbat-F" was a development of the MiG-25RB dedicated to suppression of enemy air defenses (SEAD). It was developed for use in the European theater against NATO radar systems as a platform for the AS-11 "Kilter" anti-radiation missile (ARM). This was the first Soviet ARM able to be carried by tactical aircraft. The MiG-25BM would have cleared a path through the defenses for MiG-25 fighters and tactical bombers. Although the prototype flew in 1976, it entered service only in 1988 after many development problems. The nose radome was painted grey to resemble that of the MiG-25PD interceptor and thus disguise the BM's true role. Behind the nose was the Yaguar (Jaguar) electronic warfare and electronic countermeasures suite.

Above: The aircraft's huge inlets and engine trunks are evident in this underside view of a MiG-25 "Foxbat-A."

Development of the MiG-25 was begun in 1961, to counter the proposed North American B-70 Valkyrie bomber. The same year the B-70 itself was cancelled, in part due to its huge cost and also because of the threat of new surface-to-air missiles. Testing of XB-70 protoytypes went ahead and Mikoyan-Gurevich continued MiG-25 development, ostensibly to counter high-altitude reconnaissance aircraft such as the Lockheed U-2 and Lockheed SR-71 Blackbird.

A prototype called the Ye-155P-1 first flew in September 1964. This was followed by several others configured as either interceptors or reconnaissance aircraft. Under the cover designation Ye-266, one was used to set a record for climbing

Above: A Libyan MiG-25PD is seen from an intercepting U.S. Navy aircraft. The missiles are AA-6 "Acrids."

Above: There were a number of specialized reconnaissance models, some with a secondary bombing capability. This is believed to be a MiG-25RBV.

to 98,400 ft (30,000 m) in 4 minutes, 3.86 seconds in 1973. The first production MiG-25s (in MiG-25R reconnaissance form) entered Soviet Air Force service in 1969, followed by MiG-25P interceptors in 1972 with the Air Defense Forces, technically a different branch of the Soviet military.

The MiG-25 had huge engine intake ducts with movable inlets to adjust airflow for different speeds. The use of twin vertical fins was one of the first on a jet fighter, although it had been seen before on the Vought F7U Cutlass. The use of heat-resistant but very expensive titanium was kept to a minimum, being used only in critical areas. Most of the structure was tempered steel, with some use of aluminium alloys.

COLD WAR DEFECTION

The West had its first close look at the MiG-25 in 1976, when pilot Viktor Belenko defected from the Soviet Union and flew an aircraft to Hakodate, Japan. The aircraft was returned, but only after it had been dismantled and thoroughly studied. U.S. technical experts discovered that the MiG-25 used old-fashioned vacuum tube electronics rather than circuit boards; the forward view was terrible; the surface finish was poor with raised rivet heads; and the aircraft had a poor combat radius and a large turning circle. All of these limitations were understood, however, when the "Foxbat" was built. Vacuum tubes were resistant to jamming or electromagnetic pulse; the radar was powerful enough to burn through enemy jamming; and the rough surfaces were in areas where they had little effect on drag. Flown correctly, the MiG-25 went a fair

distance very quickly, reaching a point where intruders could be destroyed by its missiles before they were in range with their own offensive weapons.

EFFECTIVE ARMAMENT

Main armament of the "Foxbat" was four to six AAMs. The most effective of these were the large AA-6 "Acrid," which was usually fitted in a mix of infrared and semi-active radar homing versions. A pair of each would be fired at a bomber target to outwit countermeasures. AA-7 "Apex" and AA-8 "Aphid" missiles were also carried, but no cannon was fitted.

The MiG-25PD "Foxbat-E" was the definitive interceptor version, with a look-down, shoot-down radar and an IRST system. A small number of MiG-25s were exported to countries including Syria, Iraq, Algeria and Libya. An Iraqi MiG-25 claimed the only aerial victory against a coalition aircraft in the 1991 Gulf War, when it shot down a U.S. Navy F/A-18.

PROPOSED REPLACEMENT

As early as 1975, an intended replacement for the MiG-25 was flying in the form of the Ye-155MP prototype for the MiG-31 "Foxhound." Although outwardly similar, the MiG-31 had few parts in common and a second seat for a radar operator. Unlike the MiG-25, the MiG-31 also had a 1.18-in (30-mm) cannon. The improved MiG-31M flew in 1983. Under its belly it could carry four R-37 "Amos" missiles, regarded as the Russian equivalent of the AIM-54 Phoenix. Few if any entered service, but many aspects were retrofitted to existing MiG-31s.

McDonnell Douglas/ Boeing F-15 Eagle

The McDonnell Douglas F-15 Eagle has become the premier air superiority fighter of the modern era. Since the 1970s, it has amassed an unequalled combat record in conflicts in the Middle East and Balkans.

F-15E SPECIFICATION

Dimensions

Length: 63 ft 9 in (19.43 m)
Height: 18 ft 5½ in (5.63 m)
Wingspan: 42 ft 9 ¾ in (13.05 m)
Wing aspect ratio: 3.01
Tailplane span: 28 ft 3 in (8.61 m)
Wheel track: 9 ft ¼ in (2.75 m)
Wheel base: 17 ft 9 ½ in (5.42 m)

Power plant

Original F-15E had power plant of F-15C/D, but with option of General Electric F110-GE-129. Aircraft from 135 onwards (90-0233), built from August 1991, have two Pratt & Whitney F100-PW-229s rated at 29,000 lb st (129 kN)

Weights

Empty operating: 31,700 lb (14,379 kg)
Normal takeoff: 44,823 lb (20,331 kg)
Maximum takeoff: 36,741 lb (81,000 kg)

Fuel and load

Internal fuel: 13,123 lb (5952 kg)
External fuel: 21,645 lb (9818 kg)
Maximum weapon load: 24,500 lb (11,113 kg)

Performance

Maximum level speed: Mach 2.5
Maximum combat radius: 685 nm (790 miles; 1270 km)
Maximum combat range: 2,400 nm (2,765 miles; 4445 km)

Armament

One 0.79-in (0.79-in (20-mm)) M61A-1 six-barrel gun, with 512 rounds, in starboard wing root. Wing pylons for AIM-9 Sidewinder, AIM-120 AMRAAM, and AIM-7 Sparrow. Single or triple rail launchers for AGM-65 Maverick on wing pylons. A wide range of guided and unguided weapons including Mk 20 Rockeye, Mk 82, MK 84, BSU-49 and -50, GBU-10, -12, -15, and-24; CBU-52, -58, -71, -87, -89, -90, -92 and -93; LAU-3A rockets; B57 and B61 nuclear weapons

Cutaway Key

1 Fiberglass radome
2 Hughes AN/APG-70 I-band pulse-Doppler radar scanner
3 Radar mounting bulkhead
4 ADF sense antenna
5 Avionics equipment bay, port and starboard
6 UHF antenna
7 Pitot head
8 AGM-130 TV-guided air-to-surface weapon
9 TACAN antenna
10 Formation lighting strip
11 Incidence probe
12 Rudder pedals
13 Instrument panel shield
14 Pilot's head-up display
15 Frameless windshield panel
16 B61 tactical nuclear weapon
17 AIM-7F Sparrow air-to-air missile
18 LANTIRN navigation pod, mounted beneath starboard intake
19 FLIR aperture
20 Terrain-following radar
21 Upward-hinging cockpit canopy
22 Pilot's ACES II ejection seat
23 Side console panel
24 Engine throttle levers
25 Boarding steps
26 Extended boarding ladder
27 Forward-retracting nosewheel
28 Landing/taxiing lights
29 Nosewheel leg shock-absorber strut

30 Underfloor control runs
31 Flying controls duplicated in rear cockpit
32 Radar hand controller
33 Weapons systems officer's ACES II ejection seat
34 Canopy hinge point
35 Cockpit air-conditioning pack
36 Port variable capture area "nodding" air intake
37 Boundary layer spill air louvers
38 Nodding intake hydraulic actuator
39 Variable-area intake ramp doors
40 Intake ramp hydraulic actuator
41 Boom-type flight refueling receptacle, open
42 Air supply duct to conditioning system
43 Ammunition magazine, 512 rounds

44 Forward fuselage fuel tanks
45 Ammunition feed chute
46 Engine intake ducting
47 Center fuselage fuel tanks (3)
48 Fuel-tank bay access panel
49 Airbrake hydraulic jack
50 Dorsal airbrake honeycomb construction
51 Upper UHF antenna
52 Starboard intake by-pass air spill duct
53 M61A-1 Vulcan 0.79-in (0.79-in (20-mm) cannon
54 Anti-collision light
55 Starboard wing pylon carrying

GBU-10, AIM-7M and AIM-120
56 Pylon mounting hard point
57 Starboard wing integral fuel tank, fire suppressant foam filled
58 Leading-edge flush HF antenna panels
59 Ventral view showing carriage of 12 Mk 82 500-lb (227-kg) bombs
60 610-gal (2309-liter) external fuel tanks (3)
61 LANTIRN navigation and targeting pods
62 Wing pylon mounted AIM-9M and AIM-120 air-to-air missiles

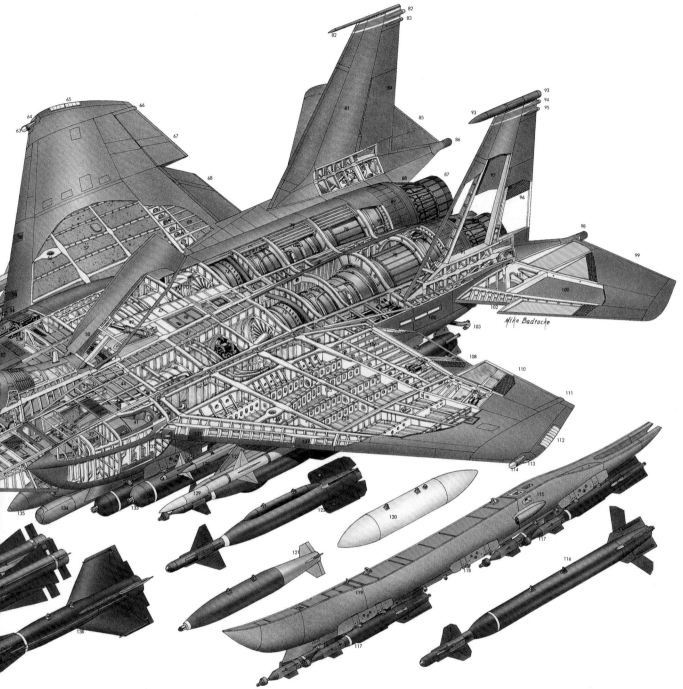

63 Forward ECM
transmitting antenna
64 Starboard
navigation light
65 Wingtip formation
light
66 Fuel jettison
67 Starboard aileron
68 Starboard plain flap
69 Trailing-edge fuel
tank
70 Engine-bay cooling
intake bleed air
louvers
71 Compressor
intake
72 Central airframe-
mounted engine
accessory equipment
gearbox
73 Machined main
fuselage/wing spar
attachment
bulkheads

74 Pratt & Whitney
F100-PW-229
afterburning
turbofan engines
75 Engine bleed air
cross-ducting
76 Forward engine
mounting
77 Main engine
mounting
"spectacle" beam
78 Afterburner ducting
79 Rear fuselage/
engine bay
diffusion-bonded all-
titanium structure
80 Tailplane hydraulic
actuator
81 Starboard fin
82 Fintip ECM antenna
83 Anti-collision light
84 Starboard rudder
85 Starboard all-
moving tailplane

86 Aft ECM
transmitting
antenna
87 Variable-area
afterburner nozzle
88 Nozzle actuating
linkage
89 Nozzle shield
panels
90 Fueldraulic
afterburner nozzle
actuators
91 Two-spar fin torsion
box structure
92 Boron-fiber fin
skin panelling
93 Radar warning
antenna
94 Port rear ECM
antenna
95 White strobe light
96 Port rudder
honeycomb core
construction

97 Tailplane pivot
mounting
98 Port aft ECM
transmitting antenna
99 Port all-moving
tailplane
100 Boron-fiber
tailplane skin
panelling
101 Machined
tailplane trunnion
mounting fitting
102 Leading edge
dogtooth
103 Runway
emergency
arrestor hook,
lowered
104 Formation
lighting strip
105 Engine bleed air
primary heat
exchangers, port
and starboard

106 Port trailing-edge
fuel-tank bay
107 Flap hydraulic jack
108 Port plain flap
109 Aileron hydraulic
actuator
110 Port aileron
honeycomb core
construction
111 Fuel jettison
112 Port formation light
113 Port navigation
light
114 Forward ECM
transmitting
antenna
115 Engine bleed air
primary heat
exchanger air
intake and
exhaust ducts
116 GBU-28 "Deep
Throat" laser-
guided bomb

117 GBU-12 laser-
guided bombs
118 CFT pylons
119 Port conformal fuel
tank (CFT)
120 AXQ-14 datalink
pod
121 Mk 84 2,000-lb
(907-kg) HE bomb
122 GBU-24 laser-
guided bomb
123 Outer wing panel
dry bay
124 Port wing integral
fuel tankage
125 Multi-spar wing
panel structure
126 Port pylon hard
point
127 Wing stores pylon
128 Missile launch
rails
129 AIM-120
AMRAAM

130 AIM-9M
Sidewinder
air-to-air missile
131 Leading-edge flush
HF antenna
132 Stores
management
system equipment
133 CBU-87
submunition
dispensers
134 Port LANTIRN
targeting pod
135 Centerline
external tank
136 AGM-65
Maverick
air-to-surface
missiles
137 Triple missile
carrier/launch rail
138 GBU-15 electro-
optical guided
glide bomb

"It's the most powerful air-superiority fighter known to man. It's exceptionally easy to fly, as easy as a Cessna." – Colonel Doug Dildy (ret.), U.S. Air Force F-15 pilot

MCDONNELL DOUGLAS F-15 EAGLE – MAJOR VARIANTS & OPERATORS

VARIANTS

F-15A: Single-seat all-weather air-superiority fighter version; 384 built 1972–79.

F-15B: Two-seat training version, formerly designated TF-15A; 61 built 1972–79.

F-15C: Improved single-seat all-weather air-superiority fighter version; 483 built 1979–85.

F-15D: Two-seat training version; 92 built 1979–85.

F-15E Strike Eagle: All-weather ground-attack strike fighter.

F-15J: Single-seat all-weather air-superiority fighter version for the Japan Air Self-Defense Force (JASDF); 139 built under license in Japan by Mitsubishi 1981–97.

F-15DJ: Two-seat training version for the JASDF.

F-15N Sea Eagle: A carrier-capable variant proposed in the early 1970s to the U.S. Navy.

F-15 Streak Eagle: One stripped and unpainted F-15A, which broke eight time-to-climb world records in January and February 1975.

F-15 S/MTD: The first F-15B was converted into a short-takeoff-and-landing maneuver-technology demonstrator aircraft.

F-15 ACTIVE: The F-15 S/MTD was later converted into an advanced flight control technology research aircraft with thrust vectoring nozzles.

F-15 IFCS: The F-15 ACTIVE was converted into an intelligent flight control systems research aircraft.

F-15 MANX: Concept name for a tailless variant of the F-15 ACTIVE, but the NASA ACTIVE experimental aircraft was never modified to be tailless.

F-15 Flight Research Facility: Two F-15A aircraft were acquired in 1976 for use by NASA's Dryden Flight Research Center.

F-15B Research Testbed: Acquired in 1993, it was an F-15B modified and used by NASA's Dryden Flight Research Center for flight tests.

OPERATORS

Israeli Air Force: Two F-15A/B squadrons and one F-15C/D squadron. The IAF had 42 F-15A/Cs, 15 F-15B/D and 25 F-15I aircraft in service as of November 2008.

Japan Air Self-Defense Force: Acquired 203 F-15Js and 20 F-15DJs from 1981. Japan had 157 F-15Js and 45 F-15DJs in use as of November 2008.

Royal Saudi Air Force: Four squadrons of F-15C/D (55/19) since 1981. The RSAF had 139 F-15C/S and 22 F-15D Eagles in operation as of November 2008.

United States Air Force: Operated 630 F-15 aircraft (499 in active duty and 131 in Air National Guard, all variants) as of September 2008.

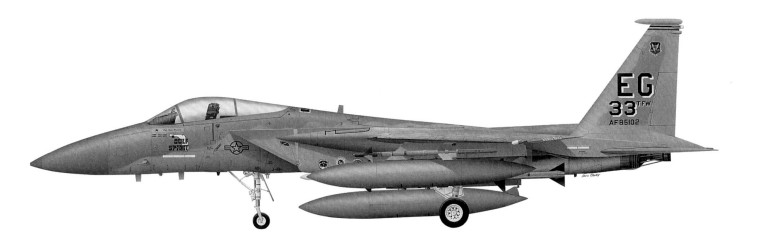

MCDONNELL DOUGLAS F-15 EAGLE

"Gulf Spirit" was the F-15C assigned to the commander of the U.S. Air Force's 33rd Tactical Fighter Wing (TFW), normally based at Eglin Air Force Base on Florida's Gulf Coast. During Operation Desert Storm, the campaign to remove Iraqi forces from Kuwait in 1991, pilots flying it destroyed three Iraqi Air Force aircraft.

On January 29, 1991, "Gulf Spirit" shot down an Iraqi Mikoyan-Gurevich MiG-23 with an AIM-7M Sparrow. The pilot was Captain David Rose. On February 7, flown by Captain Anthony Murphy, it destroyed two Sukhoi Su-22M fighter-bombers, again with Sparrows. Colonel Rick Parsons, CO of the 33rd TFW, scored a victory against an Su-22 while flying another F-15, and this is shown by a green star by his name.

The TFX (Tactical Fighter Experimental) requirement that led to the F-15 was issued in 1968. Experience in Vietnam had shown the need for a fighter with far better maneuverability than McDonnell Douglas's F-4 Phantom; improved visibility, particularly to the rear; and a radar that could identify and track targets to be destroyed well beyond visual range. The requirement evolved to specify Mach 2-plus top speed as a counter to Mikoyan-Gurevich's MiG-25 "Foxbat," regarded as a huge threat even though little was factually known about it at the time.

McDonnell Douglas won the TFX contest, and its YF-15A Eagle prototype flew in July 1972, followed in November 1974 by deliveries to the U.S. Air Force.

KEEPING THE WEIGHT DOWN

The F-15A had the same armament as the F-4E Phantom: four AIM-7 Sparrows, four AIM-9 Sidewinders and an M61 Vulcan cannon. Ground attack was very much a secondary consideration, to the extent that "not a pound for air to ground" – in other words, no extra structural weight should be added so that the Eagle could carry bombs – was a frequently heard remark during the design phase.

The F-15A's cockpit was equipped with conventional round dial instruments, but unlike the F-4 had a head-up display (HUD) that displayed flight, radar and weapons information in the pilot's forward vision. Many radar, weapons and communications functions could be controlled by buttons and switches on the throttles and control stick. This was the first application of hands-on-throttle-and-stick, or HOTAS, controls that allowed the pilot to keep his eyes on the enemy without the need to look down.

Avionics equipment was made as accessible as possible, and many items were fitted in line replaceable units or LRUs, which could simply be pulled out and

replaced with a fresh unit if the aircraft's built-in test equipment (BITE) detected a fault.

OVERSEAS INTEREST

Israel became the first export customer in 1976 and the only one for the F-15A and two-seat B, which it named Baz (eagle). Later Israeli F-15Cs were the Akef (buzzard) and the F-15I strike aircraft the Ra'am (thunderbolt). In June 1979, Israeli Defense Force/Israeli Air Force Eagles destroyed five Syrian MiG-21s in a skirmish and went on to shoot down many more in 1982 during the Israeli invasion of Lebanon.

Saudi Arabia bought F-15Cs in 1981 and later the F-15S version of the Strike Eagle, eventually acquiring over 140 in total. Saudi Eagles shot down two Iranian Phantoms in 1984. Mitsubishi in Japan built the F-15J and two-seat F-15DJ under license, while South Korea and Singapore have taken versions of the F-15E designated F-15K and F-15SG, respectively.

In the 1991 Gulf War, U.S. Air Force Eagles were credited with 33 Iraqi aircraft, and a Saudi F-15 destroyed two more. Most kills were scored with the AIM-7. Four MiG-29s fell to U.S. Air Force F-15s over the former Yugoslavia in 1999.

Production of the fighter Eagle has ended, but Boeing has proposed a version of the F-15E called the "Silent Eagle," with canted vertical fins, internal weapons carriage and other stealth features for countries unable to afford or not cleared to receive advanced stealth aircraft such as the F-35 Lightning II.

Above: In the F-15E Strike Eagle, computer screens have replaced many of the dials found in the F-15A and F-15C.

Above: An F-15C of the U.S. Air Force's 1st Fighter Wing launches an AIM-7 Sparrow. The majority of the F-15s kills have been with AIM-7s.

Above: The F-15 is similar in size to a World War II North American B-25 bomber. Its large wing area is evident here on this Alaska-based aircraft.

Lockheed Martin F-16 Fighting Falcon

F-16C FIGHTING FALCON SPECIFICATION

Dimensions

Fuselage length: 49 ft 4 in (15.03 m)
Wingspan with tip-mounted AAMs: 32 ft 9¾ in (10.00 m)
Wing area: 300.00 sq ft (27.87 m²)
Wing aspect ratio: 3.0
Tailplane span: 18 ft 3¾ in (5.58 m)
Vertical tail surfaces: 54.75 sq ft (5.09 m²)
Height: 16 ft 8½ in (5.09 m)
Wheel track: 7 ft 9 in (2.36 m)
Wheel base: 13 ft 1½ in (4.00 m)

Power plant

One General Electric F110-GE-100 turbofan rated at 28,984 lb st (128.9 kN) with afterburning, or a Pratt & Whitney F100-PW-220 23,770 lb st (105.7 kN) in Blocks 40/42

Weights

Empty operating: 19,100 lb (8663 kg)
Typical combat takeoff: 21,585 lb (9791 kg)
Max. takeoff for air-to-air mission without drop tanks: 25,071 lb (11,372 kg)
Max. takeoff with max. external load: 42,300 lb (19,187 kg)
g limits: Max. symmetrical design g limit with full internal fuel load ±9

Performance

Max. level speed "clean" at altitude: 1,146 kt (1,320 mph; 2124 km/h)
Max. level speed at sea level: 795 kt (915 mph; 1472 km/h)
Max. rate of climb at sea level: 50,000 ft (15,240 m) per minute
Service ceiling: more than 50,000 ft (15,240 m)
Combat radius: 295 nm (340 miles; 547 km) on a hi-lo-hi mission with six 1,000-lb (454-kg) bombs

Armament

One internal M61 Vulcan 0.79-in (0.79-in (20-mm)) cannon; max. ordnance of 15,200 lb (6894 kg) on one fuselage pylon and six underwing pylons

Cutaway Key

1 Pitot head/air data probe
2 Fiberglass radome
3 Lightning conducting strips
4 Planar radar scanner
5 Radome hinge point, opens to starboard
6 Scanner tracking mechanism
7 ILS glideslope antenna
8 Radar mounting bulkhead
9 Incidence vane, port and starboard
10 IFF antenna
11 GBU-12B laser-guided bomb
12 AN/APG-68 digital pulse-Doppler multimode radar equipment bay
13 Forward oblique radar warning antennas, port and starboard
14 Front pressure bulkhead
15 Static ports
16 Fuselage forebody strake fairing
17 Forward avionics equipment bay
18 Canopy jettison charge
19 Instrument panel shield
20 Instrument panel, multifunction CRT head-down displays
21 Sidestick controller, fly-by-wire control system
22 Video recorder
23 GEC wide-angle head-up display
24 CBU-52/58/71 submunition dispenser
25 LAU-3A 19-round rocket launcher
26 2.75-in (68-mm) FFAR
27 CBU-87/89 Gator submunition dispenser
28 Starboard intake flank (No. 5R) stores pylon adaptor
29 LANTIRN (FLIR) targeting pod
30 One-piece frameless cockpit canopy
31 Ejection-seat headrest
32 McDonnell-Douglas ACES II zero-zero ejection seat
33 Side console panel
34 Canopy frame fairing
35 Canopy external emergency release
36 Engine throttle lever incorporating HOTAS (hands-on throttle-and-stick)
37 radar controls
Canopy jettison handle
38 Cockpit section frame structure
39 Boundary layer splitter plate
40 Fixed-geometry engine air intake
41 Nosewheel, aft retracting
42 LANTIRN (FLIR/TFR) navigation pod
43 Port intake flank (No. 5L) stores pylon adaptor
44 Port position light
45 Intake duct framing
46 Intake ducting
47 Gun gas suppression muzzle aperture
48 Aft avionics equipment bay
49 Cockpit rear pressure bulkhead
50 Canopy hinge point
51 Ejection-seat launch rails
52 Canopy rotary actuator
53 Conditioned-air delivery duct
54 Canopy sealing frame
55 Canopy aft glazing
56 600-gal (2271-liter) external fuel tank
57 Garrett hydrazine turbine emergency power unit (EPU)
58 Hydrazine fuel tank
59 Fuel-tank bay access panel
60 Forward fuselage bag-type fuel tank, total internal capacity 6972 lb (3162 kg)
61 Fuselage upper longeron
62 Conditioned-air ducting
63 Cannon barrels
64 Forebody frame construction
65 Air system ground connection
66 Ventral air-conditioning system equipment bay
67 Centerline fuel tank, capacity 300 gal (1136 liters)
68 Mainwheel door hydraulic actuator
69 Mainwheel door
70 Hydraulic system ground connectors
71 Gun-bay ventral gas vent
72 GE M61A1 Vulcan 0.79-in (20-mm) rotary cannon
73 Ammunition feed chute
74 Hydraulic gun drive motor
75 Port hydraulic reservoir
76 Center fuselage

77 integral fuel tank
Leading-edge flap drive hydraulic motor
78 Ammunition drum with 511 rounds
79 Upper position light/refueling floodlight
80 TACAN antenna
81 Hydraulic accumulator
82 Starboard hydraulic reservoir
83 Leading-edge flap drive shaft
84 Inboard, No. 6 stores station, capacity 4,500 lb (2041 kg)
85 Pylon attachment hard point
86 Leading-edge flap drive shaft and rotary actuators
87 No. 7 stores hard point, capacity 3,500 lb (1588 kg)
88 Starboard forward radar warning antenna
89 Missile launch rails
90 AIM-120 AMRAAM medium-range AAMs
91 MXU-648 baggage pod, carriage of essential ground equipment and personal effects for off-base deployment

92 Starboard leading-edge maneuver flap, down position
93 Outboard, No. 8 stores station, capacity 700 lb (318 kg)
94 Wingtip, No. 9 stores station, capacity 425 lb (193 kg)
95 Wingtip AMRAAM
96 Starboard navigation light
97 Fixed portion of trailing edge
98 Static dischargers
99 Starboard flaperon
100 Starboard wing integral fuel tank
101 Fuel system piping
102 Fuel pump
103 Starboard wing root attachment

fishplates
104 Fuel-tank access panels
105 Universal air refueling receptacle (UARSSI), open
106 Engine intake centerbody fairing
107 Airframe mounted accessory equipment gearbox
108 Jet fuel starter
109 Machined wing attachment bulkheads
110 Engine fuel management equipment
111 Pressure refueling receptacle ventral

adaptor
112 Pratt & Whitney F100-PW-229 afterburning turbofan engine
113 VHF/IFF antenna
114 Starboard flaperon hydraulic actuator
115 Fuel-tank tail fins
116 Sidebody fairing integral fuel tank
117 Position light
118 Cooling air ram air intake
119 Finroot fairing
120 Forward engine support link
121 Rear fuselage integral fuel tank
122 Thermally insulated tank inner skin
123 Tank access panels

124 Radar warning system power amplifier
125 Finroot attachment fittings

126 Flight control system hydraulic accumulators
127 Multi-spar fin torsion box structure
128 Starboard all-moving tailplane (tailplane panels interchangeable)
129 General Electric F110-GE-129 alternative power plant
130 Fin leading-edge honeycomb core
131 Dynamic pressure probe
132 Carbon-fiber fin skin panelling
133 VHF comm antenna (AM/FM)
134 Fintip antenna fairing
135 Anti-collision light

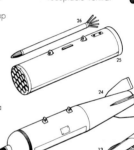

Originally conceived as a "no-frills" lightweight fighter, the F-16 has morphed into a potent multirole aircraft and one of the great sales successes of the modern era. Constant updating will see this 1970s design remain effective well into the twenty-first century.

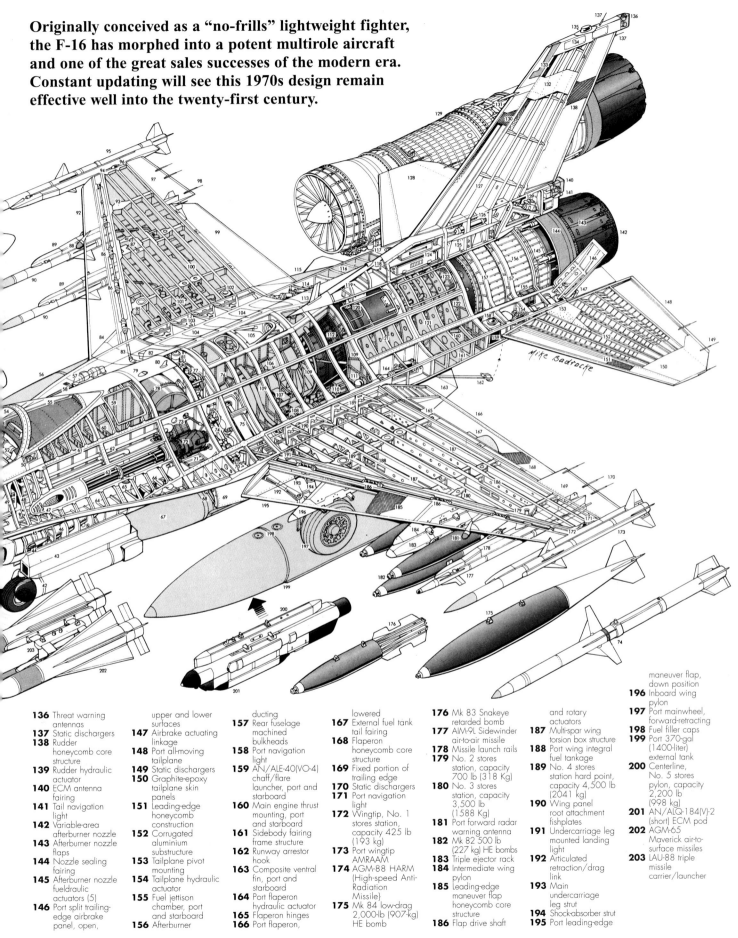

Mike Badroche

136 Threat warning antennas
137 Static dischargers
138 Rudder honeycomb core structure
139 Rudder hydraulic actuator
140 ECM antenna fairing
141 Tail navigation light
142 Variable-area afterburner nozzle
143 Afterburner nozzle flaps
144 Nozzle sealing fairing
145 Afterburner nozzle fuel/hydraulic actuators (5)
146 Port split trailing-edge airbrake panel, open, upper and lower surfaces
147 Airbrake actuating linkage
148 Port all-moving tailplane
149 Static dischargers
150 Graphite-epoxy tailplane skin panels
151 Leading-edge honeycomb construction
152 Corrugated aluminium substructure
153 Tailplane pivot mounting
154 Tailplane hydraulic actuator
155 Fuel jettison chamber, port and starboard
156 Afterburner
157 Rear fuselage machined bulkheads
158 Port navigation light
159 AN/ALE-40(VO-4) chaff/flare launcher, port and starboard
160 Main engine thrust mounting, port and starboard
161 Sidebody fairing frame structure
162 Runway arrestor hook
163 Composite ventral fin, port and starboard
164 Port flaperon hydraulic actuator
165 Flaperon hinges
166 Port flaperon, lowered
167 External fuel tank tail fairing
168 Flaperon honeycomb core structure
169 Fixed portion of trailing edge
170 Static dischargers
171 Port navigation light
172 Wingtip, No. 1 stores station, capacity 425 lb (193 kg)
173 Port wingtip AMRAAM
174 AGM-88 HARM (High-speed Anti-Radiation Missile)
175 Mk 84 low-drag 2,000-lb (907-kg) HE bomb
176 Mk 83 Snakeye retarded bomb
177 AIM-9L Sidewinder air-to-air missile
178 Missile launch rails
179 No. 2 stores station, capacity 700 lb (318 Kg)
180 No. 3 stores station, capacity 3,500 lb (1588 Kg)
181 Port forward radar warning antenna
182 Mk 82 500 lb (227 kg) HE bombs
183 Triple ejector rack
184 Intermediate wing pylon
185 Leading-edge maneuver flap honeycomb core structure
186 Flap drive shaft
187 Multi-spar wing torsion box structure
188 Port wing integral fuel tankage
189 No. 4 stores station hard point, capacity 4,500 lb (2041 kg)
190 Wing panel root attachment fishplates
191 Undercarriage leg mounted landing light
192 Articulated retraction/drag link
193 Main undercarriage leg strut
194 Shock-absorber strut
195 Port leading-edge and rotary actuators
196 Inboard wing pylon
197 Port mainwheel, forward-retracting
198 Fuel filler caps
199 Port 370-gal (1400-liter) external tank
200 Centerline, No. 5 stores pylon, capacity 2,200 lb (998 kg)
201 AN/ALQ-184(V)-2 (short) ECM pod
202 AGM-65 Maverick air-to-surface missiles
203 LAU-88 triple missile carrier/launcher

maneuver flap, down position

"The F-16 makes you think there is nothing you can't do. As one [evaluation] pilot said: 'If I'm here and I want to be there, I just sort of *think* there and I *am* there!'"
– Phil Oestricher, F-16 test pilot

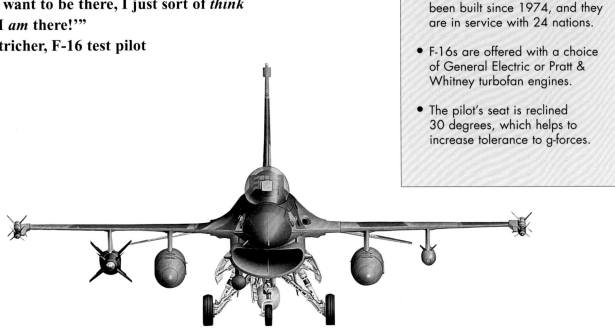

LOCKHEED MARTIN F-16 FIGHTING FALCON – MAJOR VARIANTS

F-16A FSD: Single-seat fighters from full-scale development batch for service testing.

F-16B FSD: Two-seat conversion trainers from full-scale development batch.

F-16A/B Block 1: Initial production version. Distinguished by their black radomes. Most Block 1 aircraft were upgraded to Block 10 standard in a program called "Pacer Loft" in 1982.

F-16A/B Block 5: Refined production version. Most Block 5 aircraft were upgraded to Block 10 standard.

F-16A/B Block 10: Slightly revised avionics equipment fit.

F-16A/B Block 15: The most numerous version of the F-16. Introduced an enlarged tailplane, which is required when carrying large bomb loads.

ADF F-16A/B Block 15: Conversion of Block 15 aircraft to dedicated Air Defense Fighter role for use by the U.S. Air National Guard.

F-16A/B Block 10/Block 15 OCU: Operational capabilities upgrade program. Improved avionics and fire-control system and provision for F100-PW-220E engine.

F-16/B MLU: Midlife update program for the original NATO F-16s.

F-16A/B Block 20: Export version for Taiwan.

F-16C/D Block 25: Introduced the ability to carry AIM-120 AMRAAM, as well as night and precision ground-attack capabilities.

F-16C/D Block 30/32: New engines: Block 30 the General Electric F110-GE-100; Block 32 the Pratt & Whitney F100-PW-220.

F-16C/D Block 40/42 "Night Falcon": Introduced the LANTIRN navigation and targeting pods and extensive air-to-ground loads. Block 40/42 production began in 1988 and went on until 1995.

F-16C/D Block 50/52: Equipped with the APG-68(V)7 radar and F110-GE-229 (Block 50) or F100-PW-220 (Block 52) Improved Performance Engine.

F-16CJ/DJ Block 50D/52D "Wild Weasel": Could carry the AGM-88 HARM and the AN/ASQ-213 HARM Targeting System (HTS) in the suppression of enemy air defenses (SEAD) mission.

F-16C/D Block 60: Export to United Arab Emirates.

F-16/79: One F-16A converted to take a General Electric J79 engine.

F-16 CCV: First YF-16 rebuild to test Control Configured Vehicle technology, with twin canards added.

NF-16D VISTA: Dedicated research aircraft.

F-16E/F: Proposed designations for single- and two-seat production versions of F-16XL.

F-16N: Version of the F-16C Block 30 for use by the U.S. Navy as an aggressor aircraft.

TF-16N: Two-seat conversion trainer version of F-16N.

LOCKHEED MARTIN F-16 FIGHTING FALCON

Israel is the largest non-U.S. user of the F-16, with more than 360 having served since 1980. These range from some of the earliest F-16As to the far more sophisticated F-16I. The aircraft illustrated here is an F-16D Block 40 of 105 "Scorpion" Tayseet (Squadron), based at Hatzor Israeli Air Force Base in central Israel. Known as the Brakeet II ("Thunderbolt"), this version was delivered in 1991 under the Peace Marble III program and features a dorsal spine containing locally designed avionics, probably associated with the "Wild Weasel" defense suppression role. It is armed with a GBU-15 glide bomb on the starboard outer wing, with a Mk 82 500-lb (227-kg) bomb for balance on the port side. Under the port fuselage is an AAW-13 datalink pod for the GBU-15 and a Litening targeting pod on the starboard side.

Above: The F-16CJ is a dedicated defense suppression variant that fulfills the "Wild Weasel" role with the AGM-88 Harm, as seen on the starboard inner pylon here.

Left: This UAE F-16 shows off its large conformal fuel tanks.

U.S. experience in Vietnam showed the need for a small, maneuverable fighter able to counter the types of threat posed by aircraft such as the MiG-17 and MiG-21 that were proliferating in Soviet-aligned countries. The trend in fighter aircraft had been toward bigger, heavier and more sophisticated aircraft such as the F-14 and F-15, which even the U.S. military could afford in only relatively small numbers.

A LIGHTWEIGHT FIGHTER

A lightweight fighter (LWF) competition was held by the U.S. Air Force, culminating in 1975 with fly-off evaluations of prototypes from Northrop (the YF-17 Cobra) and General Dynamics (the YF-16). General Dynamics' F-16 design was the victor, while the YF-17 was further developed to become the F/A-18 Hornet for the U.S. Navy and Marine Corps.

Key to the F-16's agility is its fly-by-wire control system, the first to be used in a production aircraft. Instead of moving the control surfaces with mechanical cables and

Above: A feature of many later block F-16C/Ds is a wide-angle holographic head-up display. Note the reclined seat.

hydraulic boosters, the pilot's inputs are carried via wires through flight-control system computers, which allow maneuvers up to but not beyond the aircraft's physical limits. Designed to be inherently unstable without the computers so that it would easily change direction when commanded to, the F-16 cannot fly without them. Instead of a conventional control column coming up from the cockpit floor, the F-16 pilot uses a sidestick controller on the right console, which has very little physical movement.

SALE OF THE CENTURY

The F-16A entered service with the U.S. Air Force simultaneously with service in several European air forces. In the so-called "fighter sale of the century," Belgium, the Netherlands, Denmark and Norway all ordered F-16s as replacements for their Lockheed F-104 Starfighters even before the program was still in the testing phase. Turkey, Portugal and Greece, and later Italy and Poland, also joined the club of European F-16 users. The Fighting Falcon, as the F-16 was eventually called, also had sales success in the Middle East (Israel, Jordan, Egypt, United Arab Emirates, Bahrain and Oman); Asia (Pakistan, Singapore, Thailand, Taiwan, Indonesia, South Korea) and South America (Venezuela and Chile). Additional countries may become users of new or used F-16s even into the design's fifth decade.

Fighting Falcons have seen action with several users. U.S., Israeli, Pakistani, Venezuelan and Dutch F-16s have all claimed air combat victories in various conflicts. In the air-to-ground role, F-16s have become one of the workhorses of close air support. Many of the NATO users have deployed their F-16s to Afghanistan since 2001.

CONTINUING SERVICE

The main production version has been the F-16C (and its two-seat counterpart the F-16D), which had structural and avionics improvements over the F-16A and B. Production for the U.S. Air Force has ended, but the Falcon is still for sale, mainly in advanced F-16E and F form. Also known as the "Block 60," the F-16E and F have electronically scanned radars, large conformal fuel tanks and the capability to carry a wider range of weapons. The E/F has sold only to the United Arab Emirates, but its features are available for other customers.

British Aerospace Sea Harrier

The Sea Harrier kept British fixed-wing naval aviation alive after the Royal Navy's last big deck carrier was retired. In 1982 it was instrumental in the fight to recover the Falkland Islands from Argentine forces.

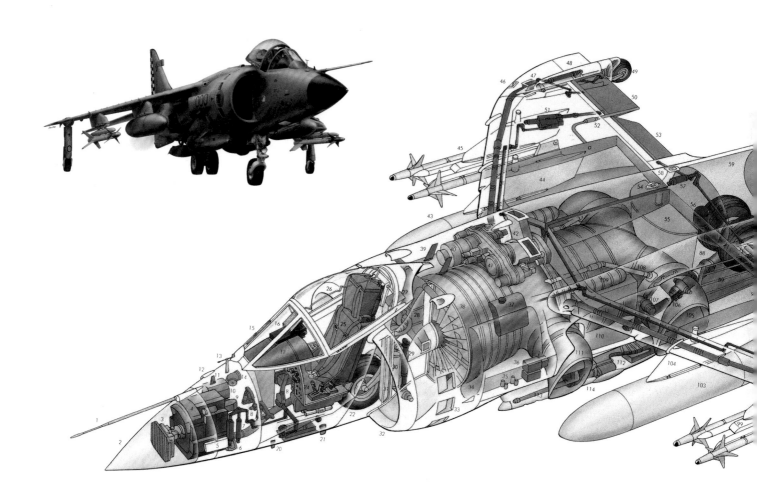

Cutaway Key

1 Pitot head
2 Radome
3 Ferranti Blue Fox radar scanner
4 Radar equipment module
5 Radome hinge
6 Nose pitch reaction control valve
7 Pitch feel and trim control mechanism
8 Rudder pedals
9 Starboard side oblique camera
10 Inertial platform
11 IFF aerial
12 Cockpit ram air intake
13 Yaw vane

14 Pressurization spill valve
15 Windshield wiper
16 Head-up display
17 Instrument panel shield
18 Control column and linkages
19 Doppler antenna
20 TACAN aerial
21 UHF aerial
22 Nose undercarriage wheel bay
23 Radar hand controller
24 Throttle and nozzle angle control levers
25 Martin-Baker Mk 10H zero-zero ejection seat

26 Miniature detonating cord (MDC) canopy breaker
27 Boundary layer spill duct
28 Cockpit air-conditioning pack
29 Nose undercarriage hydraulic retraction jack
30 Hydraulic accumulator
31 Boundary layer bleed duct
32 Engine air intake
33 Intake suction relief doors (spring-loaded)

34 Forward fuselage flank fuel tank
35 Hydraulic system ground connectors
36 Engine monitoring and recording equipment
37 Engine oil tank
38 Rolls-Royce Pegasus Mk 104 turbofan engine
39 UHF homing aerials
40 Alternator
41 Accessory equipment gearbox
42 Gas turbine starter/auxiliary power unit (GTS/APU)

43 Starboard external fuel tank
44 Starboard wing integral fuel tank
45 Twin missile pylon
46 Starboard navigation light
47 Roll control reaction air valve
48 Outrigger wheel fairing
49 Starboard outrigger wheel
50 Starboard aileron
51 Aileron hydraulic actuator
52 Fuel jettison valve
53 Starboard plain flap
54 Anti-collision light

55 Water methanol tank
56 Engine-fire suppression bottle
57 Flap hydraulic actuator
58 Water-methanol filler cap
59 Rear fuselage fuel tank
60 Emergency ram air turbine extended
61 Ram air turbine actuator
62 Heat exchanger air intake
63 HF tuner
64 HF notch aerial
65 Rudder control linkage

66 Starboard all-moving tailplane
67 Temperature probe
68 Forward radar-warning antenna
69 VHF aerial
70 Rudder
71 Rudder trim tab
72 Rear rudder-warning antenna
73 Tail pitch control reaction air valve
74 Yaw control reaction air valves
75 Port all-moving tailplane
76 IFF notch aerial
77 Tail bumper

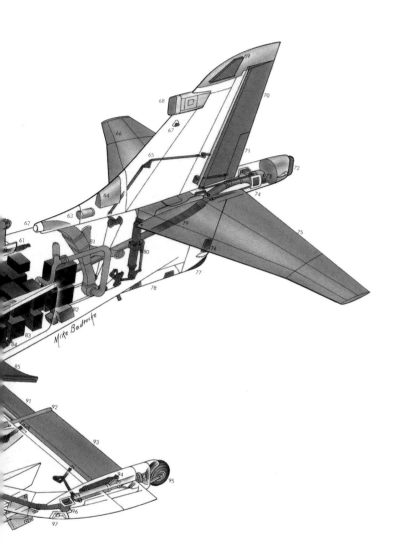

Mike Badrocke

SEA HARRIER FRS1 SPECIFICATION

Dimensions

Overall length: 47 ft 7 in (14.50 m)
Length with nose folded: 41 ft 9 in (12.73 m)
Wingspan: 25 ft 3 in (7.70 m)
Wingspan with ferry tips: 29 ft 8 in (9.04 m)
Wing area: 202.10 sq ft (18.68 m²)
Wing aspect ratio: 3.175

Power plant

One Rolls-Royce Pegasus Mk 104 vectored thrust
turbofan rated at 21,500 lb st (95.6 kN)

Weights

Basic empty: 13,000 lb (5897 kg)
Operating empty: 14,502 lb (6374 kg)
Maximum takeoff weight: 26,200 lb (11,884 kg)

Fuel load

Maximum internal fuel: 5,060 lb (2295 kg)
Maximum external fuel: 5,300 lb (2404 kg) in two
    120-gal (455-liter) drop tanks or two 396- or 228-gal
    (1500- or 864-liter) ferry tanks; maximum ordnance
    8,000 lb (3629 kg)

Performance

Maximum speed at high altitude: 825 mph
    (1328 km/h)
Maximum speed "clean" at sea level: more than
    736 mph (1185 km/h)
Cruising speed at 36,000 ft (10,975 m):
    528 mph (850 km/h)
Maximum rate of climb at sea level: 50,000 ft
    (15,240 m) per minute
Service ceiling: 51,000 ft (15,545 m)
Takeoff run: 1,000 ft (305 m) at maximum takeoff
    weight without "ski jump"; landing run 0 ft (0 m) at
    normal landing weight

Range

Combat radius: 460 miles (750 km) on a hi-hi-hi
    interception mission with four AAMs, or 288 miles
    (463 km) on a hi-lo-hi attack mission.
g limit: +7.8/-4.2

Armament

Underfuselage mounts for two 1.18-in (30-mm) ADEN
    cannon, and four underwing hard points stressed for
    up to 8,000 lb (3629 kg). Standard carrying
    capabilities as follows: underfuselage and inboard
    wing hard points 2,000 lb (907 kg) each; outboard
    wing pylons 650 lb (295 kg) each. Cleared for
    carriage of standard British 1,000-lb (454-kg) free-fall
    and retarded HE bombs, BAe Sea Eagle ASM, AGM-
    84 Harpoon ASM, WE177 tactical nuclear free-fall
    bomb, Lepus flare units, CBLS 100 practice bomb
    dispenser and most NATO-standard bombs, rockets
    and flares. Air-to-air armament can comprise four
    AIM-9L Sidewinders on twin-rail launchers, or MATRA
    Magic missiles on Indian aircraft.

78 Radar altimeter aerials
79 Reaction control air duct
80 Tailplane hydraulic actuator
81 Rear equipment bay air-conditioning pack
82 Chaff/flare dispensers
83 Avionics equipment bay
84 Airbrake hydraulic jack
85 Ventral airbrake
86 Liquid oxygen converter
87 Hydraulic system nitrogen pressurizing bottle
88 Main undercarriage stowage
89 Nozzle blast shield
90 Port wing integral fuel tank
91 Port plain flap
92 Fuel jettison
93 Port aileron
94 Outrigger wheel hydraulic retraction jack
95 Port outrigger wheel
96 Roll control reaction air valve
97 Port navigation light
98 AIM-9L Sidewinder air-to-air missiles
99 Twin missile carrier/launcher
100 Outboard stores pylon
101 Reaction control air duct
102 Port aileron hydraulic actuator
103 External fuel tank
104 Inboard wing pylon
105 Rear (hot-stream) swivelling exhaust nozzle
106 Main undercarriage hydraulic retraction jack
107 Pressure refueling connection
108 Nozzle bearing cooling air duct
109 Hydraulic system reservoir, port and starboard
110 Center fuselage flank fuel tank
111 Fan air (cold-stream) swivelling nozzle
112 Ammunition magazine
113 ADEN 1.18-in (30-mm) cannon
114 Ventral gun pack, port and starboard

"The Sea Harrier with the AIM-9L
Sidewinder was a very bad system for us,
a very good system for the British."
– Argentine Navy pilot Bernado Rotolo

BAE SEA HARRIER – VARIANTS & OPERATORS

VARIANTS

Harrier T4N: Two-seat naval training version of the Harrier T2.

Sea Harrier FRS1: Initial production version of a navalized Harrier. 57 built survivors converted to Sea Harrier FA2.

Sea Harrier FRS51: Indian Navy variant of the FRS1. Single-seat fighter, reconnaissance and attack aircraft. Fitted with Matra R550 Magic air-to-air missiles. The first of 23 FRS51s were delivered in 1983.

Harrier T60: Export version of the T4N two-seat training version for the Indian Navy. At least four Harrier T60s were purchased by the Indian Navy for land-based training.

Sea Harrier FA2: Upgrade incorporating increased air-to-air weapons load, look-down radar, increased range, and improved cockpit displays. The first aircraft was delivered on April 2, 1993, and the first operational deployment was in April 1994 as part of the UN force in Bosnia. The final new-build Sea Harrier FA2 was delivered on January 18, 1999.

Harrier T8: Seven Harrier T4s two-seat trainers updated with Sea Harrier FA2 instrumentation but no radar. Retired from service in March 2006.

OPERATORS

India
Indian Navy
300 Naval Squadron
Still in service.

United Kingdom
Royal Navy
Fleet Air Arm
800 Naval Air Squadron
Operated 12 Sea Harrier FRS1s aboard HMS *Hermes* during the Falklands War (1982).
Disbanded 2006.

801 Naval Air Squadron
Operated eight Sea Harrier FRS1s aboard HMS *Invincible* during the Falklands War (1982).
Disbanded 2006.

809 Naval Air Squadron
Operated Eight Sea Harrier FR1s across HMS *Hermes* and HMS *Invincible* during the Falklands War (1982) and served with HMS *Illustrious* after the Falklands War.
Disbanded 1982.

899 Naval Air Squadron
12 Sea Harriers (10 loaned to 801 Naval Air Squadron and 809 Naval Air Squadron during the Falklands War).
Disbanded 2006.

BAE SEA HARRIER

The Sea Harrier FA2 first saw operational service flying patrols over Bosnia in August 1994 with the Royal Navy's Operational Evaluation Unit, No. 899 Squadron. Shown here with two Sidewinders and fuel tanks, the FA2 could carry AIM-9s on double launchers or up to four AIM-120 AMRAAMs on the wing pylons and in place of the cannon pods seen fitted here. One drop tank has also been modified to carry a camera. As a Sea Harrier FRS1, Sea Harrier XZ455 shot down two Argentine Daggers in the Falklands War in 1982. It crashed into the Adriatic Sea in February 1996 when returning from a mission over Bosnia, but the pilot was rescued.

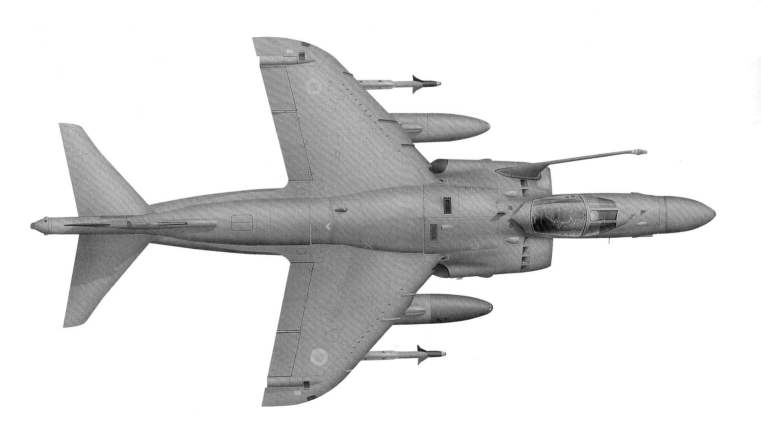

Even before the Hawker Siddeley Harrier GR1 Vertical Take-Off and Landing (VTOL) strike aircraft entered Royal Air Force service in 1969, its potential as a shipboard aircraft had been tested on a variety of platforms. Despite factions that said every new fighter had to be large and Mach 2–capable, design work began in 1972 on a basic adaptation of the RAF Harrier into a fighter for operation from light carriers.

The new naval Harrier was intended to be multirole, able to defend the fleet against Soviet Navy "Bear" bombers, conduct anti-shipping and ground-attack missions, and perform photo-reconnaissance duties. As such, it was designated Sea Harrier FRS1, for "fighter," "reconnaissance" and "strike." The Sea Harrier had a new nose section with a raised canopy and a pointed radome containing a Ferranti Blue Fox radar. A new navigation system and completely revised cockpit were other changes from the GR3, as was a folding nose to allow it to use standard aircraft-carrier elevators.

FALKLANDS FIGHTERS

By the time the Sea Harrier flew in 1978, the last "big deck" Royal Navy carrier, HMS *Ark Royal*, was being retired. The Admiralty had commissioned three so-called "through-deck cruisers" as a way of retaining a carrier capability. The first

Top: The nozzle control lever common to Harriers can be seen on the left console of this Sea Harrier FRS1 cockpit.

Above: One modification made after the 1982 Falklands War was to fit double AIM-9 launchers to Harrier FRS1s such as these No. 800 Squadron aircraft.

of these, HMS *Invincible*, and the older carrier HMS *Hermes* were the only means of providing air protection for the task force that was sent to reclaim the Falkland Islands from Argentina in 1982. Both ships were fitted with "ski-jump" ramps that allowed rolling takeoffs and vertical landings, saving fuel and increasing range.

Flying from HMS *Invincible* and HMS *Hermes*, Sea Harriers destroyed 23 Argentine aircraft with their AIM-9L Sidewinders and 1.18-in (30-mm) cannon pods during Operation Corporate, the British name for the Falklands campaign. To keep the carriers safe from Argentine air attack, they had to operate well to the east of the Falklands, giving them little time on station over the islands, and Argentine aircraft were able to successfully attack a number of ships.

VERY LIMITED EXPORT

India became the only export customer for the Sea Harrier when its navy ordered 24 FRS51s, in 1978. Today, the remaining aircraft fly from INS *Vikrant*, the former HMS *Hermes*, and are being upgraded to take newer weapons such as the Rafael Derby AAM.

In 1988 an upgraded version, the Sea Harrier FRS2 (later renamed FA2) was flown. This replaced the Blue Fox radar with the multimode Blue Vixen in a new, bulged radome. Four Sidewinders or AIM-120 AMRAAMs replaced the two AIM-9s of the Falklands era. A mix of conversions and new-build aircraft were made for a total of just over 50 aircraft. These served on the "Invincible"-class ships from the mid-1990s and saw action over the Balkans in Operation Deliberate Force in 1995 and Operation Allied Force in 1999, flying both combat air patrol and bombing missions.

The Royal Navy's Sea Harriers were retired somewhat prematurely in 2006 as a money-saving measure, and the Fleet Air Arm's strike capability was merged with the RAF's Harrier GR7 units to form Joint Force Harrier. The Royal Navy will have a "capability gap" in organic air defense until the Joint Combat Aircraft (F-35 Lightning II) enters service in the mid-2010s.

Above: A Sea Harrier FA2 makes a vertical landing on a Royal Navy "Invincible"-class carrier.

Sukhoi Su-27 "Flanker"

The massively powerful, maneuverable and long-ranged Su-27 helped to change Western perceptions of Soviet aircraft. Since the end of the Cold War, exports of Su-27s have helped to keep both Sukhoi and the Russian aerospace industry alive.

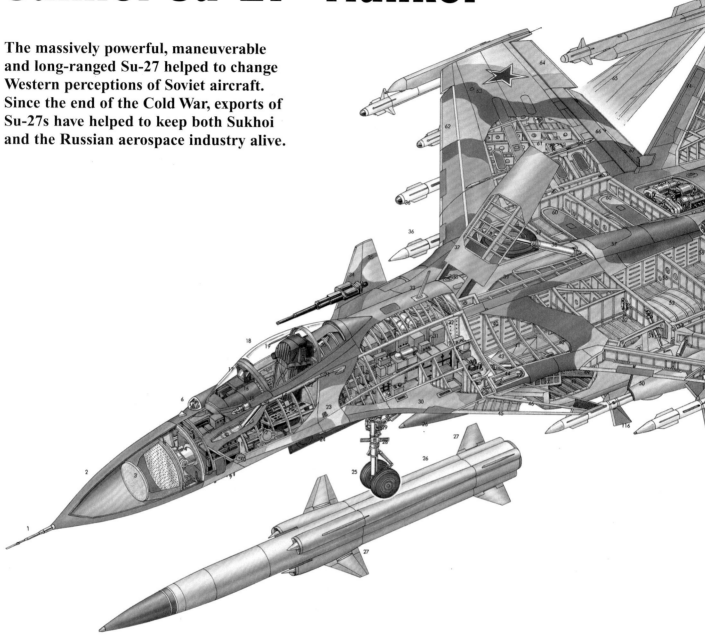

Cutaway Key

1 Pitot head
2 Upward-hinging radome
3 Radar scanner
4 Scanner mounting
5 Radome hinge point
6 Infrared search and tracking scanner
7 Refueling probe housing
8 Radar equipment module; tilts down for access
9 Lower SRO-2 "Odd-Rods" IFF aerial
10 Incidence transmitter
11 Cockpit front pressure bulkhead

12 Retractable spotlight, port and starboard
13 Cockpit side console panel
14 Slide-mounted throttle levers
15 Flight-refueling probe, extended
16 Instrument panel shield
17 Pilot's head-up display
18 Upward-hinging cockpit canopy
19 K-36MD "zero-zero" ejection seat
20 Canopy hydraulic jack

21 Dynamic pressure probe, port and starboard
22 Cockpit rear pressure bulkhead
23 Temperature probe
24 Nosewheel door
25 Twin nosewheels, forward-retracting
26 ASM-MSS long-range ramjet and rocket-powered anti-shipping missile
27 Missile folding fins
28 Nosewheel hydraulic steering jacks
29 Deck approach "traffic lights"

30 Leading-edge flush EW aerial
31 Avionics equipment bay
32 Ammunition magazine, 149 rounds
33 HF aerial
34 Starboard fuselage GSh-30-1 1.18-in (30-mm) cannon
35 Canard foreplane
36 Starboard wing missile armament
37 Dorsal airbrake
38 Gravity fuel-filler cap
39 Center fuselage fuel tank

40 Forward lateral fuel tanks
41 ASM-MSS missile carrier on fuselage centerline station
42 Variable-area intake ramp doors
43 Ramp hydraulic jack
44 Foreplane hydraulic actuator
45 Port canard foreplane
46 Engine air intake
47 Boundary layer bleed air louvers
48 Segmented ventral suction relief doors
49 Retractable intake FOD screen

50 Mainwheel door
51 Door hydraulic jack
52 Port mainwheel bay
53 Intake trunking
54 Wing panel attachment joints
55 Engine compressor face
56 Wing center-section integral fuel tanks
57 ADF antenna
58 Airbrake hydraulic jack
59 Starboard mainwheel, stowed position
60 Fuel-tank access panels

61 Wing-fold hydraulic jack
62 Leading-edge flap, down position
63 Starboard outer, folding, wing panel
64 Outboard plain flap, down position
65 Starboard wing, folded position
66 Inboard double-slotted flap segments
67 Engine bleed air pre-cooler air intake
68 Engine accessory equipment gearbox
69 Central auxiliary power unit

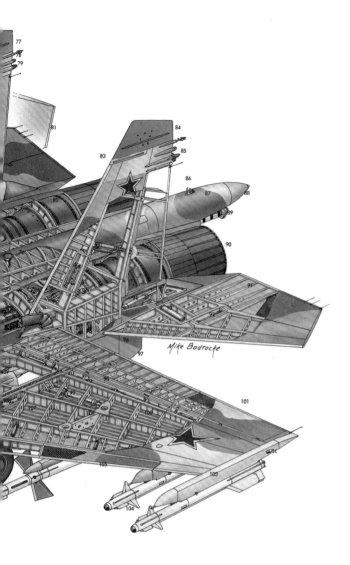

Mike Badrocke

70 Chaff/flare launchers
71 Rear fuselage integral fuel tank
72 Engine oil tank
73 Fin structure
74 Leading-edge HF aerial
75 Rudder hydraulic actuator
76 Fintip UHF/VHF aerial
77 ILS aerial
78 Tail navigation light
79 Radar warning antenna
80 Starboard rudder
81 Starboard tailplane folded position
82 AL-31F afterburning turbofan engine
83 Port tail fin

84 ILS aerial
85 ECM antenna
86 Upper SRO-2 "Odd Rods" IFF aerial
87 Tailcone fairing
88 Rear EW antenna fairing
89 Deck arrestor hook
90 Variable-area afterburner nozzle
91 Port tailplane
92 Tailplane fold joint rotary actuator
93 Tailplane pivot bearing
94 Hydraulic actuator
95 Hydraulic accumulator
96 Ventral fin
97 Port inboard double-slotted flap segments

98 Flap hydraulic actuators
99 Wing-fold hydraulic jack
100 Outer wing panel structure
101 Outboard plain flap segment
102 Port navigation light
103 Wingtip missile launch rail
104 Vympel R-73 (AA-11 "Archer") air-to-air missiles
105 Leading-edge flap
106 Pylon attachment hard points
107 Port wing integral fuel tank
108 Wing-fold locking mechanism jack

109 Main undercarriage hydraulic retraction jack
110 Mainwheel leg strut
111 Wing-fold hinge joint
112 Leading-edge flush EW aerial panels
113 Missile pylon
114 Vympel R-27 (AA-10 "Alamo-B") infrared-homing air-to-air missile
115 Port mainwheel
116 Vympel R-27 (AA-10 "Alamo-C") radar-homing air-to-air missile

SU-27P "FLANKER-B" SPECIFICATION

Dimensions

Fuselage length (including probe): 72 ft 0 in (21.94 m)
Wingspan over tip missile launch rails: 48 ft 3 in (14.70 m)
Wing aspect ratio: 7.76
Tailplane span: 32 ft 5 in (9.88 m)
Wing area: 667.8 sq ft (62.04 m²)
Horizontal tail area: 131.75 sq ft (12.24 m²)
Total fin area: 165.76 sq ft (15.40 m²)
Distance between fintips: 14 ft 1¼ in (4.30 m)
Overall height: 19 ft 6 in (5.93 m)
Wheel track: 14 ft 3 in (4.34 m)
Wheel base: 19 ft 4 in (5.88 m)
Maximum wing loading: 93.4 lb/sq ft (456.2 kg/m²)

Power plant

Two Saturn Lyul'ka AL-31F afterburning turbofans each rated at 16,755 lb st (74.53 kN) dry and 27,558 lb st (122.59 kN) with afterburning

Weights

Empty operating: 36,112 lb (16,380 kg)
Normal takeoff: 50,705 lb (23,000 kg)
Maximum takeoff: 62,391 lb (28,300 kg)

Fuel and load

Internal fuel: normal 11,620 lb (5270 kg); maximum 20,723 lb (9400 kg) or 3,170 gal (12,000 liters) in three main fuselage tanks, with additional tanks in outer wing panels; the basic Su-27 has no provision for inflight refueling or for the carriage of external fuel tanks (see under individual variant briefings for exceptions)
Maximum theoretical weapon load: 17,636 lb (8000 kg)
Normal weapon load: 8,818 lb (4000 kg)
g limits: 8–9 at basic design gross weight

Performance

Maximum level speed at sea level (estimated): 743 kt (850 mph; 1370 km/h)
Maximum level speed "clean" at altitude: 1,236 kt (1,418 mph; 2280 km/h)
Limiting Mach number: 2.35
Absolute ceiling: 60,700 ft (18,500 m)
Practical service ceiling (est.): 58,070 ft (17,700 m)
Takeoff run: 1,640 ft (500 m) or 1,476 ft (450 m)
Landing roll: 1,968 ft (600 m) or 2,297 ft (700 m)
Landing speed: 121–124 kt (140–143 mph; 225–230 km/h)

Range

Maximum range: 1,987 nm (2,285 miles; 3680 km) at altitude; 740 nm (851 miles; 1370 km) at low level
Radius of action (high-altitude): 590 nm (677 miles; 1090 km)
Radius of action (low-altitude): 227 nm (261 miles; 420 km)

Armament

One 1.18-in (30-mm) GSh-30-1 cannon with 275 rounds
Up to 8,000 kg (17,600 lb) on ten external pylons
Up to six medium-range R-27 missiles, two short-range heat-seeking R-73 missiles

"Those who design, develop or fly fighters know that Sukhoi has succeeded at Paris in making Western fighter aerodynamics look very conventional."
– British test pilot John Farley, at the 1989 Paris Air Show

SUKHOI SU-27 "FLANKER" – VARIANTS

T10 ("Flanker-A"): Initial prototype configuration.

T10S: Improved prototype.

P-42: Special version built to beat climb time records.

Su-27: Pre-production series built in small numbers with AL-31 engine.

Su-27S (Su-27/"Flanker-B"): Initial production single-seater with improved AL-31F engine.

Su-27UB ("Flanker-C"): Initial production two-seat operational conversion trainer.

Su-27SK: Export Su-27 single-seater.

Su-27UBK: Export Su-27UB two-seater.

Su-27K (Su-33/"Flanker-D"): Carrier-based single-seater with folding wings.

Su-27PD: Single-seat demonstrator with improvements such as inflight refueling probe.

Su-27PU (Su-30): Limited-production two-seater.

Su-30M/Su-30MK: Next-generation multirole two-seater.

Su-30MKA: Export version for Algeria.

Su-30MKI ("Flanker-H"): Substantially improved Su-30MK for the Indian Air Force, with canards, vectored-thrust engines, new avionics provided by several nations, and multirole capability.

Su-30MKK ("Flanker-G"): Su-30MK for the Chinese Air Force, with updated Russian-built avionics and multirole capability.

Su-30MKM: Copy of Su-30MKI with special configuration for Malaysia.

Su-30KN ("Flanker-B" Mod. 2): Improved single-seater.

Su-30KI ("Flanker-B" Mod. 2): Improved single-seater with Su-30MK.

Su-27M (Su-35/-37, "Flanker-E"/"Flanker-F"): Improved demonstrators for an advanced single-seat multirole Su-27S derivative.

Su-27SM ("Flanker-B" Mod. 1): Upgraded Russian Su-27S, featuring technology evaluated in the Su-27M demonstrators.

Su-27SKM: Single-seat multirole fighter for export.

Su-27UBM: Comparable upgraded Su-27UB two-seater.

Su-32 (Su-27IB): Two-seat long-range strike variant with side-by-side seating in "platypus" nose. Prototype of Su-32FN and Su-34 "Fullback."

Su-27KUB: Essentially an Su-27K carrier-based single-seater with a side-by-side cockpit, for use as a naval carrier trainer or multirole aircraft.

Su-35BM/Su-35S: Also dubbed the "Last Flanker." The latest development from the "Flanker" family. It features newer avionics and new radar.

SUKHOI SU-27 "FLANKER"

This Su-27 "Flanker-B" served with the Russian Air Forces Training Center at Lipetsk in the 1990s. The unit mainly trains qualified weapons and tactics instructors. The so-called "Lipetsk Shark" was one of the first Russian aircraft to be seen in the West with nonstandard markings, although they were not unknown in the Soviet era. Other "Flankers" of the unit wore a shark's mouth on the intake, but not the full-length shark silhouette seen here. The aircraft is armed with AA-11 "Archer" dogfight missiles on the wingtip and outer pylons, and the AA-10 "Alamo-A" semi-active radar-homing missile on the underfuselage pylons. The infrared-guided "Alamo-B" is fitted on the inner wing pylons.

FACTS

- The Su-27 had the first fly-by-wire system in an operational Russian aircraft.

- The Su-27 has been the mount of the "Russian Knights" and "Test Pilots" display teams.

- The engines are protected from foreign objects by intake screens that close when the wheels are on the ground.

In 1969, the Soviet military formulated a requirement for a new fighter, calling for a long-range interceptor to replace various older types, a counter to airborne warning and control system (AWACS) aircraft and something that could meet the McDonnell Douglas (now Boeing) F-15 Eagle on equal terms. At the time, the F-15 all-weather tactical fighter was still in development, as was Boeing's E-3 Sentry AWACS aircraft.

The desire for extreme maneuverability combined with long range could not be met in one airframe. The requirement was split into heavy and lightweight projects, the latter eventually leading to the Mikoyan-Gurevich MiG-29. Sukhoi proceeded with its T10 design – a large aircraft with plenty of internal fuel capacity, two widely spaced engines and large leading-edge root extensions that blended into the wings, which had curved tips.

The T10-1 prototype flew in May 1977, followed by several others that differed in detail. These proved less than completely satisfactory, but the revised T10S series of prototypes, which began test flights in April 1981, were to become the true predecessors of the Su-27. The T10S-3 prototype was stripped of all uneccessary weight. Also known as the P-42 "Streak Flanker," it set a number of records for the fastest climb to altitude, beating those set by a similarly modified F-15.

TEETHING PROBLEMS

There were further developmental troubles before the production Su-27, by now known in the West as "Flanker-B," began to enter service in 1986. The wing planform had changed to a more squared-off shape and the nose profile had altered, with a large radome housing a multimode radar. An infrared search-and-track sensor ball was mounted ahead of the windshield. ECM equipment was fitted in a large tail "stinger" that protruded from between the engines.

Above: Two prototypes of the Su-35 show the wide range of armament available on modernised "Flankers," as well as the canard foreplanes.

Armament included an internal 1.18-in (30-mm) cannon and ten pylons for missiles, including AA-10 "Alamo" beyond-visual-range weapons and AA-11 "Archer" dogfight AAMs.

The Su-27 first appeared in Western skies at the 1989 Paris Air Show, impressing observers with its agility for such a large aircraft and by not crashing, unlike the MiG-29. When the Soviet Union collapsed shortly afterwards, several former republics such as the Ukraine, Belarus and Uzbekistan inherited sizable numbers of "Flankers." Some of these aircraft, as well as Russian examples, found their way to places such as Angola, Eritrea and Syria. In fighting between Ethiopia and Eritrea that began in 1998, the former country's Su-27s got the better of the latter's MiGs on a number of occasions.

NAVAL VERSION

Russia developed a naval version, the Su-27K (later redesignated Su-33), for use on its first conventional aircraft carriers. In the end, only the *Admiral Kuznetsov* was completed by Russia, but China, which acquired its sister ship *Varyag* and is refurbishing it for service, plans to purchase further Su-33s. China bought a number of Su-27s for its air force and is building more under license as the Shenyang J-11.

The Su-30 is a fully combat-capable version of the two-seat Su-27UB with added strike capabilities. India's Su-30MKIs incorporate thrust-vectoring engines and canards for extra maneuverability. The Su-35 designation was initially used for a relatively modest upgrade plan; however, a new model Su-35BM with many internal and external improvements flew in 2008 and is to form the basis of a production model for use by the Russian Air Force.

Above: The baseline Su-27's cockpit was a product of the 1970s, with a plethora of conventional instruments.

Above: Late 1980s appearances at Farnborough and Paris air shows of Sukhoi's Su-27 demonstrators gave the West its first close views of the new "superfighter."

Panavia Tornado ADV

The Tornado Air Defense Variant (ADV) is a fighter derived from a bomber design, which perhaps made it less efficient than a purpose-built fighter. Still, it has served well as the United Kingdom's principal air-defense asset for more than two decades.

TORNADO F3 SPECIFICATION

Dimensions

Length: 61 ft 3½ in (18.68 m)
Height: 19 ft 6¼ in (5.95 m)
Wingspan spread: 45 ft 7½ in (13.91 m)
Wingspan swept: 28 ft 2½ in (8.60 m)
Aspect ratio spread: 7.73
Aspect ratio swept: 2.96
Wing area: 286.33 sq ft (26.60 m²)
Tailplane span: 22 ft 3½ in (6.80 m)
Wheel track: 10 ft 2 in (3.10 m)

Power plant

Two Turbo-Union RB.199-34R Mk 104 turbofans each rated at 9,100 lb st (40.48 kN) dry and 16,520 lb st (73.48 kN) with afterburning

Fuel and load

Internal fuel: 12,544 lb (5690 kg)
External fuel: up to 12,800 lb (5806 kg) in two 594-gal (2250-liter) and two 476-gal (1500-liter) or four 396-gal (1500-liter) drop tanks
Maximum ordnance: 18,740 lb (8500 kg)

Weights

Empty operating: 31,970 lb (14,502 kg)
Maximum takeoff: 61,700 lb (27,986 kg)

Performance

Maximum level speed "clean" at 36,000 ft (10,975 m): 1,262 kt (1,453 mph; 2238 km/h)
Operational ceiling: 70,000 ft (21,335 m)
Combat radius: more than 300 nm (345 miles; 556 km) supersonic or more than 1000 nm (1,151 miles; 1852 km) subsonic

Armament

One 1.06-in (27-mm) IWKA Mauser cannon fitted to the starboard side. Main armament is four BAe SkyFlash semi-active radar-homing or four AIM-120 AMRAAM active-radar AAMs with a range of 31 miles (50 km), carried semi-recessed under the fuselage. Four AIM-9L Sidewinders or four ASRAAMS are also carried for short-range combat. Self-defense is provided by a Bofors Phimat chaff dispenser carried on starboard outer Sidewinder pylon or Celsius Tech BOL integral chaff/flare dispenser in Sidewinder rail. Vicon 78 chaff/flare dispensers under rear fuselage. GEC-Marconi Ariel towed-radar decoy can be carried on outboard wing pylon.

Cutaway Key

1 Starboard taileron construction
2 Honeycomb trailing-edge panels
3 Compound sweep taileron leading edge
4 Taileron pivot fixing
5 Afterburner ducting, extended 14 in (36 cm)
6 Thrust-reverser bucket door actuator
7 Afterburner nozzle jack
8 Starboard fully variable engine exhaust nozzle
9 Thrust-reverser bucket doors, open
10 Dorsal spine and fairing
11 Rudder hydraulic actuator
12 Honeycomb rudder construction
13 Rudder
14 Fuel jettison pipes
15 Tail navigation light
16 Aft passive ECM housing/radar warning antenna
17 Dielectric fintip antenna housing
18 VHF aerial
19 Fuel jettison and vent valve
20 ILS aerial, port and starboard
21 Underside view showing semi-recessed missile positions
22 Extended fuselage section
23 Extended radar equipment bay
24 Radome
25 Secondary heat exchanger intake
26 Wing pylon-mounted missile rails
27 External fuel tanks
28 Port taileron
29 Fin leading edge
30 Fin integral fuel tank
31 Tailfin construction
32 Vortex generators
33 Heat shield
34 Fin spar root attachment joints
35 Engine bay central firewall

36 Starboard airbrake, open
37 Airbrake hydraulic jack
38 Taileron actuator, fly-by-wire control system
39 Turbo-Union RB.199-34R Mk 104 three-spool afterburning turbofan
40 Hydraulic reservoir
41 Hydraulic system filters
42 Engine bay bulkhead
43 Bleed air duct
44 Heat exchanger exhaust duct
45 Primary heat exchanger
46 Ram air intake
47 HF aerial fairing
48 Engine compressor faces
49 Rear fuselage bag-type fuel tank
50 Intake trunking
51 Wing root pneumatic seal
52 KHD/Microtecnica/Lucas T312 APU
53 Engine-driven auxiliary gearbox
54 APU exhaust
55 Flap drive shaft
56 Starboard full-span double-slotted flaps, extended
57 Spoiler housings
58 Starboard wing, fully swept position
59 Flap guide rails
60 Flap screw jacks
61 Wingtip fairing
62 Starboard navigation light
63 Structural provision for outboard pylon attachment
64 Full-span leading-edge slats, extended
65 Starboard external fuel tank, capacity 594 gal (2250 liters)
66 Fuel-tank stabilizing fins
67 Swivelling wing stores pylon
68 Missile launching rail
69 AIM-9L Sidewinder air-to-air missiles

70 Leading-edge slat screw jacks
71 Slat guide rails
72 Wing rib construction
73 Two-spar wing torsion box construction
74 Swivelling pylon mounting
75 Starboard wing integral fuel tank
76 Main undercarriage leg strut
77 Starboard mainwheel
78 Mainwheel door
79 Undercarriage breaker strut
80 Wing pivot sealing fairing
81 Telescopic control linkages
82 Pylon swivelling link
83 Main undercarriage hydraulic retraction jack
84 Wing sweep actuator attachment joint
85 Starboard wing pivot bearing

86 Flexible wing seals
87 Wing pivot carry-through (electron beam—welded titanium box construction)
88 Wing pivot box integral fuel tank
89 Pitch and roll control non-linear gearing mechanism
90 Air-conditioning supply ducting (Normalair Garrett system)
91 Dorsal spine fairing
92 Anti-collision light
93 UHF aerials
94 Port wing pivot bearing
95 Flexible trailing-edge seals
96 Spoiler actuators
97 Port spoilers, open
98 Port wing, fully swept back position
99 Full-span double-slotted flaps, extended
100 Port wing, fully forward position

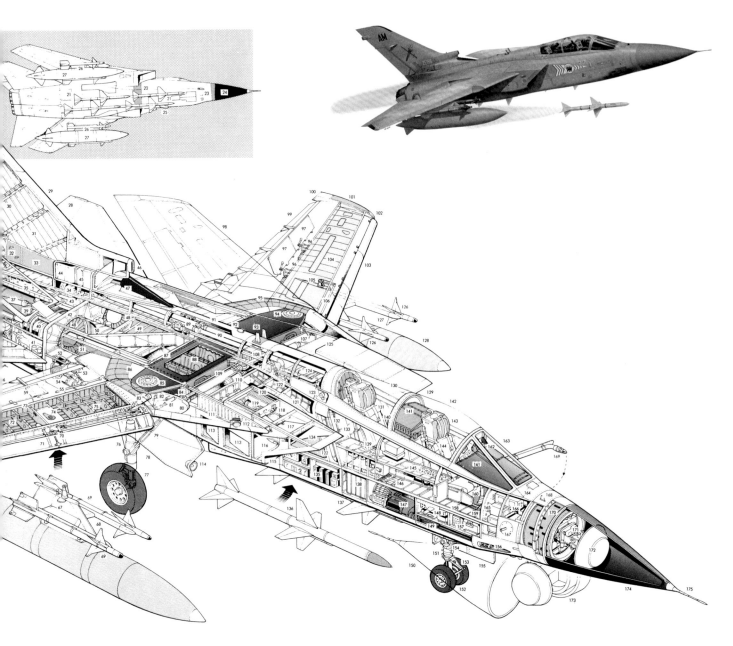

101 Wingtip fairing
102 Port navigation light
103 Full-span leading-edge slats, extended
104 Port wing integral fuel tank
105 Swivelling pylon mounting
106 Pylon angle control link
107 Port wing sweep actuator
108 Wing flap and leading-edge slat drive motors
109 Starboard wing sweep actuator
110 Hydraulic drive motor and gearbox
111 Extended wing root glove fairing

112 Forward radar-warning receiver, port and starboard
113 Supplementary "blow-in" intake doors
114 Landing lamp, port and starboard
115 Starboard fully variable engine air intake
116 Navigation light
117 Variable-intake ramp
118 Ramp control linkage
119 Ramp hydraulic jack
120 Bleed air exit louvers
121 Boundary layer spill duct

122 Enlarged forward fuselage bag-type fuel tank
123 Cockpit canopy pivot mounting
124 Air and fuel system ducting
125 Port intake bleed air outlet fairing
126 AIM-9L Sidewinder air-to-air missiles
127 Missile launching rail
128 Port external fuel tank
129 Intake lip
130 Navigator's cockpit enclosure
131 Navigator's ejection seat (Martin-Baker Mk 10A "zero-zero" seat)

132 Canopy jack strut
133 Cockpit rear pressure bulkhead
134 Engine air intake curved inboard sidewall
135 Starboard avionics equipment and flight control system equipment bay
136 BAe SkyFlash air-to-air missile
137 Ventral semi-recessed missile housing
138 Cartridge case and link collector box
139 Navigator's side console
140 Canopy center arch

141 Navigator's instrument console
142 One-piece cockpit canopy cover
143 Ejection-seat headrest
144 Pilot's ejection seat
145 Side console panel
146 Ammunition feed chute
147 Mauser 1.06-in (27-mm) cannon, starboard only
148 Instrument pressure sensor
149 Cannon barrel
150 Radome, open position
151 Nosewheel leg strut
152 Twin nosewheels
153 Torque scissor links

154 Taxiing lamp
155 Nosewheel doors
156 Cannon muzzle blast tube
157 Electrical system equipment and ground test panels
158 Cockpit pressure floor
159 Rudder pedals
160 Control column
161 Instrument panel shield
162 Pilot's head-up display
163 Windshield panels
164 Windshield rain-dispersal duct
165 Cockpit front pressure bulkhead
166 Avionics equipment, communications

and navigation systems
167 Angle-of-attack transmitter
168 Blade antenna
169 Inflight refueling probe, extended
170 Marconi-Elliot "Foxhunter" airborne interception radar
171 Scanner tracking mechanism
172 Cassegrain radar antenna
173 Radar unit hinged to starboard for replacement of line replaceable units (LRUs)
174 Extended radome
175 Pitot tube

133

"As a pure interceptor, the F3 performs well against medium and low-level non-agile threats. Where it falls down is against high-flying targets or agile fighters."
– Ian Black, former RAF Tornado F3 pilot

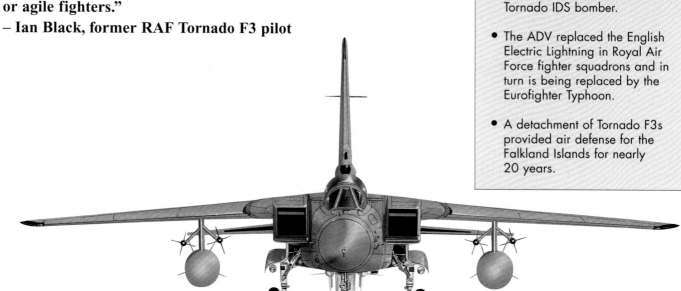

PANAVIA TORNADO ADV – VARIANTS & OPERATORS

VARIANTS

Tornado F2: Two-seat all-weather interceptor fighter aircraft, powered by two Turbo-Union RB.199-34R Mk 103 turbofan engines. Initial production version. 18 built.

Tornado F2A: F2 upgrade to F3 standard, but retaining F2 engines. One built.

Tornado F3: Improved version, powered by two Turbo-Union RB.199-34R Mk 104 engines, with automatic wing sweep control, increased AIM-9 carriage and avionics upgrades.

Tornado EF3: Unofficial designation for F3 aircraft modified with ALARM missile capability.

OPERATORS

Italy

12° Gruppo, 36° Stormo, Aeronautica Militare, 1995–2003.

1° Gruppo, 53° Stormo, Aeronautica Militare, 1995–2001.

Saudi Arabia

No. 29 Squadron, Royal Saudi Air Force, 1989–present.

United Kingdom
Operational

No. 111 Squadron RAF – F3. Based at RAF Leuchars, Fife, Scotland, 1990–present.

Disbanded

No. 5 Squadron RAF — F3. RAF Coningsby, Lincolnshire, England, 1987–2003.

No. 11 Squadron RAF — F3. RAF Leeming, North Yorkshire, England, 1988–2005.

No. 23 Squadron RAF — F3. RAF Leeming, North Yorkshire, England, 1988–1994.

No. 25 Squadron RAF — F3. RAF Leeming, North Yorkshire, England, 1989–2008.

No. 29 Squadron RAF – F3. RAF Coningsby, Lincolnshire, England, 1987–1998.

No. 43 Squadron RAF — F3. RAF Leuchars, Fife, Scotland, 1989–July 2009.

No. 56 (Reserve) Squadron RAF — F3. RAF Coningsby, England and RAF Leuchars, Scotland, 1992–2008 (Operational Conversion Unit).

No. 229 Operational Conversion Unit (No. 65 [Reserve] Squadron) RAF — F2 and F3. RAF Coningsby, Lincolnshire, England, 1984–1992.

No. 1435 Flight RAF— F3. RAF Mount Pleasant, Falkland Islands, 1992–2009.

TORNADO ADV

As part of a giant arms deal with the United Kingdom in the 1980s, Saudi Arabia purchased 24 Tornado ADV fighters and 48 Tornado IDS bombers, as well as spare parts and a training and maintenance package. The ADVs served initially with No. 29 Squadron, Royal Saudi Air Force, at Tabuk. Delivered from 1989 onwards, they flew patrols in the 1991 Gulf War, but did not see combat with any Iraqi aircraft. Unlike the RAF's Tornados, the Saudi aircraft had a working automatic wing sweep system. They used the same armament of four Skyflash semi-active radar-homing AAMs and four Sidewinders. The ADVs are being replaced with an order of 72 Eurofighter Typhoons and were withdrawn from use in 2007.

Above: Seen on an East Asia sales tour, this F3 has its wings in the forward position and its leading-edge flaps down. The Tornado was built with an automatic wing sweep system, but this was disconnected on the Royal Air Force's F3s.

The Tornado Air Defense Variant (ADV) came about as a development of the Tornado Interdictor Strike (IDS), a dedicated bomber designed to meet the needs of Germany, Italy and the United Kingdom. The Germans and Italians had a requirement for only a ground-attack aircraft, but the United Kingdom wanted to replace the English Electric Lightning F 6 and the McDonnell Douglas Phantom FG1 and FGR2 in the air defense role. The British solution was to stretch the basic airframe, adding an air interception (AI) radar in a lengthened nose radome and medium-range missiles in recesses under the aircraft's fuselage.

The original Tornado prototype flew in 1974 and the ADV in October 1979. The first fighter version was intended to be the Tornado F2, but there were significant delays with radar development and the 18 F2s built did not enter full RAF service. Some of them flew with ballast in the nose instead of radars. Once problems with the Marconi AI24 Foxhunter radar were worked out, the ADV was delivered to the Royal Air Force as the Tornado F3 from 1986.

Above: The ADV's primary weapons were four Skyflash missiles recessed into the belly, as seen on this F3 of No. 229 Operational Conversion Unit.

Like the Phantom, the ADV can carry eight missiles: four semi-active radar-homing Skyflash or AIM-7 Sparrow rounds semi-recessed under the belly and four AIM-9 Sidewinders on wing pylons. On RAF aircraft, the AIM-9s have been replaced by the AIM-132 ASRAAM (Advanced short-range air-to-air missile). The integration of the AIM-120 AMRAAM (advanced medium-range air-to-air missile) was delayed until quite late in the F3's RAF career. Unlike the baseline IDS, the ADV has one 1.06-in (27-mm) Mauser cannon, rather than two. A retractable refueling probe was fitted on the port side of the forward fuselage, unlike the removable starboard-side probe used on the IDS. The ALARM (air-launched anti-radiation missile) has been cleared for use on the F3 for the SEAD (suppression of enemy air defenses) role, but it is not thought that any squadrons are currently trained in its use.

VARIABLE GEOMETRY

The Tornado ADV is a variable-geometry, or "swing-wing," design, which allows the aerodynamic configuration to be changed for high- and low-speed flight. The wings sweep from 25 degrees to 67 degrees, allowing a maximum speed of more than Mach 2, while providing good handling characteristics for takeoff and landing.

The ADV is regarded as something of a compromise as a fighter. Its intended function was as an interceptor, able to meet incoming Soviet bombers approaching the United Kingdom at a distance greater than the bombers' missile ranges. As such, it emphasized speed, climb rate and endurance, rather than dogfighting ability, and usually comes off second-best in air combat training with more modern fighters.

RAF F3s were deployed in Saudi Arabia for the 1991 Gulf War, and in Italy for operations over the Balkans in the 1990s, but have never engaged in actual combat.

OPERATORS OUTSIDE THE UK

Saudi Arabia was the only country to purchase the ADV outright, taking 24 in 1989 as part of the huge al-Yamamah weapons deal with Britain. They serve alongside McDonnell Douglas (now Boeing) F-15Cs in the air-defense role with the Royal Saudi Air Force. Despite not being a part of ADV development, Italy acquired surplus F3s from Britain in a lease deal to bridge the gap between the phasing out of the Lockheed F-104 and service entry of the Eurofighter Typhoon. The F3s served the Aeronautica Militare from 1995–2004, before being returned to the United Kingdom and replaced by leased Lockheed Martin F-16As.

Above: The ADV was one of the last Western fighters built without multifunction display screens and hands-on-throttle-and-stick (HOTAS) controls.

Eurofighter Typhoon

The Eurofighter Typhoon is an example of successful international industrial cooperation, although its development has not been without problems – most of them political, rather than technical.

EUROFIGHTER TYPHOON SPECIFICATION

Dimensions

Length: 52 ft 5 in (15.96 m)
Height: 17 ft 4 in (5.28 m)
Wingspan: 35 ft 11 in (10.95 m)
Wing area: 538 sq ft (50 m²)

Power plant

Two Eurojet EJ200 afterburning turbofan rated at 13,500 lbf (60 kN) dry and 20,250 lbf (90 kN) with afterburner

Weights

Empty operating: 24,250 lb (11,000 kg)
Normal takeoff: 34,280 lb (15,550 kg)
Maximum takeoff: 51,800 lb (23,500 kg)

Fuel and load

Internal fuel: 1,506 gallons (5700 liters)
External fuel: two 264-gal (100-liter) tanks
Maximum weapon load: 16,500 lb (7500 kg)

Performance

Maximum level speed: In excess of Mach 2 (1,550 mph/2495 km/h)
Maximum combat radius: Ground attack, lo-lo-lo: 373 miles (601 km); ground attack, hi-lo-hi: 863 miles (1389 km); air defense with 3-hr CAP: 115 m (185 km); air defense with 10-minute loiter: 863 miles (1389 km)
Maximum combat range: 1,840 nm (1802 miles; 2900 km)
Service ceiling: 65,000 ft (19,810 m)

Armament

One 1.06-in (27-mm) Mauser BK-27 cannon with 150 rounds. 13 hard points: eight underwing; five underfuselage stations. Air-to-air missiles: AIM-9 Sidewinder, AIM-132 ASRAAM, AIM-120 AMRAAM, IRIS-T. Air-to-surface missiles: AGM-84 Harpoon, AGM-88 HARM, ALARM, Storm Shadow, Brimstone, Taurus KEPD 350, Penguin. Also carrying bombs, flares, and electronic countermeasures.

Cutaway Key

1 Glass-reinforced plastic radome
2 Air data sensors
3 Starboard canard foreplane
4 Port canard foreplane
5 Foreplane pivot mounting
6 Single-piece windshield
7 Wide-angle head-up display (HUD)
8 Martin-Baker Mk 16A zero-zero ejection seat
9 Upward-hinging canopy
10 Cockpit pressurization valves
11 Lower VHF antenna
12 Starboard engine intake
13 Fuselage strake
14 Intake ramp bleed air spill louvers
15 Conditioning systems heat-exchanger exhaust
16 Formation lighting strip
17 Nosewheel
18 Starboard leading-edge maneuvering flap
19 Wingtip defensive aids system pod
20 Fixed inboard leading edge
21 Port mainwheel and tire
22 Undercarriage scissor link
23 Port main undercarriage door
24 Port navigation light
25 Carbon-fiber composite wing skin
26 Auxiliary power unit (APU) exhaust
27 Fuel filler cap
28 Carbon-fiber composite fuselage panels
29 Port leading-edge maneuvering flap
30 Dorsal airbrake (closed)
31 Anti-collision strobe light
32 Starboard outboard elevon
33 Starboard inboard elevon
34 Heat exchanger ram air intake
35 Engine compressor intake
36 Eurojet EJ200 low-bypass turbofan engine
37 Engine fuel control system
38 Wing root trailing-edge fairing
39 Laser warning receiver (LWR)
40 Tailpipe sealing plates
41 Engine nozzle shield panels
42 Variable afterburner nozzle
43 Port inboard elevon
44 Port outboard elevon
45 Brake parachute door
46 Missile approach warning sensor
47 Engine bleed air heat exchanger outlet
48 Rudder
49 Fuel jettison outlet
50 UHF/IFF antennas in fintip
51 Carbon-fiber composite fin skin
52 Metal alloy fin leading edge
53 Formation lighting strip
54 AIM-9L Sidewinder infrared-guided air-to-air missile
55 Air-launched anti-radiation missile (ALARM)
56 GBU-16 1,000-lb (454-kg) laser-guided bomb
57 AIM-120 advanced medium-range air-to-air missile (AMRAAM)

"The plane flies with one finger. I took the controls myself and I can tell you that this plane is like a drug. I didn't want to come down."
– Antonio Martino, Italy's Secretary of Defense, November 1, 2005

F A C T S

- All Typhoons are fitted with a 1.06-in (27-mm) Mauser cannon. Initially, the United Kingdom chose not to make its own operational for cost reasons but has since done so.

- The Typhoon has a direct voice input system that allows hands-off control of many systems, although not weapons launch.

- A helmet-mounted sight system projects flight and radar information anywhere the Typhoon's pilot looks.

EUROFIGHTER TYPHOON – VARIANTS

DEVELOPMENT AIRCRAFT
DA1 (Germany): DA1's main role was handling characteristics and engine performance. DA1 first flew on March 27, 1994. The aircraft was retired on December 21, 2005.

DA2 (United Kingdom): DA2 undertook envelope expansion, flight control assessment and load trials. The aircraft first flew on April 6, 1994. The flight control assessment included development of the Eurofighter's "carefree handling."

DA3 (Italy): Weapons systems development.

DA4 (United Kingdom): Radar and avionics development.

DA5 (Germany): Radar and avionics development, being upgraded to Tranche 2 standard.

DA6 (Spain): Airframe development and handling. DA6 was lost in a crash in Spain in November 2002 after both engines failed.

DA7 (Italy): Navigation, avionics and missile carriage.

INSTRUMENTED PRODUCTION AIRCRAFT (IPA)
IPA1 (United Kingdom): Defensive Aids Sub System (DASS).
IPA2 (Italy): Air-to-surface weapons integration.
IPA3 (Germany): Air-to-air weapons integration.
IPA4 (Spain): Air-to-surface weapons integration and environmental development.
IPA5 (United Kingdom): Air-to-surface and air-to-air weapons integration.

IPA6 (United Kingdom): Converted Series Production Aircraft (BS031) – Tranche 2 Computer Systems.
IPA7 (Germany): Converted Series Production Aircraft (GS029) – Full Tranche 2 Standard.

SERIES PRODUCTION AIRCRAFT
EdA aircraft
The Spanish Air Force (Ejército del Aire) has one squadron of aircraft. The aircraft is designated the C16 Typhoon.

Luftwaffe aircraft
Germany has two active EF-2000 fighter wings, Jagdgeschwader 73 and Jagdgeschwader 74. JG 73 began converting to the Eurofighter in April 2004. JG 74 received its first aircraft on June 25, 2006.

RAF aircraft
T1: The Typhoon will replace the Royal Air Force's Panavia Tornado F3 (fighter) and SEPECAT Jaguar (ground-attack) forces.

T1A: A two-seat trainer.

F2: Single-seat fighter variant.

T3: Two-seat Block 5 or later aircraft (built or upgraded from T1).

FGR4: Single-seat Block 5 or later aircraft (built or upgraded from F2). Feature increased capabilities of fighter/ground-attack/reconnaissance aircraft. The FGR4 has from June 2008 achieved the required standard for multirole operations.

EUROFIGHTER TYPHOON

Rather than a single prototype, the Eurofighter partners built a series of instrumented production aircraft (IPA) for development work. The first to be completed was DA2, the first British aircraft, although Germany's DA1 made the first flight in March 1994. DA2, serial ZH588, flew in April 1994 and is seen here fitted with a pair of AIM-9L Sidewinders. A sensor for the PIRATE infrared tracking system is mounted below the left of the windshield, although this was not fitted to production aircraft until the end of the first tranche. An air data probe above the radome was used for measurements as part of the test program. It continued flying on various trials until January 2007, after which it was retired to the Royal Air Force Museum at Hendon in London.

As far back as the early 1970s, studies were under way in Britain and Germany for a highly maneuverable fighter aircraft along the lines of the U.S. F-16 and F/A-18 Hornet. These, together with French, Italian and Spanish requirements, merged in 1983 as the Future European Fighter Aircraft program. Politics interceded at every stage, and France dropped out in 1985 to pursue development of its Rafale technology demonstrator into an operational fighter. Across the Channel, British Aerospace flew its own Experimental Aircraft Prototype (EAP) in August 1986.

The eventual industrial agreement followed the model of the Panavia Tornado program, where aircraft were assembled in each of the partner nations using components built in different countries. For example, the Eurofighter Typhoon's forward fuselage, canards and tail fin are built in the United Kingdom; the central fuselage is made in Germany; the starboard wing and both leading-edge flaps are Spanish; and the port wing and flaperons come from Italy. The major systems include EJ200 engines from Eurojet and the CAPTOR radar from Euroradar. Each of these suppliers are consortiums of partner nation companies.

Workshare is allocated based on aircraft to be ordered: 232 for the United Kingdom; 180 for Germany; 121 for Italy; and 87 for Spain. Each partner nation has sales responsibility for a particular part of the world. For example, Saudi Arabia's 72 Typhoons will be built by BAE Systems (48 of them in collaboration with a local partner), while Austria's 15 jets have come from German production.

THREE-PART PRODUCTION

Known as the EFA 2000 at the time of the first (German) aircraft's maiden flight in March 1994, the name "Typhoon" was adopted in 1998 for the Royal Air Force and export aircraft. The first country to order the Typhoon outside of the partner nations was Greece, but it withdrew from the deal due to the cost pressures of the 2004 Olympic Games.

The Typhoon has a cropped delta wing, canard foreplanes and a ventral air intake with hinged flaps to regulate the airflow to the engines. There are a total of 13 weapons stations under the wings and fuselage. A sophisticated fly-by-wire control system allows carefree handling throughout the flight envelope.

Production is divided into three distinct groups, or tranches, each adding new capabilities. Tranche 1 offers basic air-to-air capabilities, with missiles including the AIM-9 Sidewinder, AIM-120 AMRAAM and AIM-132 ASRAAM. Later Tranche 1 aircraft have the PIRATE (Passive Infra Red Airborne Tracking Equipment) sensor forward of the cockpit. Tranche 2 aircraft will have a wide range of air-to-surface and air-to-air weapons options, and Tranche 3 may incorporate features such as electronically scanned radar and thrust-vectoring engines.

COMING TO FRUITION

Budgetary considerations led to delays in signing contracts for the later tranches. The nature of the original agreement

Above: Weapons, navigation, radar and systems data can be shown on any of the Typhoon's MFD screens.

means that there are large penalties for the respective countries not taking the originally allocated share of production, but it is possible that Tranche 3 aircraft will not be delivered to some or all of the partner air forces.

Typhoons have seen operational service in the air-defense role, providing combat air patrols over the Turin Winter Olympics in 2006, as well as during several international summits. They have also performed quick reaction alert (QRA) duties over the partner nations and the Falkland Islands. In addition to this, Typhoons have supplied air cover for Albania and the Baltic States, which currently have no operational fighter aircraft of their own.

Right: The Typhoon F2 was the RAF's initial single-seat version. Tranche 2 aircraft are designated FGR4, emphasizing their multirole capabilities.

Above: Weapons options have expanded during Typhoon production. Even the "austere" capability allows carriage of precision weapons such as these LGBs.

Lockheed Martin/Boeing F-22 Raptor

The F-22 "Air Dominance Fighter" outclasses all previous and existing fighters. Its enormous price tag, however, means that it will not be fielded in great numbers and politics means that it cannot be sold to the United States' allies.

LOCKHEED MARTIN/BOEING F-22 RAPTOR SPECIFICATION

Dimensions

Length: 62 ft 1 in (18.9 m)
Height: 16 ft 8 in (5.08 m)
Wingspan: 44 ft 6 in (13.56 m)
Wing area: 840 ft² (78.04 m²)

Power plant

Two Pratt & Whitney F119-PW-100 Pitch Thrust vectoring turbofans each rated at 29,300 lb (130 kN) dry thrust and 35,000 lb (156 kN) thrust with afterburner

Weights

Empty operating: 43,430 lb (19,700 kg)
Normal takeoff: 64,460 lb (29,300 kg)
Maximum takeoff: 83,500 lb (38,000 kg)

Performance

Maximum speed at altitude: Mach 2.25 (1,500 mph/ 2410 km/h)
Maximum combat radius: 410 nm (471 miles; 759 km)
Maximum combat range: 1,600 nm (1,840 miles; 2960 km) with two external fuel tanks

Armament

One 0.79-in (20-mm) M61A2 Vulcan Gatling gun with 480 rounds. Air-to-air missiles: six AIM-120 AMRAAM and two AIM-9 Sidewinder. Air-to-ground: two AIM-120 AMRAAM and two AIM-9 Sidewinder and either two 1,000-lb (450-kg) JDAM or two Wind Corrected Munitions Dispensers (WCMDs) or eight 250-lb (110-kg) GBU-39 Small Diameter Bombs. Four hard points to carry for 600-gal (2271-liter) drop tanks or weapons, each with a capacity of 5,000 lb (2268 kg)

Cutaway Key

1 Composite radome
2 Northrop Grumman/Raytheon AN/APG-77 radar (hidden)
3 Composite fuselage chine skin panels
4 Pitot head
5 Formation lighting strip
6 Nosewheel door
7 Nosewheel and tire
8 Forked nosewheel strut
9 Instrument panel shield
10 Head-up display (HUD)
11 Starboard engine intake
12 Pilot's ACES II ejection seat
13 Canopy actuator strut
14 M61A2 Vulcan 0.79-in (20-mm) cannon
15 Flush starboard electronic warfare antenna
16 Starboard communication/ navigation/ identification (CNI) antenna
17 Starboard leading-edge flap
18 Starboard wingtip navigation light
19 Port rear EW antenna
20 Formation lighting strip
21 Starboard aileron
22 Starboard flaperon

23 Fin leading edge containing CNI antenna
24 Starboard fin
25 Fin trailing edge containing CNI VHF antenna
26 Starboard all-moving tailplane
27 Rudder lower fixed fairing
28 Starboard rear CNI antenna (hidden)

29 Two-dimensional thrust vectoring afterburner nozzle
30 Runway arrestor hook fairing
31 Pratt & Whitney F119-PW-100 afterburning turbofan engine
32 Port rudder
33 Port fin
34 Rudder lower fixed fairing
35 Port rear CNI antenna (hidden)

36 Port all-moving tailplane
37 Port flaperon
38 Port aileron
39 Formation lighting strip
40 EW antenna (hidden)
41 Port navigation light
42 EW equipment (hidden)
43 Carbon-fiber wing skin
44 Port leading-edge flap

45 Inboard stores pylon
46 Port mainwheel tire
47 Port CNI UHF antenna
48 Auxiliary power unit (APU) exhaust
49 Engine bleed air heat exchanger
50 GPS antenna
51 Inflight refueling receptacle (covered)
52 Weapons bay rear bulkhead
53 Flush port EW antenna

54 Mainwheel retraction strut
55 Mainwheel retraction jack
56 Lateral weapons bay door
57 Ventral weapons bay doors
58 Weapons bay door retraction strut
59 Port engine intake
60 Throttle controls
61 Port side cockpit console

62 Ventral weapons bay
63 Missile launch trapeze
64 AIM-9X Sidewinder short range air-to-air missile
65 GBU-39 Small Diameter Bomb
66 AIM-120 AMRAAM medium-range air-to-air missile

"**The F-22 is a revolutionary, not evolutionary, leap very, very far forward.**"
– Lieutenant Colonel Mike "Dozer" Shower, U.S. Air Force F-22 pilot

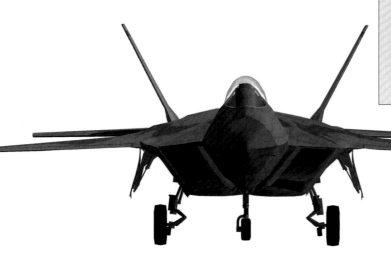

LOCKHEED MARTIN/BOEING F-22 RAPTOR – OPERATORS

The U.S. Air Force is the only operator of the F-22 Raptor, with a total of 145 aircraft in inventory at the time of writing. These are operated by the following commands:

Air Education and Training Command
325th Fighter Wing, Tyndall Air Force Base, Florida
43rd Fighter Squadron – The first squadron to operate the F-22 and continues to serve as the Formal Training Unit. Known as the "Hornets," the 43rd was reactivated at Tyndall in 2002.

Air Combat Command
1st Fighter Wing, Langley Air Force Base, Virginia
27th Fighter Squadron – The first combat F-22 squadron. Began conversion in December 2005 and flew the first operational mission (January 2006 in support of Operation Noble Eagle).
94th Fighter Squadron
49th Fighter Wing, Holloman Air Force Base, New Mexico
7th Fighter Squadron
8th Fighter Squadron
53rd Wing, Eglin Air Force Base, Florida
422rd Test and Evaluation Squadron – The "Green Bats" are responsible for operational testing, tactics development and evaluation for the F-22.
57th Wing, Nellis Air Force Base, Nevada
433rd Weapons Squadron

Air Force Materiel Command
412th Test Wing, Edwards Air Force Base, California
411th Flight Test Squadron – Conducted competition between YF-22 and YF-23 from 1989–91. Continues to conduct flight test on F-22 armaments and upgrades.

Pacific Air Forces
3rd Wing, Elmendorf Air Force Base, Alaska
90th Fighter Squadron – Converted from McDonnell Douglas/Boeing F-15Es; first F-22A arrived August 8, 2007.
525th Fighter Squadron
477th Fighter Group, Elmendorf Air Force Base, Alaska – Air Force Reserve Command (AFRC) unit.
302nd Fighter Squadron – Associate AFRC squadron to the 3rd Wing.

Air National Guard
192nd Fighter Wing, Langley Air Force Base, Virginia
149th Fighter Squadron – Associate Air National Guard squadron to the 1st Fighter Wing.

Future bases and units will include:
154th Wing, Hickam Air Force Base, Hawaii (2009/2010)
199th Fighter Squadron, Hawaii Air National Guard
531st Fighter Squadron, Hickam Air Force Base, Hawaii – Associate squadron to the 199th Fighter Squadron
44th Fighter Group, Holloman Air Force Base, New Mexico – Air Force Reserve Command (AFRC)
301st Fighter Squadron – Associate AFRC squadron to the 49th Fighter Wing

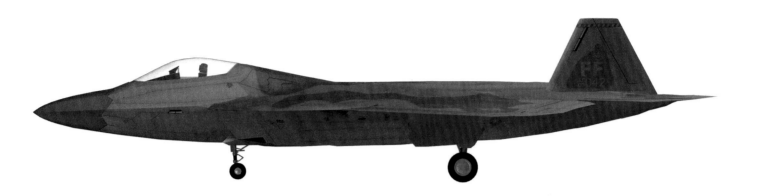

LOCKHEED MARTIN/BOEING F-22 RAPTOR

The U.S. Air Force's 1st Fighter Wing at Langley Air Force Base, Virginia, became the first operational unit to receive the F-22A Raptor in March 2006. The wing shares its 40 F-22s with the pilots of the Virginia Air National Guard's 149th Fighter Wing. The two units were declared operational in December 2007. This F-22A wears the "FF" ("First Fighter") tail codes of 1 TFW. With weapons mounted internally in bays, the armament configuration can be kept secret until the moment of use. An F-22 carrying bombs appears no different nor does it give away any performance to one equipped only with air-to-air missiles. The only stores regularly seen on F-22s are external fuel tanks for ferry missions.

The Advanced Tactical Fighter (ATF) requirement issued in 1981 set in motion a long process that led to the service entry of the F-22 Raptor some 26 years later. In that time, the world and technology changed greatly. Computer modelling of the 1970s and 1980s could guarantee stealth performance only for faceted shapes and straight lines. The F-117 "stealth fighter" was not a fighter at all, with no provision for air-to-air weaponry. Its defense was not to be detected at all, but even before 1999, when one was brought down by an older-generation surface-to-air missile over Kosovo, it was clear that future combat aircraft would need stealth protection of a whole different magnitude, without having their combat capability compromised by the stealth features.

In 1986, Lockheed (partnered with Boeing) and Northrop (with McDonnell Douglas) were invited to build two airframes each to demonstrate and validate their concepts. In August 1990, the Northrop/McDonnell Douglas YF-23 flew and the Lockheed/Boeing YF-22 was unveiled. The YF-22 flew a month later. Many observers believe that the larger YF-23 was technically better, and "won" the fly-off part of the evaluation. In April 1991, however, Lockheed/Boeing were chosen to build the ATF, as much for their perceived ability to manage and deliver a complex program as on technical merit.

FULL-SCALE DEVELOPMENT

The journey from the YF-22 to the full-scale development (FSD) F-22, which bore only a passing resemblance to the original, took until 1997. In the meantime, the Cold War had ended. In stages, the Pentagon cut planned production rates and the total requirement from the original 750 to 339.

On first viewing, the F-22A does not appear radically different to the F-15 that preceded it, but just on the surface

Above: Getting in the cockpit of the F-22 is the goal of most American fighter pilots. With fewer than 200 to be built, it will be a position of privilege.

Above: The sun catches the unique surface finish of a U.S. Air Force 1st Fighter Wing F-22A. The Raptor's coatings have unique and expensive radar and infrared absorption characteristics.

and under it are many unique features. Key to its incredible maneuverability are the Pratt & Whitney F119 engines with two-dimensional thrust-vectoring engines, which work in the vertical plane. Used in a turn, they allow the pilot instantly to turn the nose onto the target. Stealth features include special coatings, diamond shapes or serrated edges on panels and doors, and alignment of intake edges and tail fins. A gold-tinted metallic coating on the frameless canopy reflects radar energy. Weapons are carried internally, in bays under the fuselage and along the intake sides.

The incredible cost per airframe, which reached $138 million by 2008, saw production eventually capped at 187. The final figure for airframes delivered is likely to be 183, to equip seven operational squadrons, plus training and test units.

FOR THE UNITED STATES ONLY

Several nations would be natural customers for the F-22, such as Japan, Israel and Saudi Arabia, and others such as Australia would consider it – if it were available. A 2007 U.S. law actually prohibits the export of the Raptor and its sensitive technology. This has boosted the export chances of aircraft such as the Eurofighter Typhoon and Dassault Rafale

Above: One of the F-22 development aircraft flies over the California desert. It took ten years from the Raptor's first flight to service entry.

in the short term, and given impetus to several nations' own fighter programs. South Korea and Japan are among those working on indigenous stealth fighter projects for the next decade, as is Russia with its own Sukhoi T-50 or PAK-FA, an aircraft with a strong outward resemblance to the F-22.

Lockheed Martin F-35 Lightning II

The F-35 Lightning II is the most ambitious fighter program in history. Designed in three distinct versions, the F-35 promises much and numerous air arms are depending on its success, but it also faces many technical and political challenges.

Cutaway Key

1. Radome
2. APG-71 AESA radar (hidden)
3. Datalink antenna
4. Distributed aperture system window
5. Nosegear door
6. Single nosewheel
7. Nosewheel torque link
8. Nosewheel leg
9. Fuselage chine
10. Forward-opening canopy
11. Electro-optical targeting system (EOTS) window
12. Starboard instrument panel
13. Canopy frame
14. Martin-Baker Mk 16 zero-zero ejection seat
15. Lift fan vertical drive shaft
16. Starboard engine intake
17. Port engine intake
18. Lift fan
19. Lift fan door
20. Starboard leading-edge flap
21. Formation lighting strip
22. Engine auxiliary air vent door
23. Engine auxiliary air vent
24. Lift fan horizontal drive shaft
25. Starboard navigation light
26. Starboard flaperon
27. Pratt & Whitney F135 afterburning turbofan engine
28. Roll post
29. Starboard horizontal tailplane
30. Starboard vertical fin
31. Starboard rudder
32. Nozzle bearings (hidden)
33. Exhaust fairing
34. Convergent/divergent exhaust nozzle in down position
35. Port vertical fin
36. Port rudder

F-35A LIGHTNING II SPECIFICATION

Dimensions

Length: 51 ft ⅔ in (15.67 m)
Height: 14 ft 2 in (4.33 m)
Wingspan: 35 ft (10.7 m)

Power plant

One Pratt & Whitney F135 afterburning turbofan rated at 28,000 lbf (125 kN) and 43,000 lbf (191 kN) with afterburner

Weights

Empty operating: 29,300 lb (13,300 kg)
Normal takeoff: 44,400 lb (20,100 kg)
Maximum takeoff: 70,000 lb (31,800 kg)

Fuel and load

Internal fuel: 18,480 lb (8382 kg)

Performance

Maximum speed: Mach 1.67 (1,283 mph; 2065 km/h)
Service ceiling: 60,000 ft (18,288 m)
Maximum combat radius: 610 nm (689.7 miles; 1110 km)
Maximum combat range: 12,000 nm (1,374 miles; 2220 km)

Armament

One GAU-22/A 0.98-in (25-mm) cannon with 180 rounds. Hard points with six external pylons on wings with a capacity of 15,000 lb (6800 kg) and two internal bays with two pylons each for a total weapons payload of 18,000 lb (8165 kg) to carry combinations of AIM-120 AMRAAM, AIM-132 ASRAAM, AIM-9X Sidewinder air-to-air missiles and AGM-154 JSOW and AGM-158 JASSM air-to-ground missiles. Bombload could include Mark 84, Mark 83 and Mark 82 GP bombs, a Mk 20 Rockeye II cluster bomb, Wind Corrected Munitions Dispenser, Paveway-series laser-guided bombs, Small Diameter Bomb (SDB) and JDAM-series

37 Port tailplane
38 Port flaperon
39 Port navigation light
40 Port leading-edge flap
41 Formation lighting strip
42 Port mainwheel and tire
43 Weapons bay door
44 Weapons bay structure
45 AIM-120 AMRAAM (advanced medium-range air-to-air missile)
46 GBU-38 Joint Direct Attack Munition (JDAM)

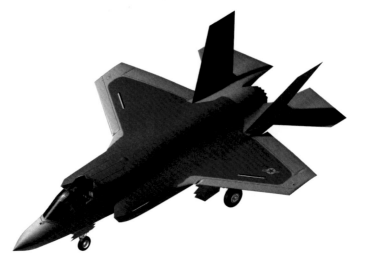

"The [F-35] brings persistent stealth over the battlefield for the first time and will enhance the lethality and survivability of American and allied combat air, sea and ground forces."
– General John Jumper,
U.S. Air Force Chief of Staff

LOCKHEED MARTIN F-35 LIGHTNING II – VARIANTS & JSF PROGRAM

VARIANTS

F-35A: Conventional takeoff and landing (CTOL) variant intended for the U.S. Air Force and other air forces. It is the smallest, lightest F-35 version and is the only variant equipped with an internal cannon, the GAU-22/A.

The A variant is primarily intended to replace the U.S. Air Force's Lockheed Martin F-16 Fighting Falcon, beginning in 2013, and replace the Fairchild-Republic A-10 Thunderbolt II starting in 2028.

F-35B: Short takeoff and vertical landing (STOVL) variant. Similar in size to the A variant, the B sacrifices some fuel volume to make room for the vertical flight system. Unlike the other variants, the F-35B has no landing hook; the "STOVL/HOOK" button in the cockpit initiates conversion instead of dropping the hook. The first test flight was on June 11, 2008. The B variant is expected to be available beginning in 2012.

F-35C: Carrier variant with a larger, folding wing and larger control surfaces for improved low-speed control, and stronger landing gear and hook for the stresses of carrier landings. The larger wing area allows for twice the range on internal fuel compared with the McDonnell Douglas (now Boeing) F/A-18C Hornet, achieving much the same goal as the heavier F/A-18E/F Super Hornet.

The U.S. Navy will be the sole user for the carrier variant. The C variant is expected to be available beginning in 2014. The first production F-35C was rolled out on July 29, 2009.

INTERNATIONAL PARTICIPATION UNDER THE JOINT STRIKE FIGHTER (JSF) PROGRAM

United Kingdom: Level 1 partner in the development of the aircraft. To purchase three F-35Bs.

Italy: Level 2 partner. To purchase 109 F-35As and 22 F-35Bs.

Netherlands: Level 2 partner. To acquire 85 F-35As.

Canada: Level 3 partner.

Turkey: Level 3 partner. Plans to order 116 F-35A CTOL versions.

Australia: Level 3 partner. Expected to order 72 or more F-35As.

Denmark: Level 3 partner. Is considering replacing F-16s with F-35s.

Norway: Level 3 partner. Has stated that it will support buying F-35s for the Royal Norwegian Air Force and will develop Joint Strike Missiles for the F-35 and other aircraft.

Israel: Security Cooperative Participant (SCP). Intends to buy more than 100 F-35A Fighters.

Singapore: Security Cooperative Participant (SCP).

LOCKHEED MARTIN F-35B LIGHTNING II

The first F-35B Lightning II flew in June 2008. Of the planned 16 flying F-35 prototypes, five are Bs, three of which would clear the flight envelope and two to test the mission systems. The front and side views depict the F-35B configured for a vertical landing, showing the lift fan doors and auxiliary doors open, and the main exhaust nozzle in the down position. In operational service, the F-35B may use a rolling vertical landing technique, rather than a pure vertical descent, when space is available, such as the on the new Royal Navy carriers. This would put less stress on the engine, increasing its lifespan, and also allow greater landing weights.

Several schemes for proposed fighters to replace a variety of fighter and attack aircraft were merged in the early 1990s to meet requirements by the U.S. Air Force, U.S. Navy, U.S. Marine Corps and the Royal Navy and Royal Air Force.

Under the banner of Joint Advanced Strike Technology (JAST), the new aircraft would be a low-cost replacement for numerous types, including the Fairchild-Republic A-10, Lockheed Martin F-16, McDonnell Douglas F/A-18C and D, Grumman A-6 Intruder and McDonnell Douglas/BAe AV-8B Harrier. The British were looking for both a Harrier and a Sea Harrier replacement. To this end, the same basic airframe would be built in three versions: a conventional takeoff and landing (CTOL) model for the air force; a version for aircraft carriers (CV); and a short takeoff and vertical landing (STOVL) variant to replace Harriers on amphibious ships and British carriers.

Above: A unique helmet-mounted sight system allows the F-35 pilot to cue weapons to any target the sensors can track, even when hidden from his view by aircraft structure.

JOINT STRIKE FIGHTER

A fly-off competition was organized in 1996 to choose a winner between competing designs by Boeing and Lockheed Martin, McDonnell Douglas having been eliminated at an earlier stage. The project was now called the Joint Strike Fighter (JSF), reflecting its joint (multiservice) procurement and multirole capabilities.

Boeing (which absorbed McDonnell Douglas in 1997) and Lockheed Martin took different approaches. Boeing built two X-32 demonstrators characterized by a huge intake under the nose. The wing was of a roughly diamond planform with large flaperons. There were no tailplanes. Lockheed Martin's X-35s were more conventional, with side-mounted intakes and tailplanes. The CV X-35A flew in October 2000, followed by the CTOL X-35C two months later. The X-35A was later modified to create the STOVL X-35B, which flew as such in June 2001. These aircraft demonstrated technologies rather than serving as strict prototypes for the JSF.

CONTRACT SUCCESS

Lockheed Martin was awarded the contract to proceed with a series of F-35A (CTOL), F-35B (STOVL) and F-35C (CV) development aircraft in October 2001. Boeing's X-32s became museum pieces (as did the X-35s).

Above: The F-35A made its maiden flight in December 2006. The flight envelope was expanded past Mach 1 in November 2008.

Above: The demonstrator X-35 underwent numerous changes in its evolution to the F-35. The more obvious ones include the shape of the nose and the tail fins, and the configuration of the canopy.

The manufacturer envisages sales of more than 4,000 F-35s, many of them replacing export F-16s. An extremely complicated industrial program was launched with the United Kingdom, Italy, the Netherlands, Canada, Turkey, Australia, Norway and Denmark sharing the development and testing, in exchange for the chance to supply components to all customers. These nations did not initially commit to purchasing any F-35s. The degree to which the United States will allow technology transfer to the partners and other customers remains an unknown and controversial factor.

Surfaces and panel edges on the production F-35 are aligned to reduce the radar cross section. Weapons will be carried internally in weapons bays. The F-35A will have an internal 0.98-in (25-mm) cannon. The other versions will carry the cannon as a gun pod. The canopy is hinged at the forward end. All versions will use the Pratt & Whitney F135 turbofan, with the addition of a Rolls-Royce lift fan and a reaction control system for the F-35B. The U.S. Marine Corps requires the F-35B for use from its amphibious ships; Italy and the United Kingdom are expected to also be customers.

DELAYED SERVICE ENTRY

The first F-35A Lightning II flew in December 2006 and began testing toward a planned service entry in 2012. Progress after that slipped greatly, however, with subsequent aircraft being late to enter testing. This has caused in-service dates for the F-35 with U.S. forces and signature of export contracts to be delayed by at least two years.

Glossary

AAM: Air-to-Air Missile.

ADV: Air Defense Variant (of the Tornado).

AEW: Airborne Early Warning.

Afterburning (reheat): Method of increasing the thrust of a gas turbine aircraft engine by injecting additional fuel into the hot exhaust duct between the engine and the tailpipe, where it ignites to provide a short-term increase of power.

Aileron: An airfoil (airplane surface) used for causing an aircraft to roll around its longitudinal axis, usually fitted near the wingtips. Ailerons are controlled by use of the pilot's control column.

ALARM: Air-Launched Anti-Radiation Missile.

All-Up Weight: The total weight of an aircraft in operating condition. Normal maximum AUW is the maximum at which an aircraft is permitted to fly within normal design restrictions, while overload weight is the maximum AUW at which an aircraft is permitted to fly subject to ultimate flying restrictions.

Altimeter: Instrument that measures altitude, or height above sea level.

AMRAAM: Advanced Medium-Range Air-to-Air Missile.

Angle of Attack: The angle between the wing (airfoil) and the airflow relative to it.

Aspect Ratio: The ratio of wing span to chord.

ASV: Air to Surface Vessel – airborne detection radar for locating ships and submarines.

ASW: Anti-Submarine Warfare.

ATF: Advanced Tactical Fighter.

AWACS: Airborne Warning and Control System

Basic Weight: The tare weight of an aircraft plus the specified operational load.

CAP: Combat Air Patrol.

Center of Gravity: Point in a body through which the sum of the weights of all its parts passes. A body suspended from this point is said to be in a state of equilibrium.

Center of Pressure: Point through which the lifting force of a wing acts.

Chord: Cross-section of a wing from leading edge to trailing edge.

Delta Wing: Aircraft shaped like the Greek letter delta.

Disposable Load: The weight of crew and consumable load (fuel, missiles, etc.).

Electronic Countermeasures (ECM): Systems designed to confuse and disrupt enemy radar equipment.

Electronic Counter-Countermeasures (ECCM): Measures taken to reduce the effectiveness of ECM by improving the resistance of radar equipment to jamming.

Elevator: A horizontal control surface used to control the upward or downward inclination of an aircraft in flight. Elevators are usually hinged to the trailing edge of the tailplane.

EW: Electronic Warfare.

FAC: Forward Air Controller. A battlefront observer who directs strike aircraft to their targets near the front line.

FGA: Fighter Ground Attack.

FLIR: Forward-Looking Infra-Red. Heat-sensing equipment fitted in an aircraft that scans the path ahead to detect heat from objects such as vehicle engines.

FRS: Fighter Reconnaissance Strike.

Gas Turbine: Engine in which burning fuel supplies hot gas to spin a turbine.

GPS: Global Positioning System. A system of navigational satellites.

GR: General Reconnaissance.

HOTAS: Hands on Throttle and Stick. A system whereby the pilot exercises full control over his aircraft in combat without the need to remove his hands from the throttle and control column to operate weapons selection switches or other controls.

HUD: Head-Up Display. A system in which essential information is projected onto a cockpit windshield so that the pilot has no need to look down at his instrument panel.

IFF: Identification Friend or Foe. An electronic pulse emitted by an aircraft to identify it as friendly on a radar screen.

INS: Inertial Navigation System. An on-board guidance system that steers an aircraft or missile over a predetermined course by measuring factors such as the distance travelled and reference to "waypoints" (landmarks) en route.

Interdiction: Deep air strikes into enemy areas to sever communications with the battlefield.

IR: Infra-Red.

Jet Propulsion: Method of propulsion in which an object is propelled in one direction by a jet, or stream of gases, moving in the other.

Laminar Flow: Airflow passes over an aircraft's wing in layers, the first of which, the boundary layer, remains stationary while successive layers progressively accelerate; this is known as laminar flow. The smoother the wing surface, and the more efficient its design, the smoother the airflow.

Landing Weight: The AUW of an aircraft at the moment of landing.

Lantirn: Low-Altitude Navigation and Targeting Infra-Red for Night. An infra-red system fitted to the F-15E Strike Eagle that combines heat sensing with terrain-following radar to enable the pilot to view the ground ahead of the aircraft during low-level night operations. The information is projected on the pilot's head-up display.

LWR: Laser Warning Radar. Equipment fitted to an aircraft that warns the pilot if he is being tracked by a missile-guiding radar beam.

Mach: Named after the Austrian Professor Ernst Mach, a Mach number is the ratio of the speed of an aircraft or missile to the local speed of sound. At sea level, Mach One (1.0 M) is approximately 762mph (1226 km/h), decreasing to about 660mph (1062 km/h) at 30,000 feet (9144 meters). An aircraft or missile travelling faster than Mach One is said to be supersonic. Mach numbers are dependent on variations in atmospheric temperature and pressure and are registered on a Machmeter in the aircraft's cockpit.

Maximum Landing Weight: The maximum AUW, due to design or operational limitations, at which an aircraft is permitted to land.

Maximum Take-Off Weight: The maximum AUW, due to design or operational limitations, at which an aircraft is permitted to take off.

MG: Machine gun (Maschinengewehr in German, hence MG 15).

NATO: North Atlantic Treaty Organization.

NBC: Nuclear, Biological and Chemical (warfare).

Operational Load: The weight of equipment necessarily carried by an aircraft for a particular role.

Phased-Array Radar: A warning radar system using many small aerials spread over a large flat area, rather than a rotating scanner. The advantage of this system is that it can track hundreds of targets simultaneously, electronically directing its beam from target to target in microseconds (millionths of a second).

Pulse-Doppler Radar: A type of airborne interception radar that picks out fast-moving targets from background clutter by measuring the change in frequency of a series of pulses bounced off the targets. This is based on the well-known Doppler Effect, an apparent change in the frequency of waves when the source emitting them has a relative velocity toward or away from an observer. The MiG-29's noted tail-slide maneuver is a tactical move designed to break the lock of a pulse-Doppler radar.

Rudder: Movable vertical surface or surfaces forming part of the tail unit, by which the yawing of an aircraft is controlled.

RWR: Radar Warning Receiver. A device mounted on an aircraft that warns the pilot if he is being tracked by an enemy missile guidance or intercept radar.

SAM: Surface-to-Air Missile.

SHF: Super High Frequency (radio waves).

Spin: A spin is the result of yawing or rolling an airplane at the point of a stall.

SRAM: Short-range Attack Missile.

Stall: Condition that occurs when the smooth flow of the air over an aircraft's wing changes to a turbulent flow and the lift decreases to the point where control is lost.

Stealth Technology: Technology applied to aircraft or fighting vehicles to reduce their radar signatures. Examples of stealth aircraft are the Lockheed F-117 and the Northrop B-2.

STOVL: Short Take-off, Vertical Landing.

Take-Off Weight: The AUW of an aircraft at the moment of take-off.

Turbofan Engine: Type of jet engine fitted with a very large front fan that not only sends air into the engine for combustion but also around the engine to produce additional thrust. This results in faster and more fuel-efficient propulsion.

Turbojet Engine: Jet engine that derives its thrust from a stream of hot exhaust gases.

Variable-Geometry Wing: A type of wing whose angle of sweep can be altered to suit a particular flight profile. Popularly called a Swing Wing.

VHF: Very High Frequency.

VLF: Very Low Frequency.

V/STOL: Vertical/Short Take-off and Landing.

Wild Weasel: Code name applied to specialized combat aircraft tasked with defense suppression.

Yaw: The action of turning an aircraft in the air around its normal (vertical) axis by use of the rudder. An aircraft is said to yaw when the fore-and-aft axis turns to port or starboard, out of the line of flight.

For More Information

Canada Aviation and Space Museum
11 Aviation Parkway
Ottawa, ON K1K 4R3
Canada
(613) 993-2010
Web site: http://www.aviation.technomuses.ca
This museum's collection focuses on the development of the aircraft, in both peace and war, from the pioneer period to the present time. More than 130 aircraft and numerous artifacts such as engines, propellers, and instruments from many nations are represented in the collection.

Canadian Warplane Heritage Museum
9280 Airport Road
Mount Hope, ON L0R 1W0
Canada
(905) 679-4183
Web site: http://www.warplane.com
This museum features the aircraft used by Canadians or Canada's military from the beginning of World War II to the present.

Commemorative Air Force (CAF) Airpower Museum
P.O Box 62000
Midland, TX 79711
(432) 567-3010
Web site: http://www.airpowermuseum.org
The CAF Airpower Museum is dedicated to preserving the history of World War II military aviation. The museum's interactive exhibits illustrate aviation concepts and events from every theater of the war.

National Museum of the U.S. Air Force
1100 Spaatz Street
Wright-Patterson AFB, OH 45433
(937) 255-3286
Web site: http://www.nationalmuseum.af.mil

The National Museum of the U.S. Air Force is dedicated to preserving U.S. military aviation history, from the Wright brothers' inventions to today's stealth and precision technology. Its collections include more than four hundred aerospace vehicles and thousands of historical items.

National Naval Aviation Museum
1750 Radford Boulevard, Suite C
Naval Air Station Pensacola, FL 32508
(850) 452-3604
Web site: http://www.navalaviationmuseum.org
This museum boasts more than 150 beautifully restored aircraft, hands-on exhibits including a Top Gun air combat simulator, and more than four thousand artifacts representing U.S. Navy, Marine Corps, and Coast Guard aviation. The Blue Angels perform practice air shows from March through November.

Smithsonian National Air and Space Museum
Independence Avenue at 6th Street SW
Washington, DC 20560
(203) 633-2214
Web site: http://www.nasm.si.edu
The Smithsonian Institution's National Air and Space Museum is home to the world's largest collection of historic airplanes and spacecraft. It is also a vital center for research into the history, science, and technology of aviation.

Web Sites

Due to the changing nature of Internet links, Rosen Publishing has developed an online list of Web sites related to the subject of this book. This site is updated regularly. Please use this link to access the list:

http://www.rosenlinks.com/wow/jets

For Further Reading

Bell, Dana, Eric F. Long, Mark A. Avino, and John Travolta. *In the Cockpit: Inside 50 History-Making Aircraft*. New York, NY: Collins Design, 2007.

Boyne, Walter J. *Beyond the Wild Blue: A History of the United States Air Force, 1947–2007*. 2nd ed. New York, NY: Thomas Dunne Books/St. Martin's Press, 2007.

Budiansky, Stephen. *Air Power: The Men, Machines, and Ideas That Revolutionized War, from Kitty Hawk to Iraq*. New York, NY: Penguin Books, 2005.

Coonts, Stephen. *Flight of the Intruder*. Twentieth anniversary ed. Annapolis, MD: Naval Institute Press, 2006.

Davies, Steve. *U.S. Multi-Role Fighter Jets*. Long Island City, NY: Osprey Publishing, 2011.

Dick, Ron, and Dan Patterson. *War & Peace in the Air* (Aviation Century). Buffalo, NY: Firefly Books, 2006.

Haney, Robert Earl, and Lee Courtnage. *Mission to Mach 2: A Fighter Pilot's Memoir of Supersonic Flight*. Jefferson, NC: McFarland & Co., 2011.

Harvey, James Neal. *Sharks of the Air: Willy Messerschmitt and How He Built the World's First Operational Jet Fighter*. Havertown, PA: Casemate, 2011.

Hearn, Chester G. *Air Force: An Illustrated History: The U.S. Air Force from the 1910s to the 21st Century*. Minneapolis, MN: Zenith Press, 2008.

Holmes, Tony. *Jane's U.S. Military Aircraft Recognition Guide* (Jane's Recognition Guides). New York, NY: Collins, 2007.

Jackson, Robert. *Aircraft of World War II*. New York, NY: Fall River Press, 2009.

Jackson, Robert. *101 Great Fighters* (101 Greatest Weapons of All Times). New York, NY: Rosen Publishing, 2010.

Landis, Tony. *U.S. Air Force Jet Fighter Prototypes: Photo Scrapbook*. North Branch, MN: Specialty Press, 2009.

Olsen, John Andreas. *A History of Air Warfare*. Washington, DC: Potomac Books, 2010.

Van Creveld, Martin. *The Age of Airpower*. New York, NY: Public Affairs, 2011.

Yenne, Bill. *The American Aircraft Factory in World War II*. St. Paul, MN: Zenith Press, 2006.

Index

About the Author

Jim Winchester is an aviation writer with many years of experience. He is the author of several books, including *A-4 Skyhawk*, *Dogfight*, and *Fighter*. He contributes to many publications, including *Air Forces Monthly* and *Aeroplane*.